The Coffin Texts

Sacred Spells of the Afterlife's Journey

Volume 2

M L Ruscsak

Trient Press
3375 S Rainbow Blvd
#81710, SMB 13135
Las Vegas,NV 89180

Ordering Information:
Quantity sales. Special discounts are available on quantity purchases by corporations, associations, and others. For details, contact the publisher at the address above.
Orders by U.S. trade bookstores and wholesalers. Please contact Trient Press: Tel: (775) 996-3844; or visit www.trientpress.com.

Printed in the United States of America

Publisher's Cataloging-in-Publication data
Ruscsak, M.L.
A title of a book : The Coffin Texts: Sacred Spells of the Afterlife's Journey Volume 2
    ISBN
Hard Cover   979-8-88990-038-2

Paper Back   979-8-88990-039-9

Ebook   979-8-88990-040-5

Disclosure for the book "Coffin Text: Sacred Spells of the Afterlife's Journey Volume 2":

In this book, we present a collection of spells, incantations, and rituals that are inspired by and closely aligned with ancient Egyptian hieroglyphs. While we have made efforts to translate and interpret these texts as accurately as possible, it is important to note that the numbers assigned to each entry are for ease of reference within this book and do not necessarily reflect a definitive chronological or organizational order. Many scholars continue to study and analyze these ancient texts, seeking to confirm their age and the periods in which they were written.

The concept of the afterlife holds a significant place in ancient Egyptian culture and religion. Therefore, numerous books with similar texts have been written throughout history to provide guidance, teachings, and inspiration that resonate with modern-day spirituality and various religions today.

It is crucial to approach these spells, incantations, and rituals with an open mind, understanding that they are rooted in the ancient Egyptian belief system and cultural context. While they may offer insights into the human quest for spiritual understanding and growth, they should be viewed as a part of the rich tapestry of human religious and spiritual exploration.

Readers are encouraged to interpret and adapt the contents of this book in a way that aligns with their personal beliefs and spiritual practices. The aim of this book is to shed light on the wisdom and traditions of ancient Egypt while providing a source of inspiration and guidance for individuals seeking to deepen their spiritual journey.

Please approach the text with respect for the ancient culture and its religious practices, and consider these spells, incantations, and rituals as tools for personal growth, reflection, and connection with the mysteries of the afterlife.

May the exploration of these ancient texts bring you insight, enrichment, and a deeper appreciation for the enduring wisdom of the ancient Egyptian civilization.

1. Spell for the protection of the deceased's body

Hear my words, O mighty guardians of the divine realm,
Inscribe upon this sacred scroll the power of protection,
For the body of the departed, a vessel of sacred essence.

By the ancient magic that spans the eons of time,
I summon the forces of strength and fortification,
To shield and guard this precious form from desecration.

With the invocation of the divine names and symbols,
I command the elements to encircle and embrace,
Forming a barrier impenetrable, a shield of divine grace.

Let the earth rise and solidify beneath the body's weight,
Like an unyielding fortress, unwavering and strong,
Preserving its sanctity, defending against all wrong.

Let the winds blow with vigor, a hurricane's fury,
Creating a whirlwind of protection, a shield unseen,
To ward off any harm, keeping the vessel serene.

Let the waters flow, a river of purity and cleansing,
Bathing the body in their soothing embrace,
Washing away any negativity, leaving not a trace.

Let the fires ignite, a blazing inferno of divine light,
Casting away darkness, consuming all impurity,
Burning with the intensity of eternal security.

Let the ether descend, a shimmering veil of ethereal power,
Cloaking the body in invisibility, beyond mortal sight,
Guarding its presence from the forces of blight.

O sacred guardians, hear my plea and heed my call,
Wrap this vessel in your celestial embrace,
Shield it from harm, safeguard it in sacred space.

By the ancient words inscribed on this sacred scroll,

I invoke the power of protection, unyielding and true,
May the deceased's body be preserved, renewed.

As it rests in eternal slumber, in the realm of the departed,
May no harm befall it, no desecration be allowed,
Protected and guarded, in the divine presence enshroud.

This is my will, let it be done,
As I speak, so mote it be.

2. Spell for the preservation of the ba in the afterlife

In the realm of the divine, where spirits take flight,
I beseech the cosmic forces to grant me their might,
To safeguard the ba, the essence of the departed,
From the trials of the afterlife, where it is charted.

By the sacred words inscribed upon this scroll,
I call upon the ancient wisdom of the soul,
To preserve the ba, to keep it whole and pure,
In the realm of eternity, where it shall endure.

Let the wings of Ma'at unfurl with grace,
Guiding the ba through the celestial space,
Carrying it on the currents of divine wind,
Away from chaos, towards serenity it shall ascend.

Let the golden scales of judgment be just and fair,
Weighing the deeds of the ba with utmost care,
May it find balance and be deemed worthy,
To traverse the realms, where it seeks its journey.

Let the waters of the sacred Nile gently flow,
Nourishing the ba with their life-giving glow,
Sustaining its essence, replenishing its vitality,
In the eternal cycle of spiritual reality.

Let the flames of the eternal hearth burn bright,
Illuminating the path, casting away the night,
May their warmth and light embrace the ba,
Keeping it safe from darkness, fear, and dismay.

Let the whispers of the ancestors guide its way,
Offering wisdom and counsel, night and day,
As the ba walks among the spirits of the past,
May their presence bring comfort that forever lasts.

O guardians of the afterlife, hear my plea,
Wrap the ba in your loving arms, set it free,
Preserve its essence, its memories and desires,

In the realm of the eternal, where it aspires.

By the power of the ancient words I speak,
Let the ba find solace, find solace that's unique,
In the everlasting realm, its essence shall dwell,
Protected, preserved, in a sacred, eternal spell.

This is my will, let it be done,
As I speak, so mote it be.

3. Invocation of the goddess Nut for safe passage

Goddess Nut, celestial canopy above,
Mistress of the starry sky, embodiment of love,
I call upon your sacred presence this day,
To grant safe passage on the afterlife's way.

With arms outstretched, you embrace the Earth,
Nurturing life, granting souls their rebirth,
Your heavenly body, adorned with countless stars,
Guides the departed on their journey afar.

O gracious Nut, hear my earnest plea,
Wrap your protective wings around me,
As I traverse the realms of the divine,
Grant me your blessings, let your light shine.

From horizon to horizon, your celestial form,
Stretches across the heavens, keeping me warm,
As I venture through the duat's shadowy veil,
May your radiance prevail, never to fail.

Your sacred breath whispers secrets of old,
Ancient wisdom and mysteries untold,
Guide me with your eternal wisdom and grace,
In this sacred journey, to find my rightful place.

Oh, Nut, mother of gods, hear my call,
By your divine power, safeguard me from all,
Grant me passage through the realms unknown,
May your protective embrace be my eternal home.

As I walk the path of the deceased,
Grant me solace, inner peace, and release,
In your loving arms, let my spirit soar,
To join the cosmic dance forevermore.

Oh, glorious Nut, I beseech thee,
Protect me with your divine decree,
With your heavenly radiance, light my way,

Through the afterlife's journey, day by day.

This invocation I speak from the heart,
In reverence and trust, I impart,
Grant me the strength, the courage to face,
The trials of the afterlife with steadfast grace.

Goddess Nut, I offer my heartfelt plea,
With gratitude and reverence, I bow to thee,
May your blessings and protection be bestowed,
As I navigate the realms where souls have flowed.

So mote it be, let it be done,
Under the watchful gaze of the moon and sun,
In the embrace of Nut, I find sanctuary,
Safe passage granted in her celestial sanctuary.

4. Spell for the union of the deceased with their ka

By the sacred power that binds us all,
I call upon the forces of the divine hall.
May the ka of the departed and their essence align,
In eternal unity, their spirits entwine.

From the depths of the duat's mystical realm,
Let the ka be summoned at the sacred helm.
May it come forth with grace, unbroken and pure,
To reunite with the deceased and endure.

Oh, ka of the departed, hear my plea,
Come forth from the heavens, set your spirit free.
Rejoin the soul that dwells in the earthly tomb,
Embrace the deceased, dispel all gloom.

As the sun rises and sets in the sky,
Let the ka and the soul be as one, on high.
In the sacred union of these two essences,
Grant them eternal bliss, divine presences.

Oh, ancient forces that govern the divine,
Guide the ka and the soul, in love intertwine.
Merge their energies, their purpose combine,
In harmony, let their essence forever shine.

With every breath and beat of the heart,
May the union of ka and soul never depart.
Bound together in a celestial embrace,
Endowing the deceased with eternal grace.

In this sacred union, let the ka be whole,
Fulfilling its purpose, fulfilling its role.
Grant the deceased eternal life and peace,
As their spirit soars, may their sorrows cease.

By the powers vested in the divine decree,
I seal this spell for all eternity.

May the union of the deceased and their ka be blessed,
In the realm of the afterlife, their spirits find rest.

So let it be written, so let it be done,
Under the watchful eyes of the moon and sun.
The union is complete, the bond is strong,
The deceased and their ka together belong.

In the realm of the divine, they shall abide,
Bound forever, side by side.
In unity and love, they transcend,
Their journey in the afterlife shall never end.

By the sacred words I have spoken,
The union of ka and soul is now awoken.
In the tapestry of eternity, their spirits entwined,
Forever united, their destinies defined.

So mote it be, let it be done,
The union of ka and soul, forever one.
In the realm of the afterlife, they shall forever dwell,
In perfect harmony, their essence will swell.

5. Ritual of purification for the journey through the Duat

In the realm of shadows, where darkness prevails,
Where souls traverse through the Duat's veiled trails,
A ritual of purification we now commence,
To cleanse the spirit, to dispel all darkness.

Gather, O spirits, in this sacred space,
As we embark on this mystical chase,
With offerings of incense and sacred flame,
We purify our souls, free from all shame.

Let the water of life, pure and divine,
Wash away our sins, make us pristine,
As we immerse ourselves, body and soul,
In the blessed waters, we become whole.

Purification of heart, purification of mind,
In this sacred ritual, seek solace to find,
Release the burdens, the weights that bind,
Let our spirits soar, leave all darkness behind.

O mighty deities, guardians of the Duat,
We call upon your guidance, we seek your support,
Through the purifying fire and sacred chant,
We cleanse our spirits, as we traverse the distant land.

With each step taken on this sacred path,
Our souls grow lighter, free from wrath,
Let the purifying flame burn bright and strong,
As we journey through the Duat, where we belong.

Blessed are the ones who seek purification's grace,
For they shall find peace in this sacred space,
May the Duat's trials be met with strength and resolve,
As we purify our spirits, our essence evolves.

By the ancient rituals and sacred rite,
We cleanse our beings, banish the night,
May the journey through the Duat be clear,

As we emerge in the realm of the divine, free from fear.

In the purifying embrace of the sacred flame,
We release all impurities, all guilt and shame,
Renewed and refreshed, our spirits ascend,
Onward we journey, to meet our eternal end.

So let the ritual of purification commence,
As we embark on the Duat's mystical dance,
With hearts purified and souls aglow,
We embrace the journey, wherever it may go.

In the realm of the Duat, our spirits shall thrive,
Through purification, we come alive,
May the path be illuminated, our souls made pure,
As we journey through the Duat, steadfast and sure.

By the sacred words we have spoken,
Our spirits purified, our journey unbroken,
In the realm of the Duat, we shall find our way,
Guided by purification, every night and day.

So mote it be, let it be done,
Through the ritual of purification, our spirits are one,
In the realm of the Duat, we shall transcend,
Purified and cleansed, until the journey's end.

6. Spell for the opening of the gates of the celestial realms

By the power vested in ancient rites,
I invoke the forces, the celestial lights.
In the realm of gods, where mysteries unfold,
I call upon the gatekeeper, wise and bold.

O gatekeeper of the celestial realms divine,
Open the gates, let the light of stars shine.
Unveil the path, reveal the sacred way,
To the realm of gods, where spirits may sway.

With sacred words, I command the gates,
To part asunder, to reveal their fates.
Grant us access to the realms above,
Where wisdom resides and mysteries are wove.

Gatekeeper, hear my earnest plea,
Unlock the gates, set our spirits free.
Through the threshold, we seek to transcend,
To the celestial realms, where eternity extends.

With offerings of incense and sacred flame,
We honor your presence, we humbly acclaim.
Open the gates wide, let the journey begin,
To the celestial realms, where gods reside within.

Gatekeeper, keeper of celestial lore,
Guide us through realms never seen before.
Grant us passage, unveil the hidden keys,
To the realms where gods dwell, with grace and ease.

As the gates swing open, the barriers fade,
The celestial realms beckon, in their glory displayed.
Through the veil of stars, our spirits ascend,
To the realms of wisdom, where our destinies blend.

Gatekeeper, we thank you for your divine aid,
For opening the gates, for this celestial crusade.

May the wisdom of the gods forever shine,
As we traverse the realms, in their presence divine.

With reverence and gratitude, we step through the gate,
To the celestial realms, where time and space await.
May the journey be blessed, our spirits aligned,
As we explore the celestial realms, unconfined.

By the power of this spell, the gates are opened wide,
The celestial realms welcome us, with arms open wide.
We embark on this sacred quest, guided by celestial gleams,
To the realms of gods, where magic and destiny streams.

So it is spoken, so it is done,
Through the opening of gates, our journey's begun.
In the celestial realms, our spirits intertwine,
As we walk the path divine, with the gods aligned.

By the ancient rites and sacred words we've spoken,
The gates of the celestial realms have awoken.
With reverence and awe, we embark on this flight,
To the realms of gods, in eternal light.

7. Incantation to ward off evil spirits in the afterlife

By the power of ancient words and sacred lore,
I call upon the gods to protect evermore.
In the realm of shadows, where darkness dwells,
I invoke their might to break the wicked spells.

Evil spirits that linger, with malicious intent,
I command you to depart, to be banished and sent.
Leave this sacred realm, retreat from this place,
For the light of divine power shall now embrace.

With words of power and gestures of might,
I summon the guardians, shining in celestial light.
They shield the deceased from the malevolent sway,
In the afterlife's realm, where souls find their way.

By the sacred names of gods and goddesses revered,
I banish the darkness, and all that is feared.
No evil spirit shall trespass this sacred space,
For the divine protection guards this eternal embrace.

I invoke the power of Ra, the sun god so bright,
To dispel the shadows, to bring forth the light.
Let his radiant rays pierce through the night,
And banish all darkness with his celestial might.

With the strength of Isis, the compassionate queen,
I call upon her to intervene.
She wraps her wings around, offering solace and care,
Shielding the deceased from all that's unfair.

Horus, the falcon-headed god of divine sight,
I seek your protection, to guide through the night.
With your piercing gaze, evil spirits you shall see,
And with your mighty wings, banish them free.

By the power of Ma'at, the goddess of truth,
I restore balance and justice, from age to youth.

Let her feather of truth weigh hearts so fair,
And keep evil spirits at bay, with her righteous glare.

Through the incantations and the sacred flame,
I ward off evil spirits, their presence I tame.
May they vanish like mist, dissipate like smoke,
As the protective powers invoke.

In the afterlife's realm, where spirits reside,
No evil shall prevail, no harm shall betide.
For the deceased shall find peace and serenity,
Protected and guarded for all eternity.

So let it be known, so let it be done,
Evil spirits are banished, their presence undone.
In this sacred realm, harmony shall prevail,
As the protective incantation sets the sail.

By the power of divine guardians, both great and small,
I ward off evil spirits, protecting one and all.
In the afterlife's embrace, the deceased shall find rest,
Safe from the clutches of evil, forever blessed.

8. Ritual for the transformation of the deceased into a divine being

In this sacred hour, when life meets its end,
We gather here to honor and transcend.
With reverence and awe, we embark on this rite,
To elevate the deceased to a celestial height.

By the ancient wisdom and sacred decree,
We invoke the gods to set the spirit free.
Through ritual and chant, we seek to bestow,
Divinity upon the deceased, that they may glow.

We call upon Osiris, the great god of the dead,
To guide the soul on its journey ahead.
Grant transformation, O lord of the divine,
As the deceased transcends mortal confines.

With each incantation and sacred gesture made,
We invoke the power of Thoth, the scribe's aid.
Let the words of knowledge and wisdom imbue,
The deceased's spirit, as it transforms anew.

Horus, the falcon-headed god of the sky,
We beseech your presence, so mighty and high.
Lend your strength and grace to this sacred rite,
As the deceased ascends to celestial light.

Isis, the compassionate goddess of love,
Wrap your wings around, like a heavenly dove.
Infuse the deceased with your nurturing care,
As they embark on a journey beyond compare.

By the sacred fire, ablaze with divine might,
We purify and cleanse, removing all blight.
Let the flames of transformation ignite the soul,
As the deceased becomes part of a greater whole.

Through the rituals of embalmment and adornment,
We prepare the body for its divine moment.

Anoint with sacred oils, with fragrances divine,
Enhancing the spirit's radiance and shine.

With each step of the ritual, we draw near,
To the moment of transformation, crystal clear.
The deceased shall transcend, their essence refined,
Into a divine being, forever enshrined.

As the ritual concludes, we stand in awe,
Witnessing the transformation, without a flaw.
The deceased, now radiant, with celestial grace,
Embarks on a journey to an eternal embrace.

May they find peace in the realm of the divine,
As a transformed being, forever to shine.
In the annals of gods, their name shall be sung,
As the deceased becomes one, with the celestial throng.

Thus, we conclude this ritual with reverence and prayer,
May the transformed deceased find eternal solace there.
Their spirit uplifted, their essence set free,
As they embrace their divine destiny.

9. Invocation of the god Thoth for wisdom and guidance

Oh Thoth, mighty god of knowledge and wisdom,
I beseech your presence in this sacred rhythm.
With heart open wide and reverence sincere,
I call upon you to lend your wisdom, oh seer.

Bearer of the written word and the celestial pen,
Guide me with your insight, again and again.
Grant me clarity of thought and a keen intellect,
Illuminate my path, your wisdom I reflect.

Oh Thoth, who knows the secrets of the universe,
I seek your counsel, I humbly rehearse.
Bestow upon me the gift of discernment,
That I may navigate life with enlightened intent.

With your ibis head and writing palette in hand,
You record the cosmic order, oh god so grand.
Your knowledge spans realms, both seen and unseen,
I implore your guidance, as I journey between.

Inscribe upon my heart the sacred hieroglyphs,
Unlock the mysteries, reveal the hidden shifts.
Let your wisdom flow through me, like a sacred stream,
Awakening my consciousness, fulfilling my dream.

Oh Thoth, I seek your wisdom, as ancient as time,
Grant me insight, let your knowledge be mine.
Illuminate my mind, expand my understanding,
With your divine guidance, my path commanding.

As I invoke your presence, may my words find flight,
And bring forth wisdom, like the stars shining bright.
In your name, Thoth, I seek wisdom's embrace,
Guide me, enlighten me, with your eternal grace.

Oh Thoth, god of wisdom, I offer my devotion,

May your presence guide me with unwavering motion.
In your divine wisdom, may I find solace and truth,
Grant me your guidance, in age and in youth.

Hail Thoth, the keeper of knowledge and light,
I honor your wisdom, with reverence so bright.
Guide me on the path of enlightenment's quest,
With your wisdom, I am eternally blessed.

10. Spell for the rejuvenation of the deceased's body in the afterlife

By the power of the sacred rites, I call upon the divine,
To restore life's vigor to this body of mine.
From the realm of the living to the realm beyond,
Grant me rejuvenation, let vitality respond.

With sacred oils and balms, I anoint my form,
Revitalizing flesh, renewing in the norm.
Let the energies of life surge through every vein,
As I traverse the realms, free from mortal chain.

O Osiris, great lord of resurrection and rebirth,
Bless me with your grace, restore my earthly worth.
In the realm of eternity, let my body thrive,
As I embrace immortality, truly alive.

From head to toe, let youthfulness unfold,
As the divine energy heals, within me it's enrolled.
Renew my skin, rejuvenate my limbs,
Grant me strength and vitality, as the light dims.

Oh, rejuvenating powers, weave your magic deep,
Awaken dormant cells, secrets you shall keep.
Let the vigor of youth flow through my being,
In the afterlife's realm, a radiant being I'm foreseeing.

Oh, sacred gods and goddesses of eternal life,
Bless me with your essence, alleviate strife.
Revive my senses, let my eyes shine bright,
In the afterlife's embrace, I reclaim my divine right.

Through the ancient rites and incantations spoken,
Let the rejuvenation process be awoken.
From the realm of the living to the realm beyond,
Grant me eternal youth, forever abscond.

As I journey through the afterlife's vast expanse,

May my body be renewed, granted a second chance.
By the power of the divine, this spell is cast,
Rejuvenation awaits, as the future becomes the past.

In the realm of eternity, I stand anew,
A vessel of youth, vibrant and true.
Forever preserved, my body shall remain,
In the afterlife's embrace, free from decay's reign.

By the divine forces of life's eternal flow,
I am rejuvenated, with radiance aglow.
Through the cycles of death and rebirth,
I transcend mortality, embracing eternal worth.

So mote it be, in the realm of the divine,
Rejuvenation's magic, forever shall shine.
In the afterlife's realm, I find eternal repose,
A rejuvenated being, forever it shows.

11. Ritual of offering to Osiris, the lord of the dead

In the sacred chamber of reverence and grace,
I come forth to offer in this sacred space.
Oh Osiris, mighty lord of the departed,
Accept my offerings, pure and wholehearted.

With reverence and devotion, I approach your shrine,
To honor your presence, divine and sublime.
I bring forth offerings, symbols of life's sustenance,
To nourish your essence in eternal continuance.

Oh Osiris, ruler of the realms unseen,
Accept these gifts, bestowed with love so keen.
As the lord of the dead, your wisdom profound,
Guide me in the afterlife, where mysteries abound.

I offer you bread, symbol of sustenance and nourishment,
To feed your divine essence, in this sacred moment.
May it provide you strength, as you guide souls on their way,
Through the depths of the Duat, where darkness holds sway.

I offer you water, pure and life-giving,
To quench your eternal thirst, as you keep on living.
May it cleanse and purify, the essence of your being,
As you preside over the souls, beyond mortal seeing.

I offer you incense, fragrant and ethereal,
Its smoke rising high, reaching realms celestial.
May its aroma carry my prayers and devotion,
To the heavens above, where you reside in motion.

I offer you flowers, symbols of beauty and bloom,
Their vibrant colors, dispelling darkness and gloom.
May their petals adorn your eternal abode,
As a testament of life, in the afterlife bestowed.

Oh Osiris, lord of the dead, accept my humble plea,
As I honor your divinity, in this sacred decree.

May my offerings be pleasing, in your divine sight,
As I seek your guidance, through eternal night.

With utmost reverence, I present these gifts to thee,
Oh Osiris, ruler of eternity's decree.
Accept my offerings, with your divine grace,
As I honor your presence, in this sacred space.

In the realm of the dead, may your blessings unfold,
Guiding me on the journey, as my destiny is told.
Oh Osiris, lord of the departed and the wise,
Accept my offerings, as I embrace the afterlife's prize.

So mote it be, with reverence and respect,
In this sacred ritual, my heart does reflect.
Osiris, accept my offerings and hear my plea,
As I honor your divinity, for all eternity.

12. Spell for protection against hostile forces in the underworld

By the power of ancient rites and sacred lore,
I call upon the guardians of the underworld's door.
In this realm of shadows and darkness profound,
I seek your protection, safe and sound.

From hostile forces that lurk in the abyss,
I invoke your power, with this heartfelt wish.
Guard my spirit with your divine shield,
As I navigate the underworld, my fate to wield.

I call upon Anubis, the jackal-headed guide,
With your wisdom and strength, stand by my side.
Keep at bay the malevolent spirits that roam,
Protect me as I journey to my eternal home.

Horus, falcon-headed deity of the sky,
Unleash your divine power, on wings that fly.
Shield me from the forces of chaos and strife,
Guard my soul on this journey, throughout my afterlife.

Isis, goddess of magic and protection divine,
Wrap your wings around me, like a celestial shrine.
With your love and compassion, keep me safe,
In this realm of shadows, where dangers chafe.

Oh Sekhmet, lioness of ferocious might,
Defend me against the terrors of the night.
With your fiery essence, burn away the foe,
Shield me from harm, wherever I may go.

I call upon Bastet, graceful and wise,
With your fierce guardianship, evils will demise.
As the lioness and the serpent intertwine,
Protect my spirit, make it eternally shine.

Great Thoth, god of knowledge and divine law,
Grant me insight and protection, without flaw.

Guide me through the labyrinthine paths I tread,
Shield me from danger, by your wisdom spread.

With the power of Ra, the radiant sun,
I am imbued with strength, as a chosen one.
Illuminate my path, banish darkness and despair,
Protect me from all harm, with your golden glare.

Oh mighty deities of the ancient realm,
Protect me with your power, steadfast and helm.
Guard me against the hostile forces that arise,
In the underworld's depths, where darkness lies.

By the ancient spells and invocations true,
I am shielded from harm, my spirit anew.
Protect me, oh guardians of the afterlife's domain,
In your embrace, may my soul forever remain.

So it is spoken, so it shall be done,
In this sacred spell, protection is won.
By the divine forces that I now invoke,
I am safeguarded from danger, in the underworld's cloak.

May this spell's power endure throughout time,
Guarding me against darkness, sublime.
With gratitude and reverence, I give my plea,
Protect me, guardians, for all eternity.

13. Incantation to pacify the gods of judgment and attain mercy

Oh, gods of judgment, hear my plea,
I stand before you, humbly on my knee.
In the realm of the afterlife, I seek your grace,
To find mercy and forgiveness in this sacred space.

I call upon Osiris, wise and just,
With your scales of truth, in you I place my trust.
May your heart be swayed by my sincere remorse,
Grant me mercy, with your divine course.

Oh, Thoth, the scribe of the gods' decree,
Let your words of wisdom intercede for me.
Guide the judgment process, with impartiality,
May your voice resonate, to grant clemency.

Isis, mother of compassion and love,
Wrap me in your nurturing wings from above.
Softened be the hearts of the gods who judge,
As I invoke your name, my soul won't budge.

Horus, falcon-eyed lord of the sky,
As I call upon you, may your justice comply.
Lend me your strength, noble and true,
To appease the gods, with a merciful view.

I offer my remorse, my plea sincere,
With contrition and repentance, let it appear.
I stand before you, ready to atone,
In your divine presence, my sins are known.

May my heart be light as a feather's weight,
Free from darkness, purified by fate.
Grant me absolution, oh gods above,
In your mercy, let me find eternal love.

As I speak these words, with utmost devotion,
May the gods be moved by my heartfelt emotion.

Pacify their judgment, let mercy prevail,
In the afterlife's realm, where souls set sail.

So it is spoken, so it shall be done,
In this sacred incantation, my fate is spun.
I seek the gods' forgiveness, with utmost plea,
Grant me mercy, in the realm of eternity.

By the power of these words, let mercy be my guide,
May the gods of judgment, my soul's destiny decide.
With reverence and contrition, I call upon your divine grace,
Pacify your judgment, and let mercy embrace.

Oh gods of judgment, hear my plea,
Grant me mercy, set my spirit free.
In this realm of the afterlife, I find solace,
As I seek your divine mercy, with unwavering grace.

14. Ritual for the merging of the ba and the ka

In this sacred rite, I stand before the divine,
To unite the ba and the ka, in a celestial design.
With reverence and devotion, I call upon the ancient powers,
To merge these essences, in this sacred hour.

Ba, the soul's unique manifestation,
Ka, the life force's vibrant incarnation,
Come together now, in harmonious embrace,
Merge as one, in this sacred space.

Oh, ba, freed from mortal strife,
Soar on wings of eternal life.
Oh, ka, essence of vitality and might,
Merge with the ba, in celestial flight.

Let the ba be a guiding star,
Leading the ka, near and far.
Together, they shall traverse the divine plane,
Bound as one, in unity's reign.

I invoke the divine essence of Osiris,
Lord of the underworld, where souls find bliss.
Grant your blessing upon this merging affair,
As the ba and the ka become a unified pair.

Isis, mother of life and magic profound,
Wrap your nurturing presence all around.
Infuse this union with your divine grace,
Embrace the ba and ka, in an eternal embrace.

Horus, falcon-eyed deity of protection and might,
Bless this merging with your celestial light.
Guide this sacred fusion, with unwavering care,
As ba and ka become one, a sacred pair.

With the power of the ancient gods combined,
Let this merging of ba and ka be signed.
In the realm of eternity, let their unity be sealed,

A transcendent union, never to be repealed.

As I speak these words with reverence and devotion,
Let the merging of ba and ka be set in motion.
In this sacred rite, their essence intertwines,
An eternal bond, where the divine aligns.

By the power of these words and the gods' decree,
Let the ba and ka become unified, eternally free.
In the realm of the afterlife, their union will endure,
A sacred fusion, pure and secure.

As I complete this ritual, with reverence and awe,
May the merging of ba and ka be forevermore.
United in spirit, in the realm of divine delight,
A harmonious blend, shining ever bright.

15. Spell for the awakening of the deceased's consciousness in the afterlife

By the power of the ancient ones, I invoke,
A spell to awaken the deceased's consciousness, evoke.
From the depths of slumber, rise and be aware,
In the afterlife's realm, let your consciousness flare.

Oh, departed soul, once bound by earthly ties,
Awaken now, let your spirit rise.
Shake off the veil of forgetfulness and sleep,
Embrace the realm of the afterlife, your secrets to keep.

Let your senses be sharp, your mind be clear,
In this sacred realm, devoid of mortal fear.
Awaken to the wonders of the celestial domain,
Where mysteries unravel, and truths remain.

By the sacred name of Ra, the sun god divine,
Let your consciousness ignite, let it brightly shine.
From the depths of darkness, emerge into the light,
Embrace the knowledge, the eternal insight.

Open your eyes to the celestial sights unseen,
Let the wisdom of the ancients, in your soul convene.
Feel the pulsating energy of the afterlife's embrace,
As your consciousness awakens, ready to embrace.

Oh, departed one, hear my fervent call,
Awaken your consciousness, stand tall.
Recall the memories of your earthly existence,
As you embark on this spiritual journey of immense significance.

Let your thoughts be clear, your understanding profound,
As your consciousness expands, let wisdom surround.
Awaken to the truths of the afterlife's lore,
With each passing moment, your consciousness restore.

By the power of this spell, by the gods' decree,

Let the deceased's consciousness awaken and be free.
In the realm of the afterlife, let awareness bloom,
A conscious existence, transcending mortal gloom.

As I speak these words with reverence and might,
Let the deceased's consciousness ignite.
Awaken, oh soul, to the realm of eternal grace,
In the afterlife's embrace, find your destined place.

So be it, by the power of this sacred decree,
Awakened consciousness, now let it be.
In the afterlife's realm, may you forever thrive,
With awakened consciousness, truly alive.

16. Invocation of the goddess Isis for healing and resurrection

Oh, mighty Isis, goddess of healing and rebirth,
I beseech thee, grace us with your divine worth.
With wings outstretched, encompassing love and care,
Bring forth your healing magic, banishing despair.

Goddess of the sacred waters, source of life's flow,
From the depths of your wisdom, let healing energies grow.
In your compassionate embrace, let all ailments be relieved,
Renew our spirits, grant us the strength to believe.

Isis, mother of all, with your nurturing touch,
Bring healing to bodies, minds, and souls, as such.
Unveil your healing wings, encompassing and wide,
Let your soothing presence be felt by our side.

Goddess of resurrection, mighty and wise,
Guide us through the darkness, where hope often dies.
With your power, bring forth renewal and rejuvenation,
Revive our weary spirits, grant us transformation.

Isis, the compassionate one, with love we implore,
Restore our health, let vitality be restored.
From illness and suffering, may we be set free,
As your healing energy flows through you and me.

Oh, great Isis, with your potent healing art,
Mend our broken bodies, mend each wounded heart.
With your divine intervention, restore us to wholeness,
Grant us the gift of healing, in your loving caress.

By the might of your sacred name, Isis, we call,
Heal us, restore us, make us whole, one and all.
With your magic and love, let healing light shine,
Resurrect us, oh goddess, with powers divine.

We offer our gratitude, our devotion, and praise,
To the goddess of healing, who guides us through haze.

With reverence and trust, we seek your intervention,
Isis, goddess of healing, bring us resurrection.

So mote it be, in the name of Isis, the goddess of healing and resurrection,
May her blessings restore us and lead us to divine perfection.

17. Ritual of embalming to preserve the body in the afterlife

In the sacred chamber, where life meets death's embrace,
We gather to perform the ancient rite in sacred space.
With reverence and care, we prepare for the final rest,
Preserving the vessel, ensuring it is truly blessed.

O Anubis, jackal-headed guardian of the necropolis,
Guide our hands, grant us your wisdom and expertise.
With precise movements and sacred tools in hand,
We embark on the ritual, a task both divine and grand.

Lay the deceased upon the sacred table, serene and still,
Anointed with oils, their essence to preserve and fulfill.
With gentle touch, cleanse the body, purify and mend,
Removing impurities, ensuring their journey won't end.

Oh, wise Thoth, with your scales of judgment in hand,
Witness our endeavor, let our actions be grand.
Guard the integrity of the spirit, the essence within,
As we honor the deceased, preserving their form, akin.

Herbs and resins, carefully selected and mixed,
Perfume the air, warding off decay, the soul bewitched.
Wrap the body in linen, layer upon layer, bound tight,
Ensuring its protection in the eternal night.

Amulets of power, placed upon the mummified chest,
Guard against malevolent forces, bring peace and rest.
With sacred words and incantations, spoken with intent,
Invoke the gods, their blessings, their divine consent.

Oh, Osiris, lord of the underworld, embrace the deceased,
Grant them passage to the afterlife, where they shall find peace.
May their body remain intact, their spirit everlasting,
Through the ritual of embalming, their journey we're casting.

In the hallowed halls of the necropolis, the process complete,
The preserved body, a vessel for the soul, a sacred feat.

May the deceased find solace in the realm beyond,
As their body rests in peace, forever to respond.

By the power of ancient rites, by the gods' decree,
The ritual of embalming fulfills its purpose, you see.
Preserving the body, honoring the spirit within,
In the afterlife's embrace, let their journey begin.

So mote it be, in the name of the gods we adore,
May this embalming ritual protect forevermore.
As the deceased traverses the realm of the divine,
May their body remain intact, their spirit ever-shine.

18. Spell for the reunion of the deceased with their loved ones in the afterlife

By the sacred veil that separates life and death,
I call upon the powers of the eternal breath.
With words of power, I summon the divine,
To bridge the realms and intertwine.

Oh, great Hathor, goddess of love and joy,
Unite the departed with those they hold dear, oh boy.
Across the realms, let their souls find each other,
Rekindle bonds, a reunion like no other.

Through the veil of eternity, let them pass,
Guided by Anubis, guardian of the sacred mass.
Lead them to their loved ones, long gone,
In the realm of the afterlife, where they belong.

Oh, beloved Osiris, ruler of the eternal realm,
Grant them the joy of reunion, overwhelm.
May their spirits dance with delight,
As they embrace, dispelling the night.

With open arms and hearts aflame,
Let their love ignite, reclaim its name.
No longer separated by earthly demise,
They find solace and love in the celestial skies.

Through the depths of the Duat, they traverse,
Finding solace in the reunion, an eternal verse.
May their spirits intertwine like vines in bloom,
Reunited, destined to forever consume.

By the power of this spell, by the gods' decree,
I call upon the cosmic forces, let it be.
Bring together the departed and their beloved kin,
In the afterlife's embrace, let the reunion begin.

So mote it be, let the spirits unite,
In the realm of the afterlife, where love takes flight.

May their bond be eternal, unbreakable, and true,
As they find each other, anew.

Through the veils of time and space, they find,
Their loved ones' presence, forever entwined.
In the afterlife's embrace, they shall remain,
United in love, never to wane.

With this spell, their reunion is sealed,
In the realm beyond, where destinies are revealed.
May their souls find peace and eternal bliss,
United forever, in love's eternal kiss.

So mote it be, in the name of the divine,
Let the reunion of souls forever shine.
In the afterlife's realm, love conquers all,
As the departed answer love's eternal call.

19. Incantation to communicate with animal spirits in the underworld

Oh, mighty Anubis, guardian of the threshold,
I beseech you to grant me the power untold.
Through the realms of the underworld I tread,
To commune with the spirits of creatures long dead.

With sacred words and reverence, I implore,
Let me speak with the animals who've gone before.
In the depths of the Duat, where their essence lies,
Grant me the gift to hear their whispers and cries.

By the power of Ma'at, the balance divine,
May my words reach the animal spirits in kind.
Through the rivers of time, let our connection be,
As I enter their world with respect and humility.

Oh, wise Thoth, god of knowledge and speech,
Guide my words as I reach for what's beyond reach.
Grant me the ability to understand their desires,
To listen to their wisdom and quench their fires.

Let the spirits of lions, proud and fierce,
Roar their stories, their strength to pierce.
May the birds, with wings spread wide,
Share their songs and secrets as my guides.

Oh, graceful gazelles and mighty elephants,
Share with me your memories, your elegant stances.
Let the snakes, with their wisdom so deep,
Teach me the secrets they've vowed to keep.

Through the veil of the afterlife's mist,
I call upon the spirits of animals, I insist.
With open heart and mind, I seek their guidance,
To learn from their spirits, in this sacred alliance.

By the sacred flame that burns bright and pure,
I summon their essence, their essence so sure.

Grant me the gift to understand their plight,
To bridge the gap between our worlds, day and night.

In the silence of the underworld's embrace,
I listen to the whispers, the echoes of their grace.
Their presence surrounds me, like a gentle breeze,
Their wisdom flows through me, putting my soul at ease.

Oh, animal spirits, I honor your existence,
I seek your guidance, your divine assistance.
In this communion, let our spirits align,
As we journey together, in harmony divine.

With gratitude and respect, I bid them farewell,
Knowing their presence in my heart shall dwell.
May their lessons and wisdom forever endure,
As I honor their spirits, pure and sure.

So mote it be, as I travel this sacred path,
Communicating with animal spirits in the aftermath.
In the underworld's depths, our connection is made,
Guided by their wisdom, in this realm and beyond, I'll wade.

20. Ritual for the guidance of the deceased through the celestial spheres

By the light of the stars, I invoke the cosmic powers,
To guide the departed through celestial hours.
With reverence and devotion, I call upon the divine,
To navigate the heavenly realms, a sacred sign.

Oh, great Ra, the radiant sun above,
Illuminate the path with your eternal love.
Guide the soul of the departed, shining bright,
Through the celestial spheres, from day to night.

Oh, celestial beings, guardians of the astral plane,
I beseech your aid, let your wisdom reign.
Lead the departed through the realms unseen,
With your celestial guidance, serene and keen.

By the power of Nut, the sky's vast embrace,
May the departed traverse with celestial grace.
Through the stars and planets, their journey unfurls,
Navigating the cosmic map, traveling in swirls.

Oh, wise Thoth, the scribe of celestial lore,
Unveil the mysteries, let them explore.
With your wisdom and knowledge, they shall ascend,
Through the celestial spheres, their journey transcend.

Let the constellation of Orion light the way,
Guiding the departed through the night and day.
The North Star, Polaris, a steadfast guide,
Leading them to their celestial destiny, far and wide.

Oh, shimmering moon, with your gentle glow,
Illuminate their path as they ascend and grow.
With each phase, a new realm to explore,
Through the celestial spheres, forevermore.

May the planets align, a celestial dance,
Guiding the departed with cosmic circumstance.

From Mercury's wisdom to Jupiter's might,
Each planet's energy aiding their celestial flight.

Oh, sacred Hathor, goddess of love and light,
Wrap the departed in your embrace, shining bright.
Let your nurturing presence guide their way,
Through the celestial spheres, where they shall stay.

With each celestial sphere they traverse and pass,
The departed find enlightenment and solace, en masse.
Guided by the celestial forces, their journey unfolds,
Through the cosmic realms, their destiny foretold.

Oh, divine cosmic beings, I offer my plea,
Guide the departed, set their spirits free.
Through the celestial spheres, their essence shall soar,
Embracing the cosmic harmony forevermore.

By the power of the celestial realms, I decree,
The departed shall find peace and serenity.
Guided by the celestial forces, their souls ascend,
Through the celestial spheres, their journey shall transcend.

So mote it be, as above, so below,
In the celestial spheres, their spirits shall glow.
With gratitude and reverence, I honor their flight,
Guided by celestial beings, into eternal light.

21. Spell for the protection of the deceased's tomb from desecration

In the sacred land where my body rests,
I call upon the gods to grant their behest.
With this incantation, I weave a shield,
To protect my tomb, my eternal field.

Oh, Anubis, guardian of the necropolis,
With your watchful eye, secure my metropolis.
Keep my tomb hidden from the profane,
Let no trespassers disturb my domain.

Oh, mighty Horus, falcon of divine sight,
Spread your wings, ward off any blight.
Guard the entrance with your majestic gaze,
Protect my tomb from intruders' craze.

By the power of Ptah, the master of creation,
Fortify the walls, a divine foundation.
Let no harm befall the sacred burial ground,
Preserve its sanctity, let serenity abound.

I call upon Osiris, the lord of the dead,
Wrap my tomb in your protective thread.
Shield it from thieves and those who defile,
Preserve its sanctity, mile after mile.

Oh, Sekhmet, fierce lioness of divine wrath,
Roar in defense of my sacred path.
Let your fiery breath consume any ill intent,
Protect my tomb, a haven heaven-sent.

By the authority of Ma'at, the goddess of truth,
Ensure that my tomb remains aloof.
Let no chaos or disorder disturb its peace,
May harmony and order forever increase.

I invoke the spirits of my ancestors past,
Stand as sentinels, steadfast and fast.

Guard my tomb with ancestral might,
Protect it from harm, both day and night.

By the sacred words I speak and decree,
I shield my tomb from desecration's glee.
May the guardians of the afterlife stand tall,
Preserving my resting place, one and all.

Let this spell bind and seal,
The protection of my tomb, its sacred appeal.
May it be guarded by ancient divine grace,
Preserving its sanctity, a hallowed space.

22. Invocation of the god Anubis for safe passage in the afterlife

Oh, Anubis, mighty guide of the deceased,
With your jackal-headed form, hear my plea.
As I journey through the realm of the dead,
Grant me your protection, a path safely led.

Guardian of the scales, judge of the heart,
I call upon you to play your sacred part.
Guide me through the Duat's treacherous way,
Keep me from straying, lead me astray.

Oh, Anubis, opener of the hidden gate,
I seek your aid, I humbly prostrate.
As I navigate the land of shadows and night,
Shine your light, dispel the darkness with might.

With your keen eyes and unwavering gaze,
Watch over me in the uncertain haze.
Guide my ka, my essence, to its destined place,
In the sacred realm, grant me solace and grace.

Anubis, protector of the embalmed heart,
Keep me safe from chaos, from evil's dart.
Shield me from the malevolent forces that lurk,
Let them not harm me, nor their presence irk.

As I embark on this otherworldly quest,
I trust in your wisdom, I feel truly blessed.
Lead me through the perils, the tests I face,
With your guidance, I find solace and embrace.

Anubis, loyal companion of the divine,
Be by my side as I cross the sacred line.
Safe passage I seek in the afterlife's domain,
Under your watchful eye, I shall remain.

I offer my reverence, my faith unwavering,
To you, Anubis, my trust unhesitating.

Guide me through the realm of eternal rest,
Grant me safe passage, as I am truly blessed.

23. Ritual of anointing with sacred oils for spiritual purification

In the sacred chamber of the temple's embrace,
Gather the oils, blessed by divine grace.
Anoint the body with reverence and care,
Let the fragrance cleanse, purify the air.

With sacred herbs and resins, blend the concoction,
Infused with prayers and profound devotion.
From lotus to myrrh, their essence combined,
A potion of purity, in which the spirit will find.

In silence and stillness, the ritual begins,
As the oils touch the flesh, a sacred hymn.
From head to toe, let the anointing unfold,
A transformation of the spirit, a story untold.

The oils, a balm, caress the weary soul,
Releasing the burdens that once took their toll.
They wash away the stains of earthly strife,
Restoring the spirit to its innate divine life.

As the fragrance rises, let it permeate the air,
A symphony of scents, a sacred prayer.
May it carry the intentions of love and light,
Lifting the spirit to celestial heights.

With each stroke, blessings are bestowed,
A sacred energy, a heavenly road.
Anoint the body, the vessel of the soul,
With oils of healing, making the spirit whole.

As the oils absorb, let the spirit awaken,
With every cell, a divine connection unshaken.
Purified, renewed, the soul's essence restored,
In this sacred ritual, the spirit is adored.

24. Spell for the transformation of the deceased into a star in the heavens

By the sacred rites of cosmic decree,
I invoke the powers that set the soul free.
In the realm of the heavens, let it be known,
A transformation divine, a celestial throne.

From earthly form to celestial light,
The soul takes flight, shining so bright.
Release the shackles of mortality's hold,
Embrace the destiny the heavens unfold.

With each breath, let the essence rise,
A radiant spark, reaching the skies.
Through the veil of eternity, the soul ascends,
Embracing the cosmic dance that never ends.

Oh, ancient stars, guide the soul's way,
Illuminate the path, night and day.
Let the celestial bodies align and proclaim,
A new star is born, forever to remain.

As the body rests in the earthly tomb,
The spirit soars, dispelling all gloom.
Transformed into stardust, forever to roam,
A luminary presence, an ethereal home.

In the heavens above, a radiant gleam,
A testament to the soul's eternal dream.
A beacon of light, a celestial art,
The deceased, now a star, forever a part.

25. Incantation to unlock the hidden knowledge of the cosmic mysteries

By the ancient words of power and might,
I call upon the cosmic realm tonight.
Open the doors to the mysteries unknown,
Reveal the wisdom that has long been sown.

From the depths of the universe profound,
Let the secrets of creation resound.
Unveil the ancient truths, hidden and veiled,
That which the mortal mind has not yet unveiled.

O cosmic forces, guardians of knowledge vast,
Grant me access to the wisdom that will last.
Remove the barriers that obscure the way,
Illuminate the path, let enlightenment sway.

Through the realms of stars and celestial light,
Guide me to the wisdom, shining so bright.
Unlock the scrolls of time, ancient and wise,
Reveal the cosmic truths, hidden in disguise.

With every word spoken, let the veil grow thin,
Allow the mysteries to enter deep within.
Transcend the boundaries of mortal sight,
Embrace the cosmic knowledge, pure and bright.

Oh, cosmic universe, grant me this request,
To delve into the mysteries that manifest.
Unlock the hidden wisdom, let it be unfurled,
As I seek the cosmic truths of this grand world.

26. Ritual of offering to the god Ra for eternal illumination

Gather before the radiant sun,
In reverence, our ritual begun.
We seek the blessings of Ra, the divine,
Whose light and warmth eternally shine.

With hearts aglow and spirits raised,
We offer our gifts, our voices praised.
Bring forth the sacred offerings bright,
Symbolic tokens of our devotion's might.

Beneath the golden rays, we stand,
A humble gesture, in awe of the grand.
Fruits of the earth, fresh and sweet,
Nourishment for the god we greet.

Incense rises, its fragrant smoke,
A bridge between mortal and divine spoke.
Its swirling tendrils reach the sky,
Carrying our prayers, as they fly high.

With words of praise, we sing and speak,
Our gratitude to Ra, we humbly seek.
For in his light, we find our way,
Guided by the sun's eternal ray.

Oh, Ra, mighty ruler of the celestial sphere,
Grant us illumination, both far and near.
Bless us with wisdom, knowledge, and might,
As we walk in your eternal light.

The Ritual of Offering to the God Ra for Eternal Illumination is a sacred ceremony dedicated to the sun god Ra, symbolizing the quest for spiritual enlightenment and eternal light. While the specifics of such a ritual may vary, here is an imaginative depiction of what it could look like:

The ritual takes place at a temple or a sacred site dedicated to Ra, ideally situated to capture the rays of the sun. The participants, dressed in elaborate white and gold robes, gather in a courtyard or an open space adorned with symbolic representations of the sun, such as solar discs and falcon motifs.

As the sun begins to rise on the horizon, casting a warm and golden glow, the priests and priestesses initiate the ceremony. They stand in a procession, carrying ornate trays filled with offerings, including fruits, flowers, incense, and precious objects symbolizing abundance and divinity.

A grand altar stands at the center of the gathering, elevated to catch the first rays of the rising sun. It is adorned with golden statues and intricate carvings representing Ra and other solar deities. The altar is also embellished with reflective surfaces like polished gold and mirrors, enhancing the brilliance of the sunlight.

The participants form a circle around the altar, facing eastward towards the rising sun. The air is filled with a sense of reverence and anticipation as they prepare to honor Ra and seek his divine illumination.

The ceremony commences with invocations and hymns, praising the majesty and power of Ra. The priests and priestesses chant ancient verses, their voices rising and falling in harmony, as they beseech Ra's benevolence and guidance.

As the sun ascends higher in the sky, its radiant rays envelop the sacred space. At this moment, the priests and priestesses begin the act of offering. They present the sacred objects and gifts to the altar, carefully arranging them in a symbolic display of devotion and gratitude.

Each offering is accompanied by prayers, expressing heartfelt intentions and aspirations for eternal enlightenment, wisdom, and spiritual illumination. The participants, guided by the priests and priestesses, offer their personal prayers and wishes, seeking Ra's blessing and the eternal light he represents.

Incense is lit, its fragrant smoke rising towards the heavens, carrying the prayers and intentions of the participants to Ra. The sun's rays, intensified by the reflective surfaces on the altar, create a mesmerizing play of light and shadows, infusing the space with an ethereal ambiance.

Throughout the ritual, the priests and priestesses perform sacred gestures and rituals, invoking the presence of Ra and symbolically merging their own divine essence with the solar deity. Their movements mimic the celestial dance of the sun, evoking a sense of unity and harmony with the cosmic forces.

As the ceremony reaches its climax, the participants collectively raise their arms towards the sun, as if embracing its radiant energy. They close their eyes and bask in its warm embrace, allowing the divine light to touch their souls and illuminate their spirits.

The ritual concludes with a final prayer, expressing gratitude to Ra for his blessings and eternal illumination. The participants depart from the sacred space, carrying the essence of the sun's divine energy within them, and the belief that Ra's light will guide them on their spiritual journey.

27. Spell for the liberation of the deceased's soul from earthly attachments

By the power of the sacred divine,
I call upon the forces, ancient and sublime.
With words of might and intentions clear,
I release the soul from earthly ties, oh seer.

Bound no longer to this mortal plane,
The soul seeks freedom, its essence to reclaim.
No chains shall hold it, no bonds confine,
For it is destined to transcend the earthly line.

I call upon the winds, wild and free,
To carry the soul to its destiny.
Away from earthly sorrows and strife,
Embracing the eternal, the afterlife.

With the sacred incantations I speak,
I sever the ties that bind the soul, so weak.
Let go of attachments, release the pain,
Embrace the light, the spiritual domain.

By the powers of the divine decree,
The soul shall soar, liberated and free.
No longer burdened by mortal desires,
It ascends to realms higher and higher.

Oh, divine forces, hear my plea,
Guide the soul to its destiny.
In the realm of eternal bliss and grace,
Let the deceased find solace in their rightful place.

28. Invocation of the goddess Sekhmet for protection and strength

Mighty Sekhmet, lioness fierce and bold,
I invoke your presence, ancient and untold.
Goddess of power, protector divine,
Grant me your strength, make it truly mine.

With fiery eyes that pierce the night,
With a roar that echoes, igniting fright,
Sekhmet, I call upon your mighty name,
Bestow upon me courage, free from shame.

Wrap me in your cloak of fiery might,
Shield me from harm, dispel the blight.
With your fierce claws and sacred flame,
Keep me safe, from fear and pain.

Oh Sekhmet, Lady of the Sun's embrace,
Grant me your protection in every place.
In battles fought, both seen and unseen,
Guide me, oh Goddess, in all I deem.

I honor you, Sekhmet, with reverence deep,
As I invoke your power, both fierce and steep.
Grant me your strength, in this mortal quest,
And with your blessing, I shall be blessed.

29. Ritual for the transfiguration of the deceased into a divine light being

In the realm of transition, where shadows dwell,
I call upon the cosmic forces, spirits to compel.
Through this sacred rite, transformation I seek,
To transcend the mortal coil, to rise and peak.

With offerings of incense, sweet and pure,
I invoke the divine light that shall endure.
I stand in reverence, in this sacred space,
To witness the ascension, the soul's embrace.

O mighty ones, guardians of the celestial plane,
Grant me passage, release from earthly chain.
In this ritual of transfiguration, I prepare,
To shed the mortal shell, and become rare.

Let the flames of transformation rise high,
As I release the limitations, bidding them goodbye.
From mortal to divine, from flesh to light,
I surrender to the currents of celestial might.

In this sacred union, body and spirit align,
As I become a radiant being, pure and divine.
Transcending boundaries, embracing the sublime,
I soar with wings of light, transcending time.

As the ritual concludes, I emerge anew,
A divine light being, shining through.
I walk the path of eternity, bathed in grace,
Embracing the cosmic dance, in every space.

The Ritual for the Transfiguration of the Deceased into a Divine Light Being is a sacred ceremony that represents the ultimate transformation of the soul into a celestial entity. While the specifics of such a ritual may vary, here is an imaginative depiction of what it could entail:

The ritual takes place in a temple or sacred space specially prepared for this profound ceremony. The atmosphere is charged with a sense of awe and reverence, as priests and attendants gather, adorned in white or golden garments symbolizing purity and divine illumination.

At the center of the sacred space stands an intricately crafted altar, adorned with sacred symbols and lit with candles and incense. It radiates a soft, ethereal glow, reflecting the divine presence invoked for the transfiguration.

The body of the deceased, carefully prepared and anointed, rests on a ceremonial bier or platform before the altar. It is positioned to face the ascending path of the sun, symbolizing the journey of the soul towards its divine destiny.

The ritual begins with melodic chants and invocations, sung by a chorus of priests and priestesses. The hauntingly beautiful melodies reverberate throughout the space, creating an atmosphere of transcendence and sacred energy.

As the chants reach a crescendo, a high priest or priestess steps forward, bearing a sacred object such as a crystal or an amulet representing divine light. They hold it aloft, allowing it to catch the light and refract radiant beams in all directions.

The high priest or priestess moves gracefully around the body of the deceased, channeling divine energy and invoking the blessings of the celestial realms. They may gently touch the body with the sacred object, infusing it with the transformative power of light.

At this pivotal moment, a beam of sunlight, carefully channeled through a precisely positioned aperture or skylight, bathes the body in a celestial glow. The radiant sunlight symbolizes the divine essence infusing the deceased, initiating their transfiguration into a luminous being.

The attending priests and priestesses raise their arms in unison, forming a sacred circle around the body. Their hands emit gentle streams of golden or white light, symbolizing their collective intention to guide and facilitate the transfiguration process.

Amidst the soft illumination and divine chants, the soul of the deceased is believed to undergo a profound metamorphosis. It transcends its mortal limitations, shedding the earthly remnants and embracing its true nature as a radiant, divine light being.

As the ritual nears its culmination, the chorus of priests and priestesses offer prayers of gratitude and invocation to the gods and goddesses associated with light, divinity, and ascension. Their words carry the collective aspirations for the deceased's elevation and union with the cosmic divine.

The ritual concludes with a final blessing, as the attending priests and priestesses collectively release the divine light energy that has been channeled into the deceased. It spreads outward, permeating the sacred space and beyond, carrying the essence of the transfigured soul into the cosmic realms.

After the ritual, the body of the deceased may be prepared for its final resting place, be it through mummification or burial. It is seen as a vessel that once housed a divine light, now released to continue its eternal journey among the stars.

30. Spell for the reunion of the deceased's ba with their earthly possessions

By the powers of the sacred realms, I call,
To bring together what was once enthrall.
May the ba of the departed swiftly find,
Its cherished possessions left behind.

In the depths of the Duat, where spirits reside,
Let the ba seek and reunite, side by side.
With this incantation, I bridge the divide,
Between the realms, where treasures abide.

O ba of the departed, heed my plea,
Guide your steps, let your essence be free.
Seek out the belongings, scattered and lost,
Reclaim what was yours, at any cost.

Through the veil of shadows, the ba shall pass,
Guided by the light of memory's steadfast.
Let no obstacle impede its sacred quest,
As it retrieves what is rightfully possessed.

I invoke the spirits of the earthly plane,
To assist the ba in its endeavor, in this arcane.
Together, we gather the scattered remains,
Restoring harmony, breaking earthly chains.

As the ba reunites with its earthly domain,
May peace and fulfillment forever remain.
In the afterlife's embrace, may joy be found,
As possessions and memories once again abound.

31. Incantation to summon the assistance of ancestral spirits in the afterlife

By the ancient spirits of bloodline and kin,
I call upon you, ancestors, to guide me within.
In the realm beyond, where spirits reside,
I seek your wisdom, your aid by my side.

From the depths of time and ancestral lore,
I beckon your presence, forevermore.
With reverence and respect, I make this plea,
To the spirits of my lineage, hear my decree.

Through the veil of existence, I summon thee,
To lend your guidance, your wisdom to me.
In the afterlife's realm, where shadows abound,
I seek your counsel, with reverence profound.

Ancestral spirits, guardians of the past,
In this sacred union, our souls are amassed.
Grant me insight, show me the way,
As I journey through the realms, night and day.

Draw near, dear ancestors, with love and grace,
Wrap me in your presence, embrace my space.
Guide me through challenges, both old and new,
With your wisdom and guidance, I shall pursue.

In this sacred union, across the great divide,
May your presence and blessings forever reside.
Ancestral spirits, I honor and invoke,
As we walk together, in this eternal yoke.

32. Ritual of purification through the sacred waters of the Nile

O mighty Nile, river of life and purity,
I stand before your flowing majesty.
With reverence and awe, I seek your embrace,
To cleanse my being, to renew my grace.

As the sun's rays dance upon your surface,
I dip my hands into your sacred purpose.
With each splash and ripple, let impurities depart,
Cleanse my body, cleanse my soul, and purify my heart.

Nile, bearer of life, from ancient times till now,
I immerse myself in your waters, to humbly bow.
May your currents wash away all that's unclean,
Leaving me renewed, a vessel serene.

As the water embraces me, I feel its gentle touch,
Removing negativity, releasing it as such.
I am reborn, like the lotus that blooms,
Emerging from your depths, dispelling all glooms.

With gratitude in my heart, I emerge anew,
Blessed by your waters, refreshed and true.
Thank you, mighty Nile, for your cleansing power,
May your sacred essence guide me every hour.

The Ritual of Purification through the Sacred Waters of the Nile is a transformative and purifying ceremony that cleanses the body, mind, and spirit of the deceased. Here is an imagined description of what it might look like:

The ritual takes place on the banks of the majestic Nile River, where the waters are believed to possess potent purifying and rejuvenating properties. The location is carefully chosen, a serene and secluded spot where the energies of the river and the surrounding nature are in harmony.

A group of priests, adorned in white linen garments symbolizing purity, gather by the water's edge. They carry sacred vessels filled with water from the Nile, which is blessed and consecrated for the ritual. The priests move with a deliberate and solemn grace, embodying the reverence and sanctity of the occasion.

The deceased's body, wrapped in linen bandages and adorned with amulets, is brought to the riverbank by family members or attendants. It is placed on a stone pedestal or a specially crafted bier, positioned to face the flowing waters of the Nile.

The priests form a semi-circle around the deceased, their faces reflecting a sense of reverence and devotion. Soft chants and invocations fill the air as they begin the ritual, calling upon the blessings of the gods and goddesses associated with the Nile and purification.

One by one, the priests step forward with their sacred vessels, gently pouring the blessed water over the deceased's body. The water cascades over the linen bandages, soaking them and carrying away impurities, both physical and spiritual. The touch of the sacred waters is believed to cleanse and renew the deceased, preparing them for the journey into the afterlife.

As the water flows over the body, the priests recite ancient prayers and invocations, beseeching the gods to purify and protect the deceased. They invoke the power of the Nile, symbolizing the eternal cycle of life, death, and rebirth, to wash away any negative energies or attachments that may linger.

The sound of the flowing water blends with the chants, creating a harmonious symphony of purification and renewal. The surrounding natural elements, the gentle breeze, and the sunlight dancing on the river's surface all contribute to the sacred ambiance of the ritual.

Throughout the ceremony, family members, friends, and mourners may join in silent prayers or offer their own words of love and farewell to the departed. Their presence adds an emotional depth and personal connection to the ritual, creating a sacred space for collective healing and closure.

Once the pouring of the sacred water is complete, the priests may gently pat dry the deceased's body, showing reverence and care for the vessel that once housed a living soul. They may adorn the body with fragrant oils or place symbolic amulets or charms to further protect and guide the deceased on their journey.

The ritual concludes with a final prayer of gratitude and blessings. The attending priests and mourners may share a moment of reflection, honoring the cleansing and transformative power of the Nile and expressing their hopes for the deceased's safe passage into the afterlife.

The body is then prepared for its final journey, be it mummification or burial, carrying the blessings and purification bestowed by the sacred waters of the Nile into the realm of the ancestors.

33. Spell for the transmigration of the deceased's soul into a new life

By the power of the cosmic forces that bind,
I call upon the ancient spirits, wise and kind.
Guide the soul of the departed on its destined way,
To find a new life, a new dawn, a brand new day.

Oh, great Ankh, symbol of eternal life and rebirth,
Open the gates of the afterlife and unearth,
A path for the soul to traverse and explore,
A new existence, a new journey to adore.

As the sun sets upon the horizon's edge,
Let the soul of the departed break free from its pledge.
Release the ties that bind to the earthly plane,
And grant the soul a chance to be born again.

May the soul find a vessel pure and true,
In which to start anew, to grow and accrue,
Wisdom and experience, lessons yet unknown,
A fresh beginning, a chance to be shown.

Guide the soul, O ancient ones, with your light,
Through the realms of transition, through day and night.
Lead it to a life filled with purpose and grace,
Where it may find its destined time and place.

With reverence and respect, I speak this plea,
Grant the soul a new life, so mote it be.
As it embarks on this wondrous quest,
May it find joy, love, and eternal rest.

34. Invocation of the god Ptah for the creation of a new reality in the afterlife

Oh Ptah, creator of worlds, master of divine art,
I call upon your mighty presence, with reverence in my heart.
In this realm of transition, where spirits find their way,
I beseech you, Ptah, to shape a new reality today.

With your divine hands, skilled and wise,
Craft a world where the deceased may rise.
In this realm of shadows, let their dreams take flight,
A canvas of possibilities, bathed in eternal light.

With your creative essence, weave a tapestry divine,
Where the deceased may find solace and peace intertwine.
Manifest a realm of beauty, a sanctuary of bliss,
Where their spirit may flourish and find eternal bliss.

Ptah, architect of creation, I beseech you now,
Lend your power and wisdom, let your presence bestow.
Mold a new reality, where the deceased may dwell,
A haven of serenity, where all troubles dispel.

Grant them a realm of purpose, where their dreams may unfurl,
A sanctuary of love, where their soul may truly swirl.
In this afterlife journey, let their spirit soar high,
With Ptah's blessing, their essence will never die.

35. Ritual for the balancing of the deceased's heart against the feather of Ma'at

In the sacred realm of judgment, where truth and balance reign,
I stand before the scales of Ma'at, where destinies are ordained.
With reverence and humility, I approach this sacred rite,
To seek the harmony of my heart, to ensure eternal light.

I offer my heart, O Ma'at, with sincerity and devotion,
May it be weighed against your feather, in perfect unison.
May my actions in life align with truth and righteousness,
May my heart be pure, untouched by falsehood's darkness.

As the scales are set in motion, let justice guide the way,
May my heart be found worthy, as it is weighed on this day.
Let the feather of Ma'at be my guide, in this moment of reckoning,
To determine my fate, my eternal awakening.

I reflect upon my deeds, my thoughts, and my intentions,
Did I live in harmony with Ma'at's divine dimensions?
Did I honor truth, justice, and compassion in all I did?
Or did I falter, and let darkness within me forbid?

O mighty Thoth, keeper of records, witness to my life,
Guide the weighing of my heart, with impartiality rife.
May my heart be free from the burden of guilt and remorse,
May it resonate with the essence of Ma'at's cosmic force.

If my heart is found pure, if it matches the feather's grace,
Let my soul ascend, to join the gods in their celestial embrace.
But if my heart is heavy, burdened with the weight of sin,
Grant me the opportunity to amend, to purify from within.

With utmost reverence, I accept the verdict of the scales,
Knowing that Ma'at's judgment, in fairness, never fails.
May I be granted eternal life, in the presence of the divine,
A soul unburdened, in Ma'at's radiant realm, forever to shine.

The Ritual for the Balancing of the Deceased's Heart against the Feather of Ma'at is a crucial moment in the journey of the soul towards the afterlife. Here is an imagined description of what it might look like:

The ritual takes place in the Hall of Judgment, a sacred space where the gods and goddesses gather to assess the worthiness of the deceased's soul. The hall is adorned with intricate carvings, murals depicting scenes of divine justice, and a grand scale with the Feather of Ma'at at one end.

The deceased's body, carefully prepared and adorned with ceremonial garments and jewelry, is brought into the hall by priests or family members. They carry the deceased on a beautifully crafted funerary bier, symbolizing the solemnity and importance of the occasion.

The attending priests, dressed in ritual attire, guide the procession towards the scale at the center of the hall. The scale is an ornate and imposing structure, meticulously designed with precision and symbolism. At one end rests the Feather of Ma'at, representing truth, harmony, and cosmic order.

As the procession arrives at the scale, the priests place the deceased's heart, which has been carefully removed during the embalming process, on the other end of the scale. The heart, preserved and protected within a small sacred vessel, represents the essence of the deceased's life and deeds.

A hushed silence fills the hall as the moment of judgment begins. An appointed deity, often the god Anubis or Thoth, takes their place beside the scale, overseeing the weighing process. The deity's presence radiates a sense of solemn authority and divine wisdom.

With great reverence, the heart is delicately balanced against the Feather of Ma'at. The deceased's heart, representing their actions, virtues, and intentions in life, is held to the highest standard of divine justice. If the heart is heavy with negativity, wrongdoing, or imbalance, it will tip the scales.

The gathered gods and goddesses, bearing witness to the ritual, closely observe the scale and the delicate balance between the heart and the feather. Their collective gaze expresses the gravity and significance of this moment.

If the heart is found to be light and in balance with the Feather of Ma'at, a sigh of relief and joy reverberates through the hall. It signifies that the deceased has lived a righteous life, aligned with the principles of truth, justice, and cosmic harmony.

In this case, the gods and goddesses bestow their blessings upon the deceased. They confer the gift of eternal life in the afterlife, where the soul will enjoy peace, bliss, and the company of divine beings.

However, if the heart proves heavy and tilts the scales, it signifies a life filled with wrongdoing, imbalance, or unresolved transgressions. In such a case, the gods and goddesses may deem the soul unworthy of a blissful afterlife and subject it to appropriate consequences or purification rituals.

The ritual concludes with prayers, invocations, and offerings to beseech the mercy and guidance of the divine. The gathered attendees, including priests, family members, and mourners, may express their hopes and wishes for the deceased's soul during this solemn moment.

Once the judgment is complete, the deceased's body is prepared for its final resting place according to the verdict of the gods. Whether granted eternal bliss or subjected to further purification, the soul's journey continues in accordance with the divine decree.

36. Spell for the liberation of the deceased's soul from karmic bonds

By the power of the cosmic forces that govern all,
I beseech the divine realms, both great and small.
In this sacred moment, I seek liberation and release,
For the departed soul burdened by karmic cease.

O mighty Anubis, guardian of the threshold divine,
Guide the soul through the realms of space and time.
Unbind the chains of past deeds and their hold,
Let the soul soar freely, as its destiny unfolds.

I call upon Osiris, lord of resurrection and rebirth,
Grant the departed soul freedom from its earthly worth.
Release it from the cycle of cause and effect's sway,
Let it transcend the karmic ties that led astray.

With sacred words and incantations spoken,
May the soul's essence be forever unbroken.
Let the karmic debts be settled, the lessons learned,
As the soul ascends to realms where it's yearned.

Let the weight of past actions be lifted and dissolved,
As the soul's journey to higher realms evolves.
May it find solace, liberation, and divine grace,
As it transcends the limitations of time and space.

By the power of this spell, I break the chains that bind,
Freeing the soul's essence, leaving no trace behind.
In the realms beyond, let it find peace and light,
Liberated from karmic bonds, shining ever bright.

37. Incantation to invoke the protective power of the Eye of Horus

Horus, great falcon of the sky,
Bearer of the sacred Eye,
I call upon your strength and might,
To safeguard me with your divine light.

Eye of Horus, watchful and wise,
With your piercing gaze, evil defies,
Unveil the truth, reveal what's concealed,
Shield me from harm, your power revealed.

With your left eye, the moon's gentle gleam,
Illumine my path, a radiant beam,
Guide me through darkness, dispel all fear,
With your wisdom and insight, keep danger clear.

With your right eye, the sun's fiery blaze,
Burn away negativity, its fiery rays,
Protect my spirit, guard my soul,
Grant me strength to achieve my goal.

Oh Eye of Horus, symbol of protection,
May your power shield me in every direction,
As I traverse the realms, both near and far,
Wrap me in your loving, celestial avatar.

By the power of Horus, the ancient sky god,
I am shielded, protected, under his nod,
With the Eye of Horus, my guardian and guide,
I am secure, in its presence, I safely reside.

38. Ritual of communion with the divine through sacred offerings

In this sacred space, I now stand,
With reverence and devotion, hand in hand,
To commune with the divine, both near and far,
I offer these gifts, as symbols of my heart's star.

With pure intention and gratitude sincere,
I present these offerings, my devotion clear,
Fruits of the earth, ripe and sweet,
Nourishment for the gods, their presence to greet.

Incense rises, carrying prayers on its smoke,
A fragrant tribute, to the deities invoked,
Its swirling tendrils, reaching the heavens high,
Carrying my intentions, beyond the sky.

Libations poured, like rivers of life,
Quenching the thirst of spirits, easing their strife,
Water as a symbol of purity and renewal,
An offering of life's essence, flowing perpetual.

Candles flicker, casting a warm glow,
Illuminating the sacred space below,
Their flames dancing, like spirits in flight,
Guiding me towards divine insight.

With each offering made, a connection is formed,
A bridge between realms, where spirits are adorned,
Through this ritual of communion, I seek to unite,
With the divine forces, shining bright.

May the gods and goddesses, with open hearts,
Accept my offerings, these sacred arts,
In this ritual of communion, may I find,
A divine presence, forever kind.

The Ritual of Communion with the Divine through Sacred Offerings is a ceremonial act of connection and reverence. Here is a description of what it might look like:

The ritual takes place in a sacred space, such as a temple or a specially prepared altar in a peaceful and dedicated area. The altar is adorned with symbolic representations of the divine, including statues or images of deities, candles, flowers, and other meaningful objects.

The practitioner, dressed in attire befitting the solemnity of the occasion, approaches the altar with deep reverence and respect. They bring forth a selection of offerings that are considered sacred and meaningful, such as fruits, grains, flowers, incense, or precious objects.

With deliberate and intentional movements, the practitioner arranges the offerings on the altar, creating a visually pleasing and harmonious display. Each item is placed with care and devotion, symbolizing gratitude, adoration, and a desire for communion with the divine.

As the offerings are arranged, the practitioner enters a state of focused meditation, quieting the mind and opening the heart to divine presence. They may recite prayers, chants, or invocations, expressing their reverence and inviting the divine to join them in the ritual.

With a sense of humility and surrender, the practitioner lights the candles and the incense, symbolizing the illumination of the sacred space and the ascent of prayers and offerings to the divine realm. The gentle fragrance of the incense fills the air, creating an atmosphere of sanctity and transcendence.

Standing or kneeling before the altar, the practitioner offers heartfelt words of gratitude, praise, and intention. They may speak softly or silently, sharing their deepest desires, seeking guidance, and expressing their love and devotion to the divine.

With reverence, the practitioner may partake in a symbolic communion with the offerings. They may take a piece of fruit, a sip of water or wine, or simply place their hands on the offerings, allowing the spiritual essence of the offerings to merge with their own being.

Throughout the ritual, the practitioner maintains a deep connection with the divine, allowing themselves to be fully present and receptive to any messages, insights, or blessings that may arise.

The ritual concludes with a sense of gratitude and a closing prayer or affirmation, thanking the divine for their presence and the communion that has taken place. The practitioner may leave the offerings on the altar for a designated period of time as a sign of continued reverence and devotion.

The practitioner carries the essence of the communion with them, integrating the divine energy and guidance into their daily life, nurturing their spiritual growth, and deepening their connection with the sacred.

39. Spell for the transformation of the deceased into a celestial traveler

Oh, ancient gods, I beseech thee this day,
Grant me passage to realms far away.
From earthly confines, I seek release,
To soar among the stars, in endless peace.

With sacred words and potent incantation,
I call upon celestial transformation.
From mortal coil, I shed my ties,
Embracing the celestial skies.

I invoke the power of cosmic might,
To guide my spirit in celestial flight.
Grant me wings of light, ethereal and free,
To traverse the heavens, eternally.

Like a shooting star across the night,
I transcend the boundaries, taking flight.
Through astral planes, I gracefully glide,
With each passing moment, my spirit amplified.

I leave behind the bounds of time and space,
Exploring celestial realms, with divine grace.
Among the constellations, I find my home,
A celestial traveler, forever to roam.

Grant me wisdom to decipher the signs,
To navigate the realms, where the divine intertwines.
With each celestial encounter, new knowledge is gained,
As a celestial traveler, my purpose ordained.

May the gods of the cosmos bestow their blessing,
As I embark on this celestial quest, never resting.
Grant me safe passage, protection from afar,
As I journey among the celestial stars.

40. Invocation of the god Sobek for protection from malevolent spirits

Mighty Sobek, fierce guardian of the Nile,
I call upon your power, strong and versatile.
Protector of the living, defender of the just,
I seek your aid, in you, I place my trust.

From the depths of the waters, you emerge,
With jaws of strength, danger you deterge.
Grant me your presence, O mighty Sobek,
Shield me from spirits, with havoc they wreck.

With scales of armor and piercing eyes,
You survey the darkness, where danger lies.
Bless me with your ferocity and might,
To repel malevolent spirits, banish their blight.

Let your sacred waters wash over me,
Cleansing my spirit, setting me free.
As you ward off evil with each mighty stroke,
I invoke your protection, as a sacred cloak.

By the power of your divine jaws, I am shielded,
From spirits and forces that seek to be wielded.
In your presence, fear and doubt fade away,
Under your watchful eye, I safely stay.

Oh, Sobek, guardian of the ancient land,
Extend your protection with your mighty hand.
Surround me with your strength, unyielding and true,
Keeping me safe from harm, as I journey through.

With your blessing, I walk the path secure,
Protected from malevolent spirits, I endure.
Thank you, Sobek, for your watchful care,
By your side, I am shielded from all despair.

41. Ritual of purification through the burning of sacred herbs and resins

In the sacred space, where spirits reside,
I light the flame, the smoke will rise.
With reverence and intention, I prepare,
To cleanse my being, release what's unfair.

I gather the herbs, with wisdom and care,
Each one selected for its sacred flare.
Sage, with its cleansing and purifying might,
Banishing negativity, restoring inner light.

Sweet lavender, soothing and serene,
Bringing peace and tranquility to the scene.
Frankincense, with its sacred perfume,
Invoking the divine, dispelling gloom.

Rosemary, herb of remembrance and strength,
Clearing the mind, purifying at length.
Cedarwood, grounding and protective power,
Creating a shield in this sacred hour.

With hands and heart, I crumble the blend,
Into the vessel, the herbs descend.
I light the flame, and watch it dance,
As smoke curls, I enter a sacred trance.

With reverence and intention, I hold my space,
I invite the spirits, with love and grace.
I walk through the smoke, letting it surround,
Cleansing my aura, shedding what's bound.

As the herbs and resins release their scent,
I release old patterns, negative intent.
I am purified, my spirit renewed,
In this sacred ritual, my essence imbued.

The smoke carries my prayers, to the divine,
A sacred connection, in this moment, mine.

I am cleansed, I am purified,
In this ritual space, I safely reside.

And as the smoke dissipates in the air,
I feel lighter, freer, without a care.
Renewed and refreshed, I step into the day,
Carrying the energy of this sacred display.

The ritual takes place in a dedicated space, perhaps a serene and quiet room adorned with symbols and images representing the divine. A small altar or table is prepared as the focal point, adorned with candles, the vessel containing the sacred herbs and resins, and any other meaningful items.

The practitioner, dressed in flowing and ceremonial attire, stands before the altar with a sense of reverence and presence. They light the candles, symbolizing the illumination of the sacred space, and take a moment to center themselves.

With purposeful movements, the practitioner carefully crumbles the selected herbs and resins, combining them into a fragrant blend. They hold the vessel close to their heart, infusing it with their intention and energy. The scent of the herbs begins to fill the air, creating an atmosphere of tranquility and purification.

Taking a deep breath, the practitioner ignites a flame, using it to light the herbs in the vessel. As the smoke rises, they use their hands or a sacred tool, such as a feather or fan, to gently guide and disperse the smoke around their body. They slowly walk through the smoke, allowing it to envelop them completely, ensuring that every part of their being is touched by the purifying essence.

With each step, the practitioner visualizes the smoke carrying away any negative energies, stagnant emotions, or impurities that may be present. They may softly chant incantations, affirmations, or prayers, invoking the divine and expressing gratitude for the cleansing process.

As the smoke swirls and dances, the practitioner enters a meditative state, allowing themselves to be fully present in the moment and deeply connected to the ritual's purpose. They may close their eyes, focusing on their breath and the sensations within their body, as they absorb the transformative energy of the smoke.

Once they feel a sense of completion, the practitioner gently waves the feather or fan to disperse any remaining smoke. They offer gratitude to the herbs, the flame, and the spirits that have joined them in this sacred act of purification.

The ritual concludes with a moment of stillness and reflection. The practitioner may choose to sit or kneel in silent contemplation, basking in the purified energy that surrounds them. They express gratitude for the cleansing, grounding, and protective qualities that the ritual has invoked, carrying this renewed energy forward into their daily life.

42. Spell for the ascension of the deceased's soul to the realm of the gods

O departed one, blessed be your journey,
May your soul soar on celestial wings.
As the sun sets upon your mortal form,
Prepare for the embrace of divine beings.

Open your heart to the wisdom of the gods,
For they hold the keys to the heavenly doors.
In the realm of eternity, your soul shall dwell,
In the presence of those who shine evermore.

Invoke the names of the ancient deities,
Let their power guide you to your destined place.
With each word spoken, with each incantation,
Your soul ascends with grace and celestial grace.

Embrace the light that leads to the heavens,
Leave behind earthly ties and mortal strife.
In the embrace of gods, find eternal solace,
As you transcend the boundaries of human life.

Oh departed one, fear not the journey,
For the gods are your guardians, steadfast and true.
May your soul find peace among the divine,
As you ascend to the realm where gods imbue.

Gathered in the sacred chamber, the priests and priestesses form a circle around the body of the deceased. Their voices resonate with reverence as they recite the ancient incantations, their words carrying the power to guide the soul on its celestial journey.

Incense fills the air, its fragrant smoke weaving a bridge between the earthly realm and the divine. The aroma rises, enveloping the space in a haze of sanctity and spiritual presence.

With hands outstretched, the priests and priestesses invoke the names of the gods and goddesses, beseeching their assistance in the soul's ascent. Their voices echo through the chamber, harmonizing with the vibrations of the universe, creating a sacred symphony of supplication.

Symbols of divinity, crafted with precision and adorned with precious gems, are placed around the body. Each symbol represents a gateway to the realms beyond, a portal through which the soul will traverse on its path towards the gods.

The priests and priestesses begin the ritual dance, their movements graceful and deliberate. They step in unison, their feet connecting with the sacred ground, establishing a rhythmic cadence that resonates with the heartbeat of the cosmos.

As the dance unfolds, the energy in the chamber intensifies. The room becomes infused with an ethereal light, casting a soft glow upon the deceased and the surrounding space. The light represents the divine grace and guidance, illuminating the path for the soul's ascent.

With every step and gesture, the priests and priestesses channel their collective energy, directing it towards the soul of the departed. Their intentions are clear - to assist the soul in transcending the boundaries of mortality and to guide it to the realm of the gods.

Amidst the dance, the chanting reaches its crescendo. The words resonate with ancient power, reverberating through the chamber and beyond. The soul, now liberated from the earthly confines, begins to ascend, drawn towards the ethereal vibrations and celestial harmonies.

The room becomes a conduit of energy, bridging the mortal and divine realms. The priests and priestesses, connected with the gods through their unwavering faith and devotion, serve as conduits for the soul's passage. Their hearts beat in synchrony with the rhythm of the universe, creating a magnetic pull towards the heavens.

As the ritual concludes, the soul's ascent is complete. It transcends the earthly plane, embarking on a celestial journey towards the realm of the gods. The priests and priestesses offer their final prayers, bidding farewell to the departed and expressing gratitude for the opportunity to facilitate their soul's ascension.

The sacred chamber now fills with a serene stillness, a testament to the profound connection forged between the earthly and divine realms. The energy lingers, an ethereal presence that reverberates in the hearts of those present.

The ritual has fulfilled its purpose - to guide the soul on its path of transcendence and unite it with the realm of the gods. The departed, now embraced by the divine, embarks on a new chapter of existence, forever connected to the eternal forces that govern the cosmos.

43. Incantation to unlock the gates of divine knowledge in the afterlife

By the sacred words I speak, by the power divine,
I call upon the ancient wisdom, secret and sublime.
O gates of knowledge, hidden and sealed,
Open wide before the deceased, revealed.

Let the veil be lifted, let the mysteries unfold,
As the soul traverses realms of stories untold.
Unlock the secrets guarded by the gods,
Where cosmic truths lie beneath the celestial sods.

Through incantations and sacred chants,
The deceased gains access to higher expanse.
From the realms of mortals to the divine abode,
Divulge the wisdom, let the hidden codes be showed.

With offerings of reverence, with fervent prayer,
The gates of divine knowledge shall declare,
Reveal the mysteries of the cosmic tapestry,
To the departed soul seeking eternal clarity.

The incantation would have been recited by a trained priest or ritual specialist. The ritual might have taken place in a specially prepared space, such as a burial chamber or temple. The priest, adorned in ritual attire, would invoke the names of the gods associated with knowledge and wisdom, offering prayers and incense as acts of devotion.

Symbols and images related to divine knowledge may have been present, such as papyrus scrolls or hieroglyphs. The priest would have chanted the incantation with precise pronunciation and rhythmic intonation, creating a sacred atmosphere. The words spoken would have been believed to have the power to unlock the gates of divine knowledge, granting the deceased access to the hidden wisdom of the afterlife.

The ritual was intended to establish a connection between the mortal realm and the divine realm, allowing the deceased to receive guidance and enlightenment from the gods. It was believed that through this ritual, the gates of divine knowledge would be opened, granting the deceased access to the secrets and mysteries of the cosmos.

44. Ritual for the protection of the deceased's soul from dark entities

In the realm of shadows where darkness dwells,
I invoke the power to protect from malevolent spells.
By the light of Ra and the divine flame's glow,
I shield the departed soul from harm below.

With sacred symbols and amulets adorned,
I form a barrier, a shield unshorn.
I summon the guardians, spirits of light,
To ward off the darkness, to banish the night.

With pure intentions and words of might,
I command the forces of evil to take flight.
By the authority of the gods, their divine decree,
No dark entity shall harm what should be free.

The soul is surrounded by a radiant glow,
A shield of protection, a luminous flow.
Guided by Horus, the falcon's keen sight,
The soul soars beyond the reach of blight.

Through sacred gestures and mystical signs,
I fortify the soul against malevolent designs.
I call upon the ancient spirits, wise and bold,
To keep the departed soul within their fold.

In this sacred ritual, a bond is made,
Between the departed and the guardians' aid.
Dark entities retreat, their powers wane,
As the soul finds solace in a protective domain.

Performed within a sacred space and time,
The ritual safeguards the soul from the sublime.
With reverence and focus, the ritual is sealed,
Protecting the departed soul, its fate revealed.

Note: The specifics of the ritual may vary depending on the time period, region, and individual beliefs.

45. Spell for the reunion of the deceased's soul with their divine essence

In the realms beyond, where spirits roam,
I call upon the forces to guide them home.
From mortal bounds, their essence is freed,
To reunite with the divine, the eternal seed.

Through sacred words and incantations sung,
I summon the cosmic energies, ancient and young.
By the power of Ma'at, the balance restored,
The soul embraces its true form, adored.

With fragrant oils and resins ablaze,
I purify the path, clearing the haze.
The deceased's soul, now ready to ascend,
To merge with the divine, its journey's end.

A sacred space prepared with utmost care,
Where the veil between worlds is thin and rare.
Guided by the gods, their divine embrace,
The soul transcends, finding solace and grace.

In this sacred rite, the soul is restored,
To its divine essence, forever adored.
United with the cosmic, the essence divine,
The soul awakens, radiant and sublime.

The ritual performed with reverence and love,
A conduit for the reunion, guided from above.
With prayers and offerings, the connection is made,
As the soul merges with the divine, unswayed.

Note: The specifics of the ritual may vary depending on the time period, region, and individual beliefs. The performance may include the presence of priests or priestesses, the use of specific symbols, offerings, and rituals aimed at invoking the gods and facilitating the reunion of the soul with its divine essence.

46. Invocation of the goddess Nephthys for guidance in the afterlife

Oh, Nephthys, goddess of the night,
I call upon your radiant light.
Guide me through the shadows deep,
In this realm where souls doth sleep.

With voice uplifted, I chant your name,
Nephthys, protector of the flame.
In this sacred space, I stand,
Seeking your guidance, hand in hand.

From the realms unseen, you come forth,
With wisdom and grace, of immeasurable worth.
With wings outspread, in darkness you soar,
Navigating the afterlife's mystical lore.

Through sacred symbols, I invoke your power,
In this ritual hour, the sacred hour.
With offerings made, fragrant incense rise,
A testament of devotion, reaching the skies.

In silence, I await your divine presence,
To receive your guidance, your luminescence.
With open heart and receptive mind,
May your wisdom and light be intertwined.

In the stillness of the sacred space,
I feel your energy, your divine embrace.
Words unspoken, but felt in my soul,
As you guide me towards my eternal goal.

The ritual performed with utmost respect,
To connect with Nephthys, profound and direct.
Through devotion and faith, our spirits entwine,
In the afterlife's journey, your guidance is mine.

47. Ritual of divination to seek guidance from the oracle of the gods

In the sacred chamber, veiled in mystery,
I invoke the power of divine prophecy.
With reverence and awe, I enter this rite,
To seek guidance from realms beyond sight.

With offerings made, the altar adorned,
Incense rises, its fragrant tendrils adorned.
A solemn hush falls upon the air,
As I prepare to commune with spirits rare.

Inscribed upon parchment, ancient symbols divine,
The oracle's language, a bridge to the divine.
With trembling hands, I cast the sacred stones,
Each one revealing secrets, in cryptic tones.

Whispers of the gods, carried on the wind,
Their wisdom, their guidance, now within.
I close my eyes, my mind focused and clear,
As the oracle's message begins to appear.

Visions and symbols, like threads woven tight,
Unraveling the tapestry of truth and insight.
The gods speak through the oracle's voice,
Their counsel and guidance, for my life's choice.

In the stillness of the chamber's embrace,
I listen intently to each word and trace.
The whispers of destiny, the echoes of fate,
Revealed through the oracle, a profound state.

With gratitude and reverence, I give thanks,
For the wisdom bestowed by the divine ranks.
The ritual concludes, the connection made,
But the guidance received will never fade.

Note: The specifics of the ritual may vary depending on the culture, tradition, and the oracle being consulted. It may involve the use of various divination tools such as tarot cards, runes, or other symbolic objects. The individual seeking guidance may enter a meditative state, ask specific questions, and interpret the messages received through the oracle's guidance. The ritual may be conducted by a skilled diviner or priest/priestess trained in the art of divination.

In the dimly lit chamber adorned with sacred symbols,
A solitary figure stands at the center, veiled in reverence.
Incense wafts through the air, carrying prayers to the gods,
As the flickering candlelight casts dancing shadows on the walls.

Before the diviner lies an intricately crafted altar,
Adorned with offerings of flowers, fruits, and precious gems.
The scent of fragrant herbs mingles with the sacred smoke,
Creating an atmosphere charged with mystic energy.

The diviner, adorned in robes of ceremonial significance,
Takes a moment to center their mind and open their spirit.
With steady hands, they take hold of the oracle's tools,
A deck of ancient cards or perhaps a set of runes.

As the diviner's fingers shuffle the cards or cast the stones,
Their focus intensifies, attuning to the unseen realms.
The room fills with a palpable anticipation,
As the diviner prepares to unlock the gateways of wisdom.

Silence descends upon the chamber, as if the universe holds its breath,
And the diviner begins to lay out the cards or interpret the symbols.
Each flip, each placement, is imbued with meaning,
As the diviner channels the whispers of the gods.

Visions and insights flow through the diviner's consciousness,
Guided by the goddess Nephthys, her presence ethereal yet potent.
Words form on the diviner's lips, spoken with reverence,
Conveying the messages received from the realms beyond.

The seeker, their heart filled with hope and curiosity,
Listens intently, absorbing each word with eager anticipation.
The diviner's voice resonates with ancient wisdom,
Navigating the labyrinthine paths of the afterlife's guidance.

With the reading complete, the diviner's hands rest upon the cards,
The symbols, once alive with energy, now quiet and still.
The seeker expresses gratitude for the divine insight received,
Their path forward illuminated by the wisdom of Nephthys.

In this sacred exchange, the seeker finds solace and direction,
Guided by the hand of the goddess, Nephthys' presence forever imprinted.
The diviner, a conduit between mortal and divine,
Honors the role entrusted to them, as the gateway to the other side.

48. Spell for the transformation of the deceased into a guardian spirit

Amidst the sacred temple, bathed in the soft glow of flickering torches,
A group of priests gathers, clad in ceremonial garments of divine significance.
Incense fills the air, carrying prayers of invocation to the gods,
Creating an atmosphere charged with reverence and spiritual energy.

At the heart of the chamber lies an intricately carved stone slab,
Symbolizing the threshold between the mortal realm and the realm of spirits.
The deceased, adorned in sacred wrappings, rests peacefully upon the altar,
Their body prepared for the transformative journey that awaits.

The lead priest, bearing a sacred amulet in hand, approaches the altar,
Chanting ancient words of power and invoking the presence of the gods.
With each resonant syllable, the energy in the room intensifies,
Creating a bridge between the earthly plane and the realm of guardians.

In unison, the priests raise their hands, palms facing upward,
Calling upon the divine forces to bless the transformation that is to come.
Their voices harmonize in a melodic chant, an invocation to the heavens,
As the vibrations reverberate throughout the sacred space.

A sacred oil, infused with potent herbs and essences, is brought forth,
Its fragrance filling the chamber, a potent elixir of spiritual transfiguration.
The lead priest carefully anoints the forehead and heart of the deceased,
Whispering words of empowerment and divine connection.

As the anointing ritual concludes, a soft luminescence envelops the altar,
Radiating from the very essence of the deceased's being.
The energy of their soul begins to stir, awakening from its slumber,
Transforming into a radiant guardian spirit, ready to fulfill its sacred purpose.

The priests form a circle around the altar, hands joined in unity,
Their voices rise in a chorus of gratitude and affirmation.
They offer blessings and prayers, honoring the newfound guardian spirit,
Acknowledging its role in the cosmic tapestry of the afterlife.

In this sacred ritual of transformation, the deceased's soul is reborn,

Elevated to the rank of guardian spirit, a protector of sacred realms.
Their essence infused with divine power, their purpose eternal,
They stand as a beacon of light, guiding and guarding those who journey beyond.

As the ceremony draws to a close, the priests offer final blessings,
Their voices carrying a solemn reverence and profound respect.
The chamber is filled with a sense of awe and divine presence,
As the guardian spirit emerges, ready to fulfill its sacred duty.

In the realm of the afterlife, the transformed guardian spirit finds purpose,
Embracing its new form and embarking on a timeless journey.
Guided by the divine forces, it watches over the realms with unwavering devotion,
A testament to the transformative power of the ancient spell of ascension.

49. Incantation to invoke the blessings of the cosmic deities

In the twilight hours, beneath the star-studded sky,
A solitary figure stands upon a sacred mountaintop.
Their voice, a whispered incantation, carries on the gentle breeze,
Reaching out to the cosmic deities, guardians of the celestial realms.

With arms outstretched, the supplicant gazes upward,
Their eyes fixed upon the vast expanse of the heavens.
Words of ancient power flow from their lips,
A rhythmic cadence that weaves a tapestry of reverence and devotion.

They call upon the primordial forces, the cosmic energies,
Invoking the blessings of celestial beings that dwell beyond mortal sight.
Each syllable resonates with divine harmony, a symphony of cosmic connection,
Drawing forth the benevolent presence of the cosmic deities.

As the incantation reverberates through the night,
The heavens respond, the stars seem to shimmer with renewed brilliance.
A cosmic radiance envelops the supplicant, a divine embrace,
As the blessings of the cosmic deities descend upon their being.

The air becomes charged with celestial energy,
Infusing the supplicant with cosmic wisdom and infinite potential.
They feel a deep connection to the vastness of the universe,
A harmonious alignment with the cosmic dance of creation.

In this sacred moment, the boundaries between the earthly and celestial realms blur,
The supplicant becomes a conduit for divine energies to manifest.
They are blessed with cosmic insight, guided by celestial whispers,
And entrusted with the wisdom and grace of the cosmic deities.

As the incantation reaches its crescendo, the supplicant's spirit soars,
Their heart filled with gratitude for the celestial blessings bestowed.
They offer thanks to the cosmic deities, expressing profound reverence,
And commit to walking the path of cosmic alignment and divine purpose.

With the final words of the incantation spoken,
The cosmic energies gently recede, returning to their celestial abodes.

The supplicant stands in the presence of cosmic majesty,
Forever changed by the blessings of the cosmic deities.

In the days and nights that follow, the supplicant carries the resonance of the incantation,
Forever connected to the cosmic web of existence.
They navigate life with celestial guidance and divine inspiration,
A testament to the power of the incantation that invoked the blessings of the cosmic deities.

50. Ritual of communion with the sacred animals of the divine realms

In the heart of a sacred temple, adorned with ancient hieroglyphs,
The seeker of divine communion prepares for an extraordinary rite.
Surrounded by the incense's sweet fragrance and flickering candlelight,
They enter a meditative state, their mind attuned to the mystical realms.

With reverent steps, they approach the sacred altar,
Where offerings of precious herbs, flowers, and fruits await.
A gentle chant rises from their lips, a melody of sacred syllables,
Creating an atmosphere of harmony and spiritual resonance.

As the incantation weaves its enchanting spell,
The veil between the mortal world and the divine realms thins.
Whispers of the ancient ones stir in the air,
Guiding the seeker's consciousness to transcend ordinary perception.

With eyes closed, the seeker envisions the celestial realms,
Where the sacred animals of the divine dwell in radiant splendor.
A sense of reverence and awe fills their being,
As they invoke the presence of these magnificent beings.

In their mind's eye, they see a procession of sacred animals,
Graceful felines, majestic birds, and powerful serpents.
Each creature embodies the essence of a divine aspect,
A manifestation of the gods and goddesses revered since time immemorial.

With open arms and a pure heart, the seeker extends an invitation,
A call to commune with the sacred animals of the divine realms.
In this sacred moment, the seeker becomes a vessel of divine harmony,
As their consciousness merges with the consciousness of the sacred beings.

As if drawn by an invisible thread of sacred energy,
The animals of the divine draw near, their presence palpable.
The seeker feels a profound connection, a merging of souls,
As they bask in the wisdom and unconditional love emanating from the sacred creatures.

In this communion, words are not necessary,
For the language of the heart transcends all barriers.
The seeker feels a deep understanding, a shared bond,
As they exchange energies, thoughts, and emotions with the sacred animals.

The seeker absorbs the wisdom and blessings bestowed,
A transformational exchange that transcends the limitations of the physical realm.
They receive insights, guidance, and healing from the sacred animals,
Empowered by the divine essence that flows through every creature.

After a timeless moment of communion, the sacred animals begin to recede,
Slowly returning to their divine abodes with a gentle grace.
The seeker remains in a state of profound gratitude and awe,
Forever touched by the mystical connection they experienced.

As they emerge from the sacred temple, their soul enriched,
The seeker carries the wisdom and blessings of the sacred animals.
They walk the earth with a deeper understanding of the interconnectedness of all life,
Honoring the divine presence within every creature they encounter.

The ritual of communion with the sacred animals of the divine realms,
A sacred dance of harmony and oneness with the natural world,
Enables the seeker to glimpse the majesty of the divine through the eyes of the sacred creatures,
And to forge an eternal bond with the spirit of the animal kingdom.

51. Spell for the liberation of the deceased's soul from earthly illusions

I have come forth, a seeker of truth,
To break the chains of illusions, aloof.
By the power of ancient incantations,
I seek liberation from earthly manifestations.

O spirits of the celestial realms, I implore,
Guide my soul through this cosmic corridor.
Grant me sight beyond veils of deception,
To perceive the essence, the divine conception.

In this earthly realm of shadows and guise,
Illusions weave their intricate ties.
But I, the enlightened one, shall not be bound,
As I awaken to truth, with clarity profound.

I call upon the winds, swift and wise,
To carry my voice to the celestial skies.
Let the celestial deities hear my plea,
To set my soul free, to break illusions' decree.

By the sacred fire, pure and bright,
I invoke its transformative light.
Burn away the veils that cloud my sight,
Reveal the path that leads to eternal light.

I release attachments to worldly desires,
Transcending illusions, my spirit aspires.
No longer swayed by falsehood and illusion,
I embrace the divine, in humble submission.

O gods and goddesses, in your divine grace,
Guide me through the realms, at a steady pace.
Illuminate my path with truth's radiant glow,
As I transcend illusions, my soul shall grow.

May the ancient wisdom of the cosmic plane,
Bless me with knowledge that shall never wane.

Liberate my soul from earthly confusion,
In this sacred journey of spiritual fusion.

As I utter these words with utmost intent,
May the barriers of illusion be rent.
My soul is liberated, soaring high,
Embracing truth's essence, no longer shy.

In the realm betwixt worlds, I am set free,
From earthly illusions that once blinded me.
With enlightened eyes, I now perceive,
The eternal truth that shall never deceive.

This spell for liberation, profound and vast,
Unbinds the soul from illusions' grasp.
The deceased's spirit finds liberation's embrace,
In the eternal realm, where illusions efface.

Note: The performance of this spell would involve the recitation of the utterance in a solemn and focused manner, accompanied by symbolic gestures and offerings. Candles may be lit to represent the illumination of truth, and incense may be burned to create a sacred atmosphere. The seeker would invoke the assistance of celestial deities and call upon the elements to aid in the liberation from earthly illusions. The spell would be performed with reverence and sincerity, with the belief that through the power of the spoken word and divine intervention, the deceased's soul would be liberated from the veils of deception.

In the realm betwixt worlds, where shadows veil the truth,
The spell unfolds, revealing paths of wisdom and verity, uncouth.
With arms outstretched and voice resolute, the seeker stands,
Seeking liberation from illusions, released from earthly strands.

The ritual begins with the lighting of sacred candles, their flames aglow,
Casting a soft, flickering light, an ethereal dance, casting shadows below.
The seeker breathes deep, inhaling the fragrant incense, divine and pure,
Awakening senses, aligning spirit and mind, ready to endure.

In the center of the sacred space, a circle is inscribed,
Traced with ancient symbols, invoking powers untamed, untied.
The seeker steps into the circle, surrounded by an unseen veil,
Protected from illusions that bind, their spirit to prevail.

With arms raised high, the seeker calls upon the celestial guides,
Entwined in the mystic dance, as the veil between worlds divides.
They chant the sacred words, resonating with divine vibration,
Seeking liberation from earthly illusions, a soul's emancipation.

The seeker envisions a web of illusions, woven with intricate thread,
Binding their soul, obscuring truth, veiling the path ahead.
With each incantation, the web begins to fray, light piercing the veil,
As illusions unravel, revealing the essence beyond the earthly trail.

The room fills with a celestial glow, a luminescence divine,
As the seeker's spirit transcends, freed from illusions' confine.
They witness truths unmasked, perceptions reshaped anew,
Embracing clarity and insight, liberation breaking through.

With a final chant, the seeker proclaims their release,
From the grip of earthly illusions, finding solace and peace.
Their soul dances in newfound freedom, unburdened and light,
Embracing the eternal truth, untethered from mortal plight.

The ritual of liberation from earthly illusions, a profound endeavor,
Unveils the hidden truths, as illusions dissolve forever.
The seeker's spirit soars, unencumbered by deceit's disguise,
Embracing the realm of authenticity, where enlightenment lies.

In the realm betwixt worlds, the liberation unfolds,
As the seeker's soul ascends, unshackled and bold.
A dance of light and shadow, a journey to be unfurled,
Liberated from earthly illusions, embraced by wisdom's world.

52. Incantation to awaken the divine spark within the deceased's heart

From the depths of the sacred flame,
I call upon the powers that bear no name.
Awaken, oh divine spark, within the heart,
Let the eternal light pierce through the dark.

By the ancient words spoken with intent,
I summon the dormant fire, radiant and unbent.
Arise, oh divine spark, from slumber deep,
Ignite the soul's fire, an eternal flame to keep.

In the realms of the divine, it lies in wait,
The divine spark within, ready to elevate.
Awaken, oh divine spark, with sacred might,
Illuminate the path, guide the soul's flight.

With every word uttered, the spark grows bright,
Pulsating, radiating, a beacon of celestial light.
Rekindle the connection to the divine source,
Ignite the flame within, let it set its course.

Through the layers of existence, let it ascend,
Reawakening the spirit, where all journeys blend.
Empower the soul with wisdom and grace,
The divine spark ignited, in its rightful place.

In the realm of the afterlife, let it shine,
A divine beacon, a sacred sign.
Awaken, oh divine spark, within the heart's core,
Merge with the cosmic energy forevermore.

Note: This incantation would be recited by a practitioner or a priest/priestess in a ceremonial setting. The focus would be on awakening the dormant divine spark within the deceased's heart, infusing it with divine energy and purpose. The words would be spoken with intention, invoking the powers of the divine and calling forth the inherent sacredness within the soul. The ritual may include gestures, symbolic objects, and an atmosphere of reverence to enhance the spiritual connection and facilitate the awakening process.

53. Invocation of the god Horus for divine protection and guidance

Hail to you, Horus, the great protector,
Mighty falcon soaring high, divine specter.
I invoke your presence, O deity of the sky,
Grant me protection as I journey on high.

With eyes keen and sharp, you see all,
From the heavens above to the earthly sprawl.
O Horus, son of Isis and Osiris renowned,
Wrap your wings around me, keep me safe and sound.

I call upon your strength, noble and true,
To guide me through challenges I must pursue.
As the falcon soars, swift and fearless in flight,
Lead me on the path of righteousness and light.

O Horus, mighty avenger, wise and just,
Defender of truth, in you I place my trust.
Protect me from darkness, shield me from harm,
With your divine presence, keep me warm.

By the power of your sacred eye, watchful and keen,
Keep me safe, even in realms unseen.
Grant me the clarity to discern wrong from right,
And the courage to fight for truth's sacred light.

As I walk in the footsteps of ancient lore,
May your guidance and protection be my core.
O Horus, god of kings, guardian of the divine,
Bestow your blessings, make them forever mine.

In times of doubt, when shadows loom,
I call upon your name, dispelling all gloom.
Guide me with your wisdom, strengthen my resolve,
In your presence, I find solace and evolve.

Horus, mighty god, I beseech you this day,
Be with me as I tread the sacred way.

Protect me from danger, lead me to my destiny,
In your embrace, may my spirit be free.

This invocation of Horus, noble and grand,
Connects the seeker to a divine hand.
With words spoken true and heart full of might,
The seeker invokes Horus, protector of light.

Note: The performance of this invocation would involve the recitation of the verses with reverence and respect. The seeker would ideally be in a quiet and sacred space, surrounded by symbols or representations of Horus, such as statues or images. The invocation would be accompanied by gestures or offerings, such as the raising of hands or the lighting of candles. The seeker would focus their intention on connecting with Horus, seeking his divine protection and guidance throughout their journey.

54. Ritual for the transformation of the deceased into a cosmic dancer

In the realm of the divine, where spirits dwell,
We gather to perform a sacred spell.
Through rhythmic movement and celestial grace,
We seek the transformation of this earthly space.

O departed soul, hear our invocation,
To become a dancer of cosmic elation.
Release the ties that bind you to this mortal plane,
Embrace the cosmic energies, let them flow through every vein.

With music as our guide, our bodies start to sway,
We surrender to the rhythm, letting it lead the way.
Our steps become a dance, a cosmic symphony,
As we embody the spirit of divine unity.

We spin and twirl, like celestial bodies in flight,
Our souls take flight, reaching celestial heights.
Through graceful gestures, we express the divine,
Transcending earthly limits, in this cosmic shrine.

Our movements embody the essence of creation,
A dance of cosmic order, a divine revelation.
We merge with the stars, the planets, and the moon,
Becoming one with the celestial harmony, attuned.

O cosmic dancer, let your spirit take flight,
Transcend the boundaries of day and night.
Embrace the cosmic rhythm, the universal song,
As you dance, may your essence forever belong.

In this ritual of transformation and grace,
We honor the spirit's eternal embrace.
The deceased soul becomes a cosmic dancer,
In the realm of the divine, a radiant enhancer.

55. Spell for the reunification of the deceased's soul with the universal soul

By the sacred words, I invoke this spell,
To reunite the departed with the universal swell.
O soul of the deceased, listen to my call,
Merge with the cosmic essence, surrendering all.

In the realm of the divine, where all souls reside,
Let the barriers dissolve, and boundaries subside.
You are not separate, but a part of the whole,
Reunite with the universal soul, become one, and console.

Release the attachments to earthly desires,
Embrace the cosmic fire, where love never tires.
Let your essence merge with the eternal stream,
Where dreams and realities intertwine like a gleam.

Through the veil of illusion, your soul shall pass,
Embracing the oneness, like a divine looking glass.
Cast away the shadows that keep you confined,
Unite with the universal soul, leaving no trace behind.

Open your heart to the cosmic symphony,
Feel the unity, the vastness, the divinity.
Let your spirit soar through cosmic realms untold,
Reunited with the universal soul, forever enfolded.

As the spell is cast, the reunion takes place,
The departed soul merges, embracing cosmic grace.
No longer bound by earthly chains, you are free,
One with the universal soul, for eternity.

Note: This spell would be performed by a practitioner or a priest/priestess in a sacred setting. They would invoke the power of the divine and speak the words of the spell with intention and reverence. The focus would be on reuniting the departed soul with the universal soul, letting go of earthly attachments, and embracing the cosmic essence. The spell would serve as a bridge between the realms, allowing the soul to transcend and merge with the universal oneness.

56. Ritual of purification through the sacred flame of the eternal light

In the sanctuary of the sacred space,
Where the eternal light holds its embrace,
I stand before the flame, pure and bright,
A beacon of cleansing, a source of divine light.

With reverence and respect, I approach the fire,
An offering of impurities, my soul's desire.
I release all that taints, all that weighs me down,
As the sacred flame dances, casting away the frown.

I hold my hands to the fire, feeling its gentle heat,
As it engulfs my being, cleansing and complete.
The flames flicker and dance, a mesmerizing sight,
Bathing me in purity, dispelling the shadows of night.

I breathe in the essence of the sacred flame,
Exhaling all impurities, releasing any blame.
The fire's radiant glow purifies my spirit and mind,
Leaving no trace of negativity behind.

As the flames rise higher, the impurities depart,
A purification of body, soul, and heart.
The sacred flame's transformative embrace,
Renews my essence, bestowing divine grace.

In this ritual of purification, I am reborn,
Free from the chains of the world's scorn.
Embraced by the eternal light's sacred fire,
I emerge purified, filled with divine desire.

Note: This ritual would involve a ceremonial space with a designated area for the
sacred flame. The practitioner would approach the flame with respect and reverence,
offering their impurities and negative energies to be consumed by the fire. The ritual
may include specific gestures, such as holding hands to the flame, and intentional
breathing exercises to facilitate the purification process. The flames serve as a symbol
of divine transformation and purification, infusing the practitioner with renewed
energy and purity.

57. Spell for the transfiguration of the deceased into a celestial musician

By the powers of the cosmic symphony,
I call upon the realms of harmony.
May my mortal form ascend and transform,
Into a celestial musician, in divine uniform.

Oh, celestial realms, hear my plea,
Grant me the gift of musical ecstasy.
Release me from earthly bonds that confine,
And let my soul with celestial melodies entwine.

With each note I play and every rhythm I beat,
May my essence transcend, reaching a heavenly feat.
Transform me into a celestial being of sound,
A musician of the heavens, forever unbound.

Grant me wings of music, soaring high,
Playing melodies that touch the sky.
Let my voice resonate with celestial choir,
Guided by celestial maestros, inspire.

My instrument, an extension of my soul,
An orchestra of cosmic vibrations, behold!
As I play, the universe dances and sings,
A symphony of love, on celestial strings.

With each melody, I transcend time and space,
Becoming one with the celestial embrace.
Let my music heal, uplift, and transform,
A celestial musician, in divine form.

Note: This spell would involve the use of musical instruments and a deep connection to the power of music. The practitioner would invoke the celestial realms, asking for the transformation into a celestial musician. The spell emphasizes the transcendent and transformative nature of music, envisioning the practitioner becoming one with the cosmic symphony. It is believed that through this spell, the deceased's soul can transcend earthly limitations and embrace the divine essence of music.

58. Ritual of anointing with sacred fragrances for spiritual elevation

In the realm of divine presence, I stand,
Seeking spiritual elevation, as planned.
With reverence and awe, I prepare this rite,
To anoint my being, to ignite my inner light.

I gather the essences, fragrances divine,
Oils of jasmine, frankincense, and pine.
With utmost care, I blend them well,
Creating a potion, a sacred spell.

In a sacred vessel, I place my creation,
A symphony of scents, a sublime sensation.
With focused intention, I anoint my brow,
Invoking the divine, I feel the sacred flow.

As I touch my temples, my pulse awakes,
Each stroke a prayer, each fragrance takes.
I anoint my throat, to speak with truth and grace,
To share my wisdom, to find my rightful place.

Next, my heart receives this sacred anointing,
To open its chambers, divine love appointing.
I anoint my solar plexus, the seat of power,
To ignite my will, to manifest my desires.

Down to my sacral center, I gently apply,
To embrace my creativity, my passion amplify.
And finally, I anoint my feet, my foundation strong,
To walk the path of spirit, where I belong.

As the fragrances merge with my being,
I feel a shift, a sacred inner freeing.
Empowered and elevated, I now reside,
In the realm of divine presence, by my side.

59. Spell for the liberation of the deceased's soul from the cycle of rebirth

O soul entwined in the cycle's embrace,
Longing for liberation, seeking sacred space,
I call upon the forces of cosmic grace,
To free you from the bonds of earthly chase.

With words of power, I chant and decree,
Release the soul, set its essence free,
From the karmic ties that bind and confine,
Let it soar on wings, in realms divine.

I summon the winds, carriers of change,
To sweep away the shackles, to rearrange,
The path of the soul, its destined flight,
Away from the cycle, into eternal light.

By the breath of life, I breathe and blow,
Dispel the illusions, let the truth flow,
The soul shall transcend, its purpose fulfilled,
No longer bound, by the cycle, stilled.

I call upon the gods, the wise and the old,
To guide the soul, to truths yet untold,
Grant it wisdom, liberation, and grace,
To transcend the cycle, find its rightful place.

With each sacred word, with each heartfelt plea,
I sever the ties that hold the soul, you see,
No longer confined by mortal desire,
It journeys onward, to realms higher.

And so, I declare, with utmost devotion,
The liberation of the soul, a divine motion,
Free from rebirth, free from the wheel,
To eternal realms, its essence shall appeal.

Note: The Spell for the Liberation of the Deceased's Soul from the Cycle of Rebirth is a powerful invocation performed with the intention of releasing the soul from the perpetual cycle of birth, death, and rebirth. The spell calls upon cosmic forces and divine assistance to free the soul from the karmic ties and illusions that bind it to earthly existence. Through chanting and the use of sacred words, the practitioner seeks to sever these ties and guide the soul towards liberation and ultimate transcendence. The spell is performed with reverence, intention, and a deep understanding of the soul's journey towards spiritual liberation.

60. Incantation to invoke the divine guidance of the sacred scarab beetle

O mighty scarab, sacred and revered,
Bearer of secrets, wisdom unfathomed,
I call upon your divine presence,
To guide me on the path of enlightenment.

With wings unfurled, you soar through the night,
Navigating the realms of shadow and light,
An emblem of transformation, rebirth, and might,
Grant me your wisdom, shining bright.

Scarab, oh scarab, divine and wise,
Unveil the truths hidden from mortal eyes,
Guide me through the labyrinth of life,
Protect me from turmoil and strife.

In your shell, the mysteries reside,
Encoded in symbols, ancient and wide,
Reveal to me the hidden truths and lore,
Let my spirit soar and explore.

As you roll the sun across the sky,
Illuminate my path, help me to defy,
The limitations of the earthly plane,
And rise above, free from mundane.

Oh sacred scarab, I seek your embrace,
To guide me on my spiritual chase,
Grant me insight, clarity, and sight,
As I journey through the realms of light.

With each beat of your wings, I feel your might,
Guiding me through the day and the night,
Your presence, a beacon of divine love,
Guiding my soul to realms above.

May your wisdom seep into my core,

Empowering me forevermore,
As I invoke your guidance, oh sacred beetle,
With gratitude and reverence, my spirit's mettle.

Note: The Incantation to Invoke the Divine Guidance of the Sacred Scarab Beetle is a powerful invocation used to seek the wisdom and guidance of the revered scarab beetle in ancient Egyptian beliefs. The scarab beetle symbolizes transformation, rebirth, and the journey of the soul. By invoking the divine presence of the scarab, one seeks its guidance and protection on the path of spiritual enlightenment. The incantation is performed with reverence and intention, calling upon the scarab to reveal hidden truths, provide insight, and illuminate the seeker's path. It is a sacred connection to the wisdom and mysteries of the scarab, empowering the individual to transcend the limitations of the earthly realm and embrace higher realms of consciousness.

61. Ritual for the transformation of the deceased into a guardian of truth

In the sacred chambers of the afterlife,
Where secrets lie veiled in eternal night,
I call upon the divine forces of truth,
To guide the soul's transformation with their might.

With hands raised high, and heart sincere,
I invoke the powers that forever adhere,
To shape the essence of the departed soul,
And fashion a guardian of truth, strong and clear.

In the presence of the divine, I stand,
With reverence and awe, I make my demand,
Grant the deceased the mantle of guardianship,
To protect the realms of truth in the spirit's command.

Let falsehoods shatter, illusions dissolve,
As the soul ascends to its destined role,
From mortal constraints, it shall break free,
Embracing the duty to safeguard truth's scroll.

Through sacred rites and incantations profound,
I beseech the gods to grace this ground,
Infuse the essence of the departed one,
With unwavering commitment, forever bound.

May their eyes see through veils of deceit,
Their voice resound with truth's heartbeat,
Their presence radiate unwavering light,
As a guardian of truth, they are complete.

This ritual, profound and sacred in its core,
Transforms the soul, forevermore,
From mortal being to celestial guide,
A guardian of truth, honored and adored.

Note: The Ritual for the Transformation of the Deceased into a Guardian of Truth
is a sacred rite performed to bestow upon the departed soul the role of a guardian in

the realms of truth. Through the invocation of divine forces, the ritual seeks to shape and elevate the essence of the deceased, imbuing them with the power to protect and uphold truth. The ritual is conducted with reverence and intention, calling upon the gods to bless and empower the soul in its new role. The transformed soul becomes a beacon of truth, seeing through illusions and falsehoods, and dedicating itself to safeguarding the integrity of knowledge and wisdom. It is a profound transformation, marking the soul's purpose in the afterlife and its eternal commitment to the pursuit of truth.

62. Spell for the reunification of the deceased's ba with their ancestral lineage

By the sacred flame of remembrance's light,
I call upon the ancient spirits of might,
To bridge the realms of the living and the dead,
And guide the ba to its ancestral height.

With words of power and reverence deep,
I summon the lineage that longs to keep,
The soul of the departed within their embrace,
United once more, never to weep.

Ancestral voices, whisper in the wind,
Guide the ba, where the threads of kin are thinned,
Across the veil, through time and space,
Let the reunion with ancestors begin.

Through the tapestry of generations past,
Let the ba's journey find solace at last,
Embraced by those who came before,
Their love and wisdom forever amassed.

From the realms of the living to the ancestral plane,
May the ba be welcomed, free from pain,
Unite the bloodline, entwined and strong,
In the embrace of the lineage's eternal reign.

This spell, spoken with love and devotion,
Opens the gates to ancestral connection,
As the ba finds its place among the revered,
Reunified, completing its soul's resurrection.

Note: The Spell for the Reunification of the Deceased's Ba with Their Ancestral Lineage is a powerful invocation performed to facilitate the reunion of the ba (soul) with its ancestral lineage. It is a sacred act of honoring and acknowledging the connection between the deceased and their forebears. Through the recitation of potent words, the spell calls upon the ancient spirits and ancestral voices to guide the ba across the realms, bridging the gap between the living and the dead. The purpose is to reunite the soul with its ancestral lineage, where it can find solace, wisdom, and love in the embrace of those who came before. This reunion is a significant step in the soul's journey, allowing it to connect with its roots, drawing strength and guidance from the accumulated wisdom of generations past.

63. Invocation of the god Seth for protection against negative energies

Mighty Seth, warrior of divine might,
I call upon you in this solemn rite,
With strength and valor, you shall stand,
As my shield against all that is dark and blight.

From the depths of chaos, you arise,
With power unmatched, you mesmerize,
I beseech you now, oh god of defense,
Guard my path, shield my soul from demise.

Seth, protector against forces malign,
With your fierce spirit, let light shine,
Banish the shadows that seek to harm,
Keep me safe in your protective design.

Unleash your rage upon negativity's sway,
Sweep away darkness, create a new day,
Empower me with your sacred flame,
As we ward off all that leads astray.

By your fierce determination and might,
Negative energies shall take flight,
With your presence, I am fortified,
Protected under your watchful sight.

Seth, god of protection and strength,
In your embrace, I find solace at length,
Thank you for safeguarding my soul,
Against the forces that would seek to wrench.

This invocation, spoken with reverence true,
Invokes the presence of Seth to imbue,
The petitioner with protection and might,
Shielding against negative energies through and through.

Note: The Invocation of the God Seth for Protection against Negative Energies is a ritualized calling upon the deity Seth to act as a powerful guardian against negative and harmful energies. Seth, known for his strength and ferocity, is invoked to provide a shield of defense and to banish darkness from the petitioner's life. By calling upon Seth's protective energies, the petitioner seeks to fortify themselves against any malevolent forces that may seek to bring harm or disruption. The invocation acknowledges Seth's power and appeals to his unwavering determination to safeguard the petitioner's well-being. Through this ritual, the petitioner establishes a connection with Seth, inviting his presence and strength into their life for protection and guidance.

64. Ritual of purification through the sacred breath of the divine wind

In the realm of the sacred, where purity resides,
I call upon the winds, the divine breath that guides,
With reverence and respect, I seek your embrace,
To cleanse my spirit and bestow your grace.

Oh, mighty wind, a vessel of the divine,
Whispering secrets from realms sublime,
Wrap me in your gentle, purifying breeze,
Carrying away impurities with ease.

As I stand in this sacred space,
I open myself to your divine embrace,
Blow away the dust of worldly strife,
And purify me with your breath of life.

Inhaling deeply, I draw in your power,
Exhaling, releasing, hour by hour,
With each breath, I shed what no longer serves,
Awakening the purity that forever preserves.

As the wind dances upon my skin,
I feel the divine touch from within,
Every gust carries away doubt and fear,
Leaving behind a spirit that is clear.

With gratitude, I honor your sacred gift,
The cleansing breeze that provides a shift,
Renewing my essence, restoring my soul,
Purifying me to be once again whole.

This ritual, performed with intention and grace,
Utilizes the sacred breath of the divine space,
Through the winds, I find purification's embrace,
And in their gentle power, I find solace and embrace.

Note: The Ritual of Purification through the Sacred Breath of the Divine Wind is a
ceremonial practice that harnesses the power of the wind as a purifying force. The

ritual involves consciously connecting with the winds and breathing in their cleansing energy to release impurities and restore spiritual purity. The practitioner acknowledges the divine nature of the wind and invites its presence to wash away negative energies and emotions, bringing clarity and renewal. By consciously inhaling and exhaling with the focus on purification, the practitioner aligns themselves with the cleansing power of the divine wind, allowing it to remove obstacles and restore inner harmony. This ritual is performed with reverence and gratitude for the elemental forces that surround us, acknowledging their role in the journey of spiritual purification.

65. Spell for the transmigration of the deceased's soul into a higher plane

By the power of the ancient ones, I invoke,
A spell of transmigration, a divine cloak,
May the soul of the departed ascend and soar,
To realms beyond, where spirits explore.

Oh, sacred energies that span the sky,
Guide this soul, as it takes its final fly,
Through the veils that separate realms unknown,
To a higher plane where true essence is shown.

May the ties to earthly existence unwind,
As the soul transcends, leaving all behind,
Shedding the limitations of mortal life,
Embracing the infinite, free from strife.

With each step taken in this cosmic dance,
Let the soul's vibration rise and enhance,
Breaking the bonds of the earthly plane,
Embracing a realm where pure light reigns.

Through the gateways of stars, the soul shall traverse,
Navigating celestial paths with grace and verse,
Untethered from time, and liberated from space,
Transcending dimensions, embracing divine grace.

Oh, divine forces of cosmic expansion,
Gather around, aiding this sacred transition,
Guide the soul through celestial gates wide,
To realms where eternal wisdom resides.

With every breath, let the soul ascend,
Into the luminous realms where destinies blend,
Transmuted and transformed, forever free,
United with the universal tapestry.

By the power of this spell and its sacred rite,
May the transmigration unfold with divine light,

As the soul finds its place in realms unseen,
Embracing its purpose, its essence serene.

Note: The Spell for the Transmigration of the Deceased's Soul into a Higher Plane is a ritualistic invocation that aims to facilitate the journey of the departed soul into elevated realms. The spell calls upon the power of the ancient forces and cosmic energies to guide and protect the soul as it transcends the earthly realm. Through the recitation of sacred words and the focus of intention, the practitioner seeks to release the soul from the limitations of physical existence, allowing it to traverse through celestial gateways and ascend to higher planes of consciousness. The spell acknowledges the divine nature of the soul and its inherent connection to the greater universe. It invites the assistance of benevolent forces to aid in the soul's transmigration, enabling it to merge with the universal tapestry and fulfill its destined purpose.

66. Incantation to awaken the dormant powers within the deceased's spirit

From the depths of the eternal abyss,
I call upon the dormant powers to arise,
Awaken, O spirit, from your slumber deep,
Unleash the hidden strength you keep.

By the ancient words of power and might,
I command the dormant energies to ignite,
Rise, O spirit, with fervor and zeal,
Reveal the gifts that within you conceal.

Awaken, O spirit, from the realms of rest,
Unlock the potential, be forever blessed,
Let the dormant powers surge and flow,
Empowering you to conquer and grow.

With each syllable spoken, the spark ignites,
Through the incantation, the spirit takes flight,
Embracing the gifts that have lain unseen,
Unleashing the power, a force supreme.

Arise, O spirit, in radiant light,
Tap into the depths of your inner might,
Let your essence shine, vibrant and strong,
As you journey through eternity's song.

By the incantation's sacred decree,
The dormant powers shall now be free,
Transformed and awakened, they shall soar,
Enhancing your being forevermore.

Note: The Incantation to Awaken the Dormant Powers Within the Deceased's Spirit is a powerful invocation that aims to activate the latent abilities and potential of the departed soul. Through the recitation of ancient words of power and the focused intention of the practitioner, the spell calls upon the dormant energies within the spirit to awaken and surge forth. It recognizes that even in death, the spirit carries untapped powers and hidden strengths, waiting to be unlocked. The incantation acts as a catalyst, igniting the dormant powers and allowing them to manifest in the spiritual realm. The awakening of these powers empowers the spirit to transcend limitations, embrace its true potential, and continue its journey with newfound strength and purpose.

67. Ritual for the communion with the spirits of the four elements

Gather in sacred space, seekers of divine,
As we embark on a journey, transcending time.
Through this ritual, we seek communion pure,
With the spirits of elements, ancient and sure.

With candles ablaze, representing the flame,
We invoke the spirit of fire, untamed.
Passion and transformation, its essence holds,
Burning away illusions, as wisdom unfolds.

Next, we turn to the tranquil waters' flow,
Calling forth the spirit of rivers that glow.
Emotions and healing, its essence brings,
Cleansing our souls, like gentle springs.

Now, we embrace the earth beneath our feet,
Summoning the spirit of grounding and retreat.
Stability and abundance, its essence thrives,
Nurturing our spirits, as roots of trees derive.

Lastly, we lift our gaze to the skies above,
Inviting the spirit of air, the breath of love.
Intellect and clarity, its essence inspires,
Expanding our minds, like celestial fires.

As the elements converge, our spirits align,
In this sacred space, transcending confines.
We open our hearts to the spirits' embrace,
Communing with energies, boundless in grace.

With reverence and respect, we offer our plea,
To the spirits of elements, hear our decree.
Grant us your wisdom, your guidance, your might,
In this sacred communion, our souls take flight.

Note: The Ritual for Communion with the Spirits of the Four Elements is a
ceremonial practice that seeks to establish a connection with the elemental forces of

fire, water, earth, and air. Through the use of candles, symbolic representations of each element, participants invoke the spirits associated with these forces. The ritual acknowledges the unique qualities and energies embodied by each element and seeks to harness their power for guidance and transformation. By communing with these elemental spirits, practitioners aim to gain insight, clarity, healing, and a deep sense of connection with the natural world. The ritual involves invoking the essence of each element, acknowledging their specific attributes, and seeking their blessings. It is a sacred and reverent act, performed with intention and respect for the elemental energies that surround and permeate our lives.

68. Spell for the liberation of the deceased's soul from the shackles of time

In the realm where time dissolves,
Where past, present, and future intertwine,
We call upon the cosmic forces,
To release the soul that seeks to shine.

By the power of eternal existence,
By the essence of boundless eternity,
We break the chains that hold the soul,
And grant it freedom for all eternity.

O Time, you are but an illusion,
A construct of mortal minds,
We now command your hold to cease,
And set the spirit free, unconfined.

Let the moments merge into one,
Let the hours and days fade away,
The soul transcends temporal bounds,
Embracing infinite realms of day.

With this incantation, we declare,
That time shall no longer hold sway,
The soul shall soar beyond its grasp,
Forever liberated, in timeless array.

Note: The Spell for the Liberation of the Deceased's Soul from the Shackles of Time is a ritual incantation performed to free the soul from the constraints of time. It acknowledges the illusionary nature of time and asserts the soul's ability to transcend temporal boundaries. The spell is a powerful invocation of cosmic forces, calling upon the timeless essence of existence to release the soul from the perceived limitations imposed by the linear progression of time. It affirms the eternal nature of the soul and invokes the divine energies to break the chains of temporal captivity, granting the soul the freedom to traverse infinite realms beyond the confines of time. The spell is performed with reverence and intention, creating a sacred space where the soul's liberation can take place.

69. Invocation of the goddess Bastet for protection and fertility

Mighty Bastet, graceful and fierce,
Goddess of protection, ever near.
I call upon your sacred name,
To shield me from harm, to bless my flame.

With the grace of a cat, swift and strong,
Wrap your loving arms, where I belong.
Guard me against all that would bring me woe,
Keep me safe wherever I may go.

Bastet, mother of the sacred feline,
Goddess of fertility, your blessings align.
Grant me abundance, in body and soul,
Fertility and prosperity, make me whole.

Like the desert sands, shifting and fine,
May your presence be with me, divine.
Guide me through life's trials and strife,
Bring me joy, love, and a fertile life.

Oh, Bastet, hear my fervent plea,
Protect me, bless me, set my spirit free.
With your presence, may my path be lit,
In your embrace, may I find my true grit.

Note: This invocation to the Goddess Bastet would be performed with reverence and respect. The practitioner would call upon Bastet for protection from harm and to bless their life with fertility and abundance. The mention of cats symbolizes Bastet's connection to feline energy and grace. It is believed that through this invocation, the practitioner seeks the goddess's guidance, strength, and blessings in various aspects of life, particularly in matters of protection and fertility.

70. Invocation of the goddess Taweret for protection and fertility in the afterlife

Mighty Taweret, Goddess of protection and fertility,
I beseech thee to hear my plea,
As I stand at the threshold of the afterlife,
Grant me your divine guidance and mercy.

With the strength of a lioness, fierce and true,
You guard the souls in the realm anew,
Shield me from harm, O powerful one,
As I navigate this journey yet to be done.

Great Taweret, who embraces the sacred river's flow,
Bring forth fertility and life's abundant glow,
Bless my spirit with your nurturing grace,
In this realm beyond, a blessed embrace.

O gentle goddess, with the head of a hippopotamus,
Your presence brings solace, dispelling all darkness,
Protect my soul from malevolent forces that may lurk,
Preserve my essence, as I traverse this spiritual work.

In the afterlife's realm, where mysteries unfold,
Guide me with your wisdom, ageless and bold,
Grant me the blessings of life's divine cycle,
And nurture my spirit with fertility's revival.

By your sacred name, I invoke your power,
Taweret, guardian of the midnight hour,
Wrap me in your loving embrace,
As I journey through this ethereal space.

Note: The Invocation of the Goddess Taweret for Protection and Fertility in the Afterlife is a reverent call to the ancient Egyptian goddess Taweret. She is invoked for her protective qualities and association with fertility, which are sought to be extended into the afterlife. The invocation acknowledges Taweret's fierce nature and ability to safeguard the souls in the afterlife realm. It calls upon her to shield the individual from harm and to provide guidance and protection throughout their spiritual journey. The invocation also seeks Taweret's blessings of fertility and abundance, ensuring the continuation of life's divine cycle in the afterlife. The ritual is performed with reverence and respect, creating a sacred space where the presence and power of Taweret can be invoked and honored.

71. Ritual of anointing with sacred waters for spiritual rebirth

In the sacred temple, where ancient secrets lie,
I stand before the waters, reflecting the sky.
With reverence and devotion, I seek rebirth,
To cleanse my spirit, to reclaim my worth.

I dip my hands into the sacred pool,
Where the divine essence sparkles and cool.
Water, pure and sacred, flowing with grace,
I anoint myself, embracing this sacred space.

With every droplet that caresses my skin,
I release the past, the shadows within.
The sacred waters wash away my strife,
Renewing my spirit, awakening new life.

As the water flows upon my brow,
I surrender to the divine, here and now.
Cleansed and purified, I am born anew,
Embracing the path that lies ahead, true.

The sacred waters, blessed by gods above,
Infuse my being with their eternal love.
They cleanse my soul, they heal my wounds,
Guiding me forward to spiritual attunements.

In this ritual of anointing, I find solace and peace,
A sacred moment of divine release.
I emerge from the waters, reborn and whole,
Ready to embark on a journey of the soul.

Note: The Ritual of Anointing with Sacred Waters for Spiritual Rebirth is a ceremonial practice that involves the use of sacred waters for purification and rejuvenation. The ritual takes place in a temple or a sacred space where the individual seeks spiritual rebirth and transformation. The sacred waters symbolize purity, renewal, and the life-giving force of the divine. By anointing oneself with the sacred waters, the person releases old patterns, burdens, and negative energies, making way for a fresh start and a renewed sense of purpose. The act of anointing represents a surrender to the divine and a willingness to let go of the past, embracing a new chapter in one's spiritual journey. The ritual is performed with intention, reverence, and a deep connection to the sacred waters, allowing for a profound spiritual experience and a sense of inner rebirth.

72. Spell for the transformation of the deceased into a vessel of divine love

In the realm of the sacred and the divine,
I call upon the powers that intertwine.
With pure intention and a heart aflame,
I seek to embody love in its highest name.

I summon the spirits of love's pure essence,
To guide me through this sacred transformation process.
From earthly bounds, I am set free,
To become a vessel of divine love, you see.

With every breath, I inhale the love divine,
Filling my being, merging with my soul's design.
Love's energy courses through every vein,
Transforming me, like a gentle summer rain.

I shed the layers of fear and despair,
Opening my heart to love's tender care.
As love flows through me, it heals and restores,
Igniting my spirit, unlocking divine doors.

I radiate love in every word and deed,
Spreading compassion, fulfilling every need.
Love is my essence, my guiding light,
Transcending boundaries, shining ever bright.

In this transformation, I become love's vessel,
A conduit of pure affection and tenderness.
I carry love's message, a beacon in the night,
Guiding souls to embrace love's infinite light.

As I leave this earthly realm behind,
Love's presence within me forever entwined.
I embrace my destiny, my purpose, my role,
To be a vessel of divine love, making the whole.

Note: The Spell for the Transformation of the Deceased into a Vessel of Divine
Love is a sacred invocation and intention-setting practice. It is performed to facilitate

the transformation of the deceased into a vessel of love, embodying the highest expression of love's essence. The spell is typically conducted with reverence and a deep connection to the divine. The individual invokes the spirits and energies of love, allowing love to flow through them and permeate their being. This transformation is seen as a shedding of lower vibrational energies and a surrender to the pure, unconditional love that exists in the spiritual realms. By becoming a vessel of divine love, the individual becomes a conduit for spreading love, compassion, and healing to others. The spell is performed with heartfelt intention, invoking the power of love to bring about a profound and lasting transformation within the deceased's soul.

73. Incantation to invoke the blessings of the celestial gods and goddesses

O mighty gods and goddesses of the celestial sphere,
I call upon your presence, both far and near.
With reverence and awe, I offer my plea,
Grant me your blessings, and set my spirit free.

From the realms of stars and galaxies above,
Descend upon me, with your divine love.
With each sacred word and utterance I make,
Let your blessings shower down, for my soul's sake.

Great Ra, sun god, radiant and bright,
Illuminate my path with your golden light.
Bless me with vitality and eternal flame,
That my spirit may forever bear your name.

Goddess Isis, embodiment of love and healing,
Wrap me in your wings, my heart revealing.
Bestow upon me your nurturing embrace,
And fill my being with boundless grace.

Mighty Horus, falcon-eyed and wise,
Guide me with your sight, beyond the skies.
Grant me protection, strength, and clarity,
As I navigate life's celestial mystery.

Osiris, lord of the underworld and rebirth,
Unite me with the eternal cycle of the earth.
Bless me with transformation, divine and true,
That I may transcend, and anew.

Goddess Hathor, beauty and joy you bring,
Infuse my life with your celestial spring.
Fill my heart with love's harmonious tune,
And let my soul dance beneath the moon.

Celestial gods and goddesses, I implore,
Pour your blessings upon me, forevermore.

Guide me on my spiritual quest and earthly strife,
That I may walk in harmony, embracing eternal life.

Note: The Incantation to Invoke the Blessings of the Celestial Gods and Goddesses is a sacred invocation and prayer. It is performed to call upon the powers and blessings of the celestial deities, such as Ra, Isis, Horus, Osiris, Hathor, and others. The incantation is recited with deep reverence and respect, with the intention of receiving divine guidance, protection, and blessings. The individual seeks to establish a connection with the celestial realm, invoking the presence and influence of the gods and goddesses in their life. By calling upon these celestial beings, the individual seeks their assistance, wisdom, and divine grace to navigate life's challenges and receive spiritual enlightenment. The incantation is performed with sincerity and devotion, allowing the blessings of the celestial gods and goddesses to flow into the individual's life, bringing forth their transformative and uplifting energies.

74. Ritual for the transfiguration of the deceased into a divine scribe

In the sacred chamber of the afterlife's realm,
Where time and space converge at the helm,
I invoke the transformation, profound and rare,
To transfigure the deceased into a divine scribe fair.

With ink of cosmic essence and parchment divine,
I embark on this ritual, invoking powers sublime.
As the deceased lies upon the sacred altar,
I prepare to awaken their spirit, never to falter.

I call upon Thoth, the god of wisdom and writing,
To bestow his blessings, the soul's journey igniting.
With quill in hand, I trace symbols in the air,
Conjuring the ancient language, the divine prayer.

I utter incantations, resonating with power,
Unveiling the mysteries of the celestial hour.
The deceased's essence begins to stir and rise,
Transforming into a scribe with awakened eyes.

Their hands become instruments of sacred art,
Transcribing cosmic wisdom, a celestial chart.
The knowledge of the ages flows through their veins,
As they become a vessel, devoid of earthly chains.

Inscribe, O divine scribe, the secrets of the divine,
Channel the cosmic wisdom, a sacred design.
Record the stories of gods, the tales of creation,
And guide the souls on their eternal migration.

Through this ritual, the deceased transcends,
Becoming a conduit, where divine knowledge descends.
Their spirit now merged with Thoth's sacred light,
A celestial scribe, in realms both day and night.

Note: The Ritual for the Transfiguration of the Deceased into a Divine Scribe is a
sacred ceremony performed to transform the deceased into a celestial being tasked

with recording and preserving the wisdom of the gods. The ritual involves invoking the presence and blessings of Thoth, the god of wisdom, writing, and the divine word. Through the recitation of incantations and the use of sacred symbols, the deceased's essence is awakened, and they are transfigured into a divine scribe. Their role is to channel cosmic wisdom, transcribe celestial knowledge, and guide the souls on their journey through the afterlife. The ritual is conducted with reverence and respect, aiming to merge the spirit of the deceased with the divine essence of Thoth, thus bestowing upon them the divine abilities of a celestial scribe.

75. Spell for the reunion of the deceased's soul with their spiritual guides

By the sacred flame, I call upon the unseen,
To guide the departed, to intervene.
Through the veils of existence, they shall traverse,
Reuniting the soul with spiritual guides, diverse.

I invoke the presence of ancestral souls,
Whose wisdom and love eternally rolls.
May their guidance shine like a beacon of light,
Leading the departed through the realm of the night.

With pure intention and heartfelt plea,
I summon the spirits, ancient and free.
Let them gather 'round, a celestial congregation,
To guide the soul in its journey's duration.

I speak the names of the beloved guides,
Whose presence in the afterlife abides.
May their voices echo through the cosmic space,
Drawing the departed to their divine embrace.

Oh, spiritual guides of wisdom and might,
Bring solace and guidance in the darkest night.
Lead the departed with compassion and care,
Through the realms of the afterlife, beyond compare.

As the departed soul seeks its destined place,
Let the reunion with guides be a moment of grace.
May they offer comfort, love, and insight,
Guiding the departed to realms of pure light.

With this spell, I forge the sacred bond,
Between the departed and their guides, beyond.
Through realms unseen, their connection is restored,
As they journey together, forevermore.

Note: The Spell for the Reunion of the Deceased's Soul with Their Spiritual Guides
is a powerful invocation performed to reunite the departed soul with their spiritual

guides and mentors. Through the recitation of sacred words and the calling upon the unseen realms, the spell seeks to draw forth the presence and guidance of ancestral souls and divine beings who serve as spiritual guides. These guides offer support, wisdom, and love to the departed as they navigate the realms of the afterlife. The spell emphasizes the importance of the departed's connection with their guides, as they provide comfort, insight, and direction on their soul's journey. Through this reunion, the departed finds solace and the assurance that they are not alone, but accompanied by benevolent spirits who are dedicated to their well-being.

76. Invocation of the god Hapi for abundance and prosperity in the afterlife

Oh, mighty Hapi, God of the Nile's flow,
I call upon you with reverence to bestow,
Your blessings upon the departed's soul,
In the realms of the afterlife, make them whole.

With your fertile waters, you bring forth life,
Nourishing the land, dispelling all strife.
I seek your presence, O generous deity,
To bless the departed with abundance and prosperity.

From your sacred river, wealth overflows,
Filling the spirit with riches that grow.
Grant the departed an eternal prosperity,
In the realms of the afterlife, where they shall be.

Pour forth your blessings, O benevolent Hapi,
Let the departed find prosperity aplenty.
May their needs be met, their desires fulfilled,
As they traverse the realms, where destinies are willed.

Guide them to the fields of plenty and wealth,
Where abundance reigns, and there's no dearth.
Let them find joy in the bounties they receive,
In the afterlife's realms, where blessings never leave.

Oh, Hapi, god of abundance and fertility,
In the afterlife, shower blessings abundantly.
May the departed soul thrive in your care,
Surrounded by prosperity beyond compare.

With this invocation, I seek your divine grace,
To bless the departed in their eternal space.
Hapi, hear my plea, as I call upon your name,
Bring forth abundance and prosperity, without blame.

Note: The Invocation of the God Hapi for Abundance and Prosperity in the Afterlife is a sacred plea to the deity Hapi, who is associated with the fertile waters of the Nile River. The invocation seeks the blessings of Hapi upon the departed soul, asking for abundance, prosperity, and wealth in the realms of the afterlife. By acknowledging Hapi's role as the bringer of life and sustenance, the invocation emphasizes the desire for the departed to experience eternal prosperity and fulfillment in their spiritual journey. It calls upon Hapi to pour forth blessings, guide the departed to fields of plenty, and ensure that their needs and desires are met in the afterlife. Through this invocation, the hope is to secure the departed's well-being and abundance, as they navigate the realms beyond.

77. Ritual of purification through the sacred movements of ritual dance

In the sacred space of divine connection,
Where spirits dwell and souls find reflection,
I invoke the power of the ancient dance,
To cleanse and purify with each graceful trance.

With reverence and intention, I begin the rite,
Moving in harmony with the sacred light,
With every step, I release what no longer serves,
Unveiling the purity that within me preserves.

Arms raised high, reaching towards the celestial sphere,
I let go of burdens, doubts, and all fear,
My body becomes a vessel, a channel of divine,
As I swirl and twirl, I leave the mundane behind.

The rhythm of the dance carries me away,
Guided by forces that lead me astray,
In the whirlwind of motion, I find my center,
Purging impurities, allowing my spirit to enter.

Each movement, a prayer, a sacred invocation,
Calling upon higher realms for purification,
With each spin and turn, I shed the old,
Embracing the purity, my spirit is enfolded.

The dance becomes a language, a sacred art,
Transmuting darkness, healing every wounded part,
As I move with grace, I am reborn anew,
In the sacred dance, my spirit finds its truest hue.

The rhythm quickens, energy surging through,
In this divine dance, I am made whole and true,
I surrender to the music, the pulsating beat,
Allowing the purification to be complete.

With the final motion, I come to stillness,

Feeling the essence of divine presence, endless,
Purified and renewed, I stand in sacred space,
Connected to the cosmic web, embraced by grace.

Note: The Ritual of Purification through the Sacred Movements of Ritual Dance is a ceremonial practice that involves using dance as a means of purifying the body, mind, and spirit. It is performed in a sacred space with the intention of releasing what no longer serves and inviting in divine purification. The dancer engages in graceful movements, invoking the power of the dance to cleanse and heal. Each step, spin, and gesture is a prayer and an invocation, connecting the dancer to higher realms and transmuting negativity into positivity. The dance is a language of the soul, a form of expression that allows for the release of impurities and the embrace of inner purity. Through this ritual, the dancer is reborn, renewed, and aligned with the sacred energies of the universe.

78. Spell for the liberation of the deceased's soul from earthly desires

In the realm between the worlds, where spirits reside,
I call upon the cosmic forces, the divine guide,
To release the shackles that bind the soul,
And free the spirit from desires taking toll.

With sacred words, I speak this spell,
To break the chains that earthly desires compel,
I summon the strength of the ancient ones,
To guide the departed from earthly attachments undone.

By the power of divine light and cosmic grace,
I sever the ties that hold the soul in chase,
No longer shall earthly cravings control,
As the spirit ascends to a higher, purer goal.

I invoke the winds to carry away the cravings deep,
The desires that bind, causing the soul to weep,
Let the flames of transformation burn them all,
As the spirit answers the divine's sacred call.

By the waters of wisdom, the soul is cleansed,
Renouncing earthly desires that once fenced,
Let the earth's grounding energy support the release,
As the spirit finds liberation, finding inner peace.

As I speak these words with intent and might,
I cut the cords that held the soul too tight,
The spirit now soars on wings of freedom's flight,
Released from earthly desires, embracing the light.

Note: The Spell for the Liberation of the Deceased's Soul from Earthly Desires is a powerful incantation performed to free the departed soul from the attachments and cravings of their earthly existence. Through the invocation of divine forces and the utilization of elemental energies, the spell aims to sever the ties that bind the soul to earthly desires. The winds carry away the cravings, the flames burn away the attachments, the waters cleanse and purify, and the grounding energy of the earth supports the release. As the spell is spoken with intention and strength, the cords that held the soul captive to earthly desires are cut, allowing the spirit to ascend to a higher state of being, free from the burdens of material cravings. The spell's purpose is to aid the deceased in finding liberation and inner peace as they journey into the realms beyond.

79. Incantation to awaken the dormant wisdom within the deceased's mind

Oh, ancient spirits of wisdom profound,
I beseech thee to gather around,
In this sacred space between worlds unseen,
Awaken the wisdom, reveal what has been.

From the depths of the soul, I call it forth,
The dormant knowledge, the secrets of worth,
With words of power and intent so pure,
I ignite the flame that will endure.

Awaken, O mind, from slumber deep,
Unveil the truths that you shall keep,
Let the veil of ignorance be torn,
As the wisdom within begins to adorn.

By the breath of the gods, the dormant shall rise,
Unveiling the mysteries before mortal eyes,
From ancient echoes, let knowledge resound,
As the deceased's mind becomes unbound.

Unlock the gates of forgotten lore,
Let wisdom flow like never before,
Ignite the spark of enlightened thought,
As the deceased's mind is now sought.

By the power of ancient texts and scrolls,
The wisdom of ages, the stories it holds,
The mind awakens, like a brilliant sun,
Revealing the truths that must be won.

With each incantation, with each sacred word,
The dormant wisdom is powerfully stirred,
Awakened, the mind is now set free,
To embrace the wisdom that eternity can see.

Note: The Incantation to Awaken the Dormant Wisdom Within the Deceased's
Mind is a powerful invocation performed to unlock the hidden knowledge and

wisdom that lies dormant within the deceased. By calling upon the ancient spirits of wisdom, the spell seeks to gather their guidance and assistance in awakening the mind's untapped potential. Through the use of words of power and intention, the spell ignites the flame of wisdom, allowing the deceased's mind to transcend the limitations of mortal understanding. As the veil of ignorance is torn, the mind becomes receptive to the ancient truths and mysteries that were once hidden. The incantation invokes the breath of the gods and the power of ancient texts to unlock the gates of forgotten knowledge. With each repetition of the incantation, the mind becomes more awakened and receptive, allowing the wisdom of the ages to flow through. The spell aims to illuminate the path of enlightenment and empower the deceased to embrace the profound wisdom that stretches beyond the boundaries of time and space.

80. Ritual for the communion with the spirits of the sacred trees

In the ancient grove where spirits dwell,
I stand amidst the trees, their stories to tell.
With reverence and respect, I approach their grace,
Seeking communion with each sacred embrace.

I open my heart to the whispers of the wood,
To the wisdom that lies within each tree's hood.
With hands outstretched, I reach for connection,
As I embark on this sacred tree communion.

First, I seek the mighty oak, ancient and wise,
A guardian of knowledge that none can disguise.
I touch its weathered bark with humble awe,
Absorbing the strength that its roots deeply draw.

Next, I turn to the graceful willow by the stream,
Its gentle branches dance, as if in a dream.
I let its soothing presence wash over me,
In its embrace, I find solace and serenity.

Then, I approach the mighty redwood, tall and grand,
Its towering presence like a sentinel, it stands.
I press my palms against its textured skin,
Feeling the energy that courses from within.

Moving on, I seek the blossom-laden cherry tree,
Its delicate petals in hues of pink and white, I see.
I inhale its sweet fragrance, a scent divine,
As its blossoms whisper secrets of beauty and time.

Finally, I come to the ancient yew, solemn and wise,
With branches reaching to the vast, endless skies.
I sit beneath its boughs, in quiet contemplation,
Absorbing the ancient wisdom of this sacred location.

With each tree, I commune, their spirits I embrace,
Listening to their voices, feeling their grace.

Through touch, breath, and stillness, we merge as one,
In this sacred ritual, our connection is spun.

In the embrace of the sacred trees' energy,
I find guidance, healing, and divine synergy.
Their spirits whisper secrets of life's mysteries,
Offering wisdom, nurturing my soul's histories.

Note: The Ritual for Communion with the Spirits of the Sacred Trees is a sacred practice that allows individuals to connect with the spiritual essence of specific trees and access the wisdom and energy they hold. This ritual involves approaching different types of trees with reverence and respect, establishing a physical and energetic connection with each one. By touching, leaning against, or sitting beneath the trees, practitioners seek to absorb their unique qualities and engage in a deep spiritual communion. Each tree represents different aspects of wisdom, strength, serenity, beauty, and ancient knowledge. Through this ritual, individuals can gain insight, guidance, and healing from the spirits of the sacred trees. It is a powerful practice of attuning oneself to the natural world and accessing the profound energies that reside within these majestic beings.

81. Spell for the transmigration of the deceased's soul into the cosmic ocean

By the shores of eternity, where the celestial waters flow,
I call upon the powers of the cosmic ocean's glow.
With words of ancient magic, I speak this sacred spell,
To guide the soul of the departed, where destiny does dwell.

In the depths of the cosmic sea, let the soul find release,
From the earthly bonds that held, now grant it eternal peace.
May the waters of the universe carry it far and wide,
To realms beyond the mortal realm, where spirits abide.

With each ripple and wave, let the soul be reborn,
Embracing the cosmic currents, its essence to transform.
As the tides ebb and flow, let it merge with the infinite,
Becoming a drop in the cosmic ocean, where all souls meet.

Let the soul dance with stardust and bathe in celestial light,
As it traverses the cosmic ocean, in its boundless flight.
May it swim with the constellations, guided by astral gleams,
Navigating cosmic currents, fulfilling its astral dreams.

O cosmic ocean, vast and profound,
Embrace this soul, forever unbound.
Carry it on your celestial tide,
To realms where cosmic mysteries reside.

In this spell's embrace, may the soul find its way,
Transmigrating through the cosmic ocean, without delay.
Grant it liberation from earthly illusions and strife,
As it journeys into the infinite, embracing eternal life.

Note: The Spell for the Transmigration of the Deceased's Soul into the Cosmic Ocean is a powerful incantation used to guide the soul of the departed into the vast expanse of the cosmic realms. By invoking the cosmic ocean and its metaphysical properties, this spell aims to release the soul from earthly attachments and enable its transmigration into higher realms of existence. The spell calls upon the cosmic forces and celestial waters to carry the soul on a transformative journey, where it can merge with the cosmic essence and find ultimate liberation. It is a ritual of transcendence and the embrace of the infinite, allowing the departed soul to connect with the universal energies and continue its spiritual evolution beyond the limitations of mortal existence.

82. Invocation of the goddess Sekhmet for protection against illness and disease

Mighty Sekhmet, lioness of divine power and healing,
I call upon your presence, your strength revealing.
In the face of illness and affliction, I seek your aid,
To shield the vulnerable, your protection displayed.

Goddess of the sun's fire, fierce and untamed,
Grant your sacred blessings, by your name proclaimed.
With your blazing radiance, banish illness away,
In your mighty presence, may health forever stay.

O Sekhmet, with eyes that pierce through the night,
With your roar, dispel sickness, restore life's light.
Invoke your sacred flame, burn away all disease,
Grant vitality and well-being, bring us ease.

In your divine embrace, let healing energy flow,
Like a gentle breeze, soothing, calming, and aglow.
Protect us from ailments, both seen and unseen,
With your divine power, may we be serene.

Goddess Sekhmet, guardian of health and life's breath,
With your grace and wisdom, ward off illness and death.
Grant us strength and vitality, fortify our souls,
In your loving care, may our bodies be whole.

As I speak your name, Sekhmet, hear my plea,
Wrap us in your healing light, set our spirits free.
Guide us on the path of wellness, with your divine grace,
In your presence, dear Sekhmet, may we find solace.

Note: The Invocation of the Goddess Sekhmet for Protection Against Illness and Disease is a sacred prayer and plea for the intervention of the fierce and powerful goddess Sekhmet. Known for her healing abilities and protection against ailments, Sekhmet is invoked to safeguard individuals from illness, disease, and physical afflictions. Through the invocation, the devotee seeks the goddess's intervention to banish sickness and restore health and vitality. It is a reverent call upon Sekhmet's divine power and healing energy, seeking her guidance and support in times of physical vulnerability.

83. Ritual of anointing with sacred powders for spiritual transformation

In a chamber adorned with symbols divine,
Where the veil between realms begins to unwind,
I gather the sacred powders, pure and rare,
To anoint and awaken the spirit's hidden flare.

With reverence and care, I hold the vessel near,
Whispers of ancient wisdom dancing in the air,
The powders, a concoction of mystical blend,
Prepared by hands blessed, their purpose to transcend.

I dip my fingers into the sacred powder's grace,
As it touches my skin, I feel its mystical embrace,
Each grain infused with energy, ancient and wise,
A conduit for transformation, a pathway to the skies.

Starting from the crown, I anoint with intention,
Tracing a path of enlightenment and ascension,
The powders bless my third eye, awakening the sight,
To perceive the hidden truths in ethereal light.

Downward I move, anointing the throat's sacred ground,
Empowering the voice, its resonance profound,
Words uttered become spells, woven with might,
A vessel for divine wisdom, shining through the night.

On the heart, I place the powder's gentle touch,
Igniting the flame of love, radiating much,
Compassion and empathy, its essence unfurled,
A sacred space where the divine resides and is heard.

The solar plexus receives the powder's gentle dust,
Awakening personal power, strength, and trust,
A fiery center, a source of divine will,
Igniting the spirit's flame, with purpose to fulfill.

Moving lower, I anoint the sacral's sacred sphere,
Stirring creativity, passion, and joy sincere,

The powders spark the fire of creative expression,
Igniting the soul's desires, boundless in their impression.

Finally, I reach the base, the root of stability,
Anointing with reverence, grounding serenity,
The powders connect to the earth's nurturing embrace,
Creating a foundation, a space of divine grace.

With each anointing, the powders merge and unite,
A catalyst for spiritual transformation's flight,
Through this ritual's act, a sacred alchemy,
The spirit awakened, dancing in harmony.

Note: The Ritual of Anointing with Sacred Powders for Spiritual Transformation is a ceremonial practice that involves the use of special powders infused with divine energy and intention. The ritual is performed in a sacred space, where the practitioner anoints specific energy centers or chakras on their body with the sacred powders. Each anointing carries a specific purpose, such as opening the third eye for heightened perception, empowering the voice for effective communication, awakening the heart for love and compassion, igniting personal power in the solar plexus, stimulating creativity in the sacral region, and grounding and stabilizing the root chakra. The act of anointing with the powders is believed to activate and align the spiritual energy centers, facilitating spiritual transformation and growth. The ritual is performed with reverence and intention, connecting the practitioner to the divine forces and their own inner power.

84. Spell for the transformation of the deceased into a vessel of divine healing

By the sacred powers that govern all,
I beseech the cosmic forces, great and small,
In this realm between worlds, I stand,
To channel healing energy, divine and grand.

Oh, spirits of ancient wisdom and grace,
Hear my plea in this sacred space,
Grant me the power to transcend the veil,
To transform the departed, and their essence unveil.

With intentions pure and heart sincere,
I call upon the energies, both far and near,
May the deceased be reborn anew,
A vessel of healing, radiating through.

From the crown to the toes, their being shall glow,
Infused with divine light, a celestial flow,
Every cell, every atom, transformed and renewed,
With healing energy, pure and imbued.

Let their hands become conduits of compassion,
Their touch a balm, soothing affliction,
Their voice a melody, healing the soul,
Restoring wholeness, making the broken whole.

May their presence bring solace and peace,
Dispelling ailments, granting release,
Their essence a beacon, a guiding light,
Leading others on the path to health's respite.

In the realms of the living, their presence felt,
An embodiment of healing, in hearts to melt,
Their spirit intertwined with divine grace,
A vessel of healing in time and space.

Note: The Spell for the Transformation of the Deceased into a Vessel of Divine
Healing is a sacred invocation performed to bestow the deceased with the ability to

become a channel for healing energies. The spell is conducted by a practitioner who seeks to harness the cosmic forces and divine wisdom to transform the departed soul into a vessel of healing. With pure intentions and a sincere heart, the practitioner calls upon the ancient spirits and cosmic energies to infuse the deceased's being with healing energy. This transformation occurs at a deep level, touching every aspect of their being, from physical to spiritual. The spell aims to empower the deceased to bring comfort, solace, and healing to those in need. Through their hands, their voice, and their very essence, they become a source of divine healing for others, acting as a guiding light on the path to wellness and wholeness.

85. Incantation to invoke the blessings of the celestial rivers and streams

Oh, mighty rivers that flow through the heavens,
Glistening streams that weave through celestial realms,
I call upon your sacred waters, pure and divine,
To bestow upon us blessings, both yours and mine.

From the celestial realm where you originate,
You carry the essence of life, a sacred mandate,
Your currents symbolize the eternal flow,
Guiding us on a journey, both high and low.

By the power of your meandering streams,
I seek your blessings in this mortal dream,
Flow through my life, like a river's gentle embrace,
Granting me wisdom, serenity, and grace.

Like the great Nile, abundant and grand,
Your blessings nourish the soul, where they land,
Wash away all that is stagnant and impure,
Purify my spirit, make it crystal clear.

I invoke your power, O rivers of the sky,
To cleanse my being, as the days go by,
Let your currents carry away all strife,
Bless me with harmony, in this earthly life.

With each ripple and wave, your blessings unfurl,
As I immerse myself in your celestial swirl,
Guide me on a path of spiritual growth,
Nourish my soul, as I take this oath.

By the celestial rivers and streams, I'm blessed,
In their sacred waters, I find solace and rest,
May their divine energy forever flow,
Granting me strength and serenity to grow.

Note: The Incantation to Invoke the Blessings of the Celestial Rivers and Streams is
a ritualistic chant performed to invoke the blessings and powers associated with

celestial waterways. The incantation calls upon the sacred rivers and streams that flow through the heavens, symbolizing the eternal flow of life and wisdom. By reciting the incantation, one seeks the cleansing and purifying qualities of these celestial waters to wash away impurities and bring serenity and harmony to their life. The rivers are seen as carriers of divine energy, and their blessings are believed to nourish the spirit and guide one on a path of spiritual growth. Through the ritual, the individual aligns themselves with the flowing currents of the celestial rivers, drawing upon their power and seeking their guidance and blessings in their earthly journey.

86. Ritual for the transfiguration of the deceased into a divine teacher

In the sacred chamber of transformation, I stand,
Before the threshold of enlightenment, I command,
To transfigure the deceased into a vessel of divine light,
A teacher of wisdom, shining with celestial might.

With reverence and purpose, I prepare the sacred space,
An altar adorned with symbols, reflecting divine grace,
Incense fills the air, carrying prayers to the heavens,
Invoking the presence of the gods, their wisdom beckons.

The deceased, prepared with utmost care and respect,
Lies upon the altar, adorned in garments select,
Anointed with oils, fragrant and pure,
Infusing the essence of divine teachings, for sure.

As the ritual commences, I chant ancient words,
Sacred verses invoking wisdom, like melodious birds,
The energy in the chamber begins to shift and sway,
A divine presence descends, guiding the way.

I call upon the cosmic forces, both near and far,
To infuse the deceased with knowledge, like a shining star,
Grant them insight, understanding, and profound clarity,
That they may become a beacon of wisdom for eternity.

The divine light envelops the deceased's form,
A transformation occurs, through a celestial storm,
Their mortal limitations now cast aside,
As a divine teacher, they shall forever abide.

Their spirit ascends to heights unexplored,
Unlocking the secrets of the universe, untoward,
With wisdom as their guide and love in their heart,
They embark on their mission, never to depart.

In the realm of the divine, they will impart,
Teachings of truth, touching souls and minds, with art,

Their presence lingers, a divine presence embraced,
Guiding seekers on the path, wisdom interlaced.

Note: The Ritual for the Transfiguration of the Deceased into a Divine Teacher is a ceremonial practice conducted to facilitate the spiritual transformation of the deceased into a vessel of divine wisdom and guidance. The ritual is performed in a sacred space, with careful preparation and reverence. The deceased is placed upon an altar, symbolically prepared and anointed with sacred oils, representing the infusion of divine teachings. Through the recitation of ancient chants and invocations, the ritual invokes the presence of cosmic forces and guides the deceased's spirit into a transfigured state. As the ritual progresses, the deceased is enveloped in a divine light, experiencing a profound transformation. Their mortal limitations are shed, and they emerge as a divine teacher, endowed with wisdom and clarity. In this transfigured state, they become a conduit for sharing divine knowledge, guiding and inspiring others on their spiritual journey.

87. Spell for the reunion of the deceased's soul with their divine purpose

By the sacred flame that burns eternal,
I call upon the cosmic forces, infernal,
To guide the departed soul, lost and adrift,
Back to their divine purpose, a precious gift.

With words of power and intention pure,
I weave a spell to reunite and assure,
That the deceased's soul aligns once more,
With their true calling, as it was before.

I summon the ancient wisdom of the stars,
To guide the soul through celestial bazaars,
Where purpose and destiny intertwine,
A cosmic tapestry, divine and sublime.

In the realm of dreams, where spirits dwell,
I enter with reverence, a mystic spell,
Through the veils of time, I navigate,
Seeking the essence, the soul's true fate.

I call upon the guardians of fate and chance,
To illuminate the path, in a celestial dance,
Let the deceased's purpose shine bright,
Guiding their journey with divine light.

In sacred silence, I speak the soul's name,
A sacred vibration, a celestial claim,
With each syllable, I stir the cosmic sea,
Awakening their purpose, setting it free.

As the spell takes hold, the soul awakens,
Remembering their purpose, no longer forsaken,
Bound by destiny, they rise and soar,
Embracing their divine purpose, forevermore.

Note: The Spell for the Reunion of the Deceased's Soul with Their Divine Purpose
is a ritual performed to guide and reunite the departed soul with their true calling and

purpose. It is conducted with the intention of assisting the soul in rediscovering its path and aligning with its higher destiny. The spell is cast with the use of sacred words and invocations, calling upon the cosmic forces and guardians of fate to guide the soul back to its divine purpose. The spell may be performed in a sacred space, where the practitioner creates an atmosphere of reverence and connection. Through the recitation of the spell, the vibration of the soul's name, and the stirring of the cosmic energy, the departed soul is awakened and reminded of its purpose. It is a transformative process that allows the soul to embrace its true calling and embark on a journey of fulfillment and spiritual growth.

88. Invocation of the god Geb for grounding and stability in the afterlife

Mighty Geb, the Earth beneath our feet,
I call upon your presence, strong and complete.
In the realm of the afterlife, I seek your aid,
To bring stability and grounding, a solid foundation laid.

Geb, the giver of life, the provider of stability,
I invoke your name with reverence and humility.
As the earth supports us in the physical realm,
Guide us in the afterlife, where spirits dwell.

With your hands, the mountains rise high,
With your breath, the valleys lie.
Grant us the strength to find our ground,
In the realms unseen, where mysteries abound.

As we journey through the realms unknown,
May your presence help us find our own.
Keep us steady amidst the swirling ethereal,
Ground our souls with your power terrestrial.

Geb, I ask for your blessings in this sacred rite,
Grant us stability and grounding, day and night.
May our spirits remain firmly rooted and strong,
In the afterlife's currents, where we belong.

With gratitude, I offer my prayers and plea,
To Geb, the god of grounding and stability.
Guide us, protect us, in this journey we undertake,
With your divine presence, our souls will never break.

Note: The Invocation of the god Geb for Grounding and Stability in the Afterlife is a ritual performed to seek the assistance of Geb, the Egyptian god associated with the earth, in providing stability and grounding in the afterlife. The invocation is done with reverence and respect, acknowledging Geb as the provider of stability and strength in both the physical and spiritual realms. Through the invocation, the practitioner seeks Geb's guidance and assistance in finding a solid foundation and stability amidst the unknown realms of the afterlife. It is performed in a sacred space, where the practitioner connects with the energy and essence of Geb, calling upon his power to support and ground the spirits in their journey. The invocation is accompanied by offerings and prayers of gratitude, expressing appreciation for Geb's assistance and presence in the afterlife.

89. Ritual of purification through the sacred sounds of chanting and music

In the realm of the sacred, where vibrations meet,
We gather to perform a rite so sweet.
With voices raised and instruments in hand,
We embark on a journey, a purification grand.

In this ritual of sound, we cleanse our souls,
Releasing all impurities that took their tolls.
Through the power of chanting and melodic tunes,
We invite divine frequencies to cleanse and attune.

In a sacred space adorned with symbols divine,
We gather in harmony, our voices intertwine.
We chant sacred mantras, ancient and pure,
Infusing the air with vibrations that endure.

The sound waves ripple through the ethereal plane,
Purging negativity, leaving no stain.
As each note reverberates, we feel the shift,
A purification, a spiritual uplift.

The beats of drums and rhythmic melodies,
Transport us to realms beyond our realities.
Instruments played with skill and devotion,
Open portals of healing and sacred emotion.

With each sacred sound, we shed layers of strife,
Revealing our true essence, the core of life.
The harmonies resonate deep within our being,
Clearing blockages, our spirits freeing.

As the music carries us to a state of grace,
We embrace the sacredness of this sacred space.
We emerge purified, refreshed, and anew,
Connected to the divine, in perfect harmony with the true.

Note: The Ritual of Purification through the Sacred Sounds of Chanting and Music
is a ceremonial practice aimed at purifying the participants' souls through the power

of sound. It takes place in a dedicated sacred space and involves the collective chanting of sacred mantras and the playing of various musical instruments. The rhythmic vibrations and melodic harmonies created during the ritual cleanse the energy field, releasing negative emotions and energetic blockages. The participants engage in harmonious chanting, allowing the sacred sounds to resonate within them, purifying their minds, bodies, and spirits. Instruments, such as drums, flutes, or bells, are also used to enhance the cleansing process and create an atmosphere conducive to spiritual transformation. The ritual concludes with a sense of renewed energy and a heightened connection to the divine.

90. Spell for the liberation of the deceased's soul from the chains of suffering

By the power of ancient wisdom and divine grace,
I call upon the forces of light in this sacred space.
With heartfelt intentions and words of power,
I seek to free the soul in its darkest hour.

O spirits of compassion, hear my plea,
Release this soul from suffering, set it free.
Break the chains that bind, remove all pain,
Let the soul transcend, its liberation to gain.

With incense burning, creating fragrant smoke,
I invoke divine mercy, invoking the sacred cloak.
Through sacred words and intentions pure,
I sever the ties that cause suffering to endure.

I call upon the guardians of the astral plane,
To guide this soul and alleviate its pain.
May the light of divine love shine bright,
Dispelling darkness, bringing respite.

As I speak the sacred words, let them resound,
Echoing through realms, with purpose profound.
May the soul's burdens be lifted, its spirit light,
Reclaiming its essence, no longer bound by plight.

In the embrace of divine grace, the soul finds peace,
Its suffering released, its anguish now cease.
Transcending the limitations of earthly woes,
It soars on wings of freedom, where true liberation flows.

Note: The Spell for the Liberation of the Deceased's Soul from the Chains of Suffering is a ceremonial invocation aimed at freeing the soul from the burdens of suffering. It is performed in a sacred space with the use of incense and sacred words. The practitioner calls upon benevolent spirits and divine forces to assist in breaking the chains of suffering that bind the deceased's soul. The intention is to alleviate the soul's pain, remove any obstacles to its liberation, and guide it towards a state of peace and freedom. The ritual is conducted with deep compassion and heartfelt intentions, seeking to bring comfort and relief to the departed soul.

91. Incantation to awaken the dormant creativity within the deceased's spirit

Oh spirits of inspiration, I call upon thee,
Awaken the dormant creativity within, set it free.
From the depths of the soul, let it rise,
Unleash the artistic essence that never dies.

By the power of the universe and cosmic might,
Ignite the creative fire, shining ever so bright.
Break the chains of stagnation and doubt,
Let creativity flow, in abundance and throughout.

With each spoken word, let the spirit ignite,
A flame of artistic expression, pure and bright.
Unleash the colors, the melodies, the forms,
Awaken the dormant creativity, let it transform.

Oh muses of old, hear my sincere plea,
Breathe life into the artistic soul, let it be.
With divine inspiration, guide its hand,
Unlock the treasures hidden, in the creative land.

Let the deceased's spirit be a vessel, a conduit,
For the artistic currents, flowing absolute.
Let the brush stroke the canvas with passion untold,
Let the pen dance upon the page, stories unfold.

By the power of creation, I call upon thee,
Awaken the dormant creativity, set it free.
From the realm beyond, let it descend,
And with artistic brilliance, let the spirit transcend.

Note: The Incantation to Awaken the Dormant Creativity within the Deceased's Spirit is a ceremonial invocation aimed at awakening the creative essence within the departed soul. It is performed with the intention of igniting the spark of artistic inspiration that may have been dormant during the earthly life. The practitioner calls upon the spirits of inspiration and the cosmic forces of creativity to infuse the deceased's spirit with renewed artistic energy. The incantation is recited with reverence and a deep desire to unleash the creative potential within the soul. The purpose is to allow the deceased to express themselves artistically in the afterlife and continue their creative journey beyond the physical realm.

92. Ritual for the communion with the spirits of the celestial bodies

In the darkest night, under the starry sky,
I stand as a humble seeker, yearning to fly.
I call upon the spirits of the celestial spheres,
To guide me on this mystical journey, free of fears.

With arms outstretched and heart open wide,
I offer my reverence to the cosmic tide.
I invoke the spirits of the moon and sun,
The planets, the constellations, every single one.

I seek communion with your divine essence,
To understand the secrets of celestial presence.
Grant me passage to your realms of light,
Illuminate my path, dispel the shadows of the night.

As I gaze upward with awe and respect,
I feel the cosmic energy, so profound and direct.
I offer my prayers to the stars above,
As vessels of wisdom, carriers of love.

In this sacred space, between Earth and sky,
I align my spirit with the celestial sigh.
I breathe in the essence of the boundless expanse,
Absorbing the cosmic wisdom, in a celestial dance.

Through this ritual of communion, I aspire,
To merge my being with the celestial fire.
To transcend earthly limitations and soar high,
Embracing the oneness with the cosmic sky.

Note: The Ritual for the Communion with the Spirits of the Celestial Bodies is a ceremonial practice aimed at establishing a connection and seeking guidance from the spirits associated with the celestial bodies. The practitioner performs this ritual under the open sky, preferably during the night, to align themselves with the energies of the stars, planets, and other celestial entities. The ritual involves invoking the spirits of the celestial bodies and offering prayers, expressing reverence, and seeking communion with their divine essence. Through this ritual, the practitioner aims to gain insight, wisdom, and guidance from the cosmic forces and to experience a profound connection with the vastness of the universe.

93. Spell for the transmigration of the deceased's soul into the realm of dreams

By the power of the midnight hour's embrace,
I call upon the realm where dreams interlace.
Oh, spirits of slumber, hear my plea,
Grant passage to the realm where souls roam free.

In the twilight between waking and sleep,
I seek to transcend this earthly keep.
With eyes closed and heart unfurled,
I surrender to the dream world's swirling twirl.

I release the ties that bind me to this plane,
Let my soul wander, untethered, untamed.
Through the gates of Morpheus, I pass with grace,
Entering the realm where dreams find their place.

O, sacred realm of visions and desire,
Ignite my spirit, let my essence aspire.
Grant me entry to your mystical domain,
Where imagination reigns, devoid of pain.

In dreams, I shall transcend the boundaries of time,
Unfolding mysteries, a journey so sublime.
I shall dance with shadows and embrace the light,
Exploring the realms of both day and night.

In this ethereal realm, I am unbound,
A spirit roaming where dreams are found.
With every slumber, my soul takes flight,
Transmigrating through the realm of dreams, bright.

By the power of this spell, I seek to explore,
The depths of my being, forevermore.
Grant me wisdom, insight, and divine sight,
As I traverse the dreamscapes, day and night.

Note: The Spell for the Transmigration of the Deceased's Soul into the Realm of
Dreams is a ritualistic practice aimed at allowing the deceased's soul to enter the

realm of dreams and explore the boundless possibilities of the dream world. The spell is performed with the intention of releasing earthly attachments and allowing the soul to transcend the physical realm, entering the domain of dreams. The practitioner recites the incantation during a meditative state, focusing on the desire to traverse the dream world and experience its wonders. Through the spell, the soul is believed to journey through the realm of dreams, where it can gain insight, wisdom, and healing, free from the limitations of the physical world.

94. Invocation of the goddess Neith for protection and guidance in the afterlife

Hail, mighty Neith, goddess of the celestial bow,
Protector of souls in the afterlife's glow.
With reverence and respect, I call upon your name,
To seek your guidance and shelter from all pain.

Oh, Neith, wise and compassionate divine,
With your keen eye, watch over me, be mine.
Guide me through the realms, both dark and bright,
Keep me safe as I journey through the night.

Goddess of weaving and skilled archery,
Grant me strength and shield me with your decree.
With your sacred arrows, ward off any harm,
Protect my soul, keep me safe from alarm.

In the afterlife's expanse, I seek your aid,
To navigate its mysteries, unafraid.
As I traverse the realms of the unknown,
Illuminate my path, let your wisdom be shown.

Neith, guardian of truth and justice fair,
Bestow upon me your unwavering care.
Lead me to the realms where my ancestors reside,
In their wisdom and presence, let me confide.

Goddess Neith, hear my heartfelt plea,
In your embrace, may my spirit forever be.
Guide me towards my destined divine place,
In your protection, find solace and grace.

As I invoke your sacred name this day,
I honor you, Neith, in every prayer I say.
May your presence be my beacon in the night,
Guiding me to eternal peace and light.

Note: The Invocation of the Goddess Neith for Protection and Guidance in the
Afterlife is a ritualistic practice aimed at seeking the protection and guidance of the

goddess Neith in the journey through the afterlife. Neith is invoked as a powerful deity known for her skills in archery and weaving, as well as her wisdom and protection. The invocation is performed with reverence and respect, acknowledging Neith's divine attributes and calling upon her for guidance, safety, and shelter from harm. The practitioner recites the invocation with sincerity and trust in Neith's power, seeking her guidance and assistance in navigating the unknown realms of the afterlife. Through this invocation, the practitioner hopes to receive the blessings and protection of Neith, allowing for a safe and guided passage in the afterlife.

95. Ritual of anointing with sacred crystals for spiritual clarity

Gather, seekers of truth, in sacred space,
With crystals of power, we embrace.
To find clarity within our souls,
Through this ritual, our spirits unfold.

Choose crystals of wisdom, pure and bright,
With energies aligning to higher light.
Amethyst, clear quartz, and selenite too,
These crystals hold vibrations that renew.

In the presence of the divine, we stand,
Holding crystals in our open hands.
Feel their energy radiate through our beings,
As we connect to higher realms, foreseeing.

Anoint the crystals with sacred oils,
Infusing them with intentions that coil.
With each drop, affirm your deepest desire,
Igniting the flame of your soul's fire.

Hold the crystals close to your heart,
Breathe in the energy, let it impart.
Feel the vibrations resonate within,
As clarity and insight begin to begin.

Place the anointed crystals upon your brow,
Opening the third eye, here and now.
Visualize a clear and expansive vision,
Guidance and wisdom, divine provision.

Meditate in stillness, allow your mind to soar,
As the crystals amplify your inner core.
Receive the messages from realms unseen,
Unveiling the truth, pure and serene.

When the ritual is complete, give thanks,
To the crystals and spirits, offering our ranks.

Carry their clarity within your soul,
As you navigate life's journey, whole.

Note: The Ritual of Anointing with Sacred Crystals for Spiritual Clarity is a ceremony that utilizes the power of crystals to enhance spiritual clarity and insight. It involves selecting crystals known for their properties of wisdom and higher consciousness, such as amethyst, clear quartz, and selenite. The crystals are anointed with sacred oils, infused with intentions and desires for clarity and spiritual growth. Participants hold the crystals close to their hearts, allowing the energy to permeate their beings and connect with higher realms. The crystals are then placed upon the brow, stimulating the third eye chakra and promoting inner vision and intuitive understanding. Through meditation and reflection, individuals open themselves to receive messages and insights from the spiritual realm, gaining clarity and guidance. The ritual concludes with gratitude and acknowledgment of the crystals' assistance. The anointed crystals can be carried or kept nearby as reminders of the clarity and wisdom attained during the ritual.

96. Spell for the transformation of the deceased into a vessel of divine wisdom

By the power of the sacred divine,
I call forth wisdom, profound and fine.
In this realm of the afterlife's embrace,
Grant me wisdom, bestowed with grace.

Let the spirit of the departed awaken,
To be a vessel of wisdom, never forsaken.
Unveil the secrets of the cosmic mind,
So divine wisdom in the soul may find.

From the depths of the ancient well,
Let wisdom's elixir within me swell.
I shed earthly ignorance and strife,
Embracing the divine wisdom of life.

With each breath, let wisdom flow,
Filling my being, radiant and aglow.
The veils of illusion are torn apart,
Revealing the wisdom that resides in the heart.

Unlock the gates of ancient lore,
Grant me access to wisdom's store.
May I be a beacon, shining bright,
Guiding others with wisdom's light.

As the deceased undergoes transformation,
Into a vessel of wisdom, divine consecration.
Let the journey of enlightenment begin,
As wisdom flows through the eternal within.

Note: The Spell for the Transformation of the Deceased into a Vessel of Divine Wisdom is a powerful invocation that seeks to awaken the dormant wisdom within the deceased's spirit. By calling upon the sacred and divine forces, the spell aims to unlock the gates of ancient knowledge and bestow profound wisdom upon the departed soul. The spell recognizes the shedding of earthly ignorance and the embrace of higher wisdom as the deceased transitions into a vessel of divine wisdom. It emphasizes the importance of wisdom flowing through the heart and guiding others on their spiritual journeys. The spell acknowledges the transformative power of wisdom and the eternal nature of the soul's quest for enlightenment.

97. Incantation to invoke the blessings of the celestial mountains and valleys

Oh, mighty mountains that touch the sky,
And valleys deep, where secrets lie,
I call upon your celestial might,
To bestow upon me blessings bright.

From lofty peaks to the depths below,
Your sacred presence, let it flow.
Grant me strength and resilience strong,
As I walk the path, steady and long.

In your grandeur, I find solace and peace,
A sanctuary where my spirit finds release.
Through towering heights and gentle slopes,
May your blessings fill my heart with hope.

Like the mountains, steadfast and true,
I seek the wisdom they imbue.
Grant me clarity, vision, and grace,
As I journey through life's endless space.

Oh, valleys deep, mysterious and serene,
Where hidden treasures remain unseen,
Guide me through the shadows and the light,
As I navigate this celestial flight.

In your depths, may I find serenity,
And unlock the secrets that set me free.
Your blessings, like streams, shall nourish my soul,
As I embrace the journey towards my goal.

Celestial mountains and valleys divine,
With reverence, I invoke your power sublime.
May your blessings shower upon me now,
As I seek harmony and wisdom, I vow.

Note: The Incantation to Invoke the Blessings of the Celestial Mountains and
Valleys is a heartfelt invocation that seeks the blessings and guidance of these sacred

natural formations. It acknowledges the awe-inspiring power and beauty of mountains, which symbolize strength, resilience, and wisdom. The incantation recognizes the importance of finding solace and peace within their grandeur and seeks the blessings of clarity, vision, and grace. It also acknowledges the significance of valleys, which represent hidden treasures and the depths of our inner selves. The incantation seeks guidance through shadows and light, with the intention to unlock the secrets that lead to serenity and nourishment for the soul. Ultimately, it honors the celestial nature of these mountains and valleys, calling upon their blessings for the journey towards personal harmony and wisdom.

98. Ritual for the transfiguration of the deceased into a divine warrior

By the power of the warrior's might,
I call upon the celestial light.
In this sacred space, I now stand,
To transform the deceased by my command.

Warrior deities, hear my plea,
Mars, Athena, and Sekhmet, I summon thee.
Grant strength, courage, and protection true,
As we embark on this sacred breakthrough.

With sword in hand, I touch this symbol,
Transferring warrior energy, now humbled.
From this moment on, let the transfiguration begin,
As the deceased's spirit becomes a warrior within.

Radiant light, golden and bright,
Envelop the deceased in your celestial might.
Transform them now, in this sacred hour,
Into a divine warrior with divine power.

Courage and strength, flow through their veins,
Protective shield, let them sustain.
Obstacles shattered, victory they'll find,
As a warrior of the divine, their spirit aligned.

Warrior's path, now open wide,
With every step, their fears subside.
Embrace their true essence, so bold and free,
As they journey through eternity.

With gratitude and reverence, I give thanks,
To the warrior deities, their divine ranks.
This ritual complete, the transformation done,
As the deceased's soul shines like the sun.

So mote it be, the ritual is sealed,
In the realms of the divine, their fate revealed.

May the deceased's spirit forever thrive,
As a divine warrior, throughout all time.

Step 1: Preparation

- ✧ Create a sacred space where the ritual will take place. This can be a dedicated altar or a designated area with spiritual significance.
- ✧ Gather ritual tools and items symbolizing strength, courage, and warrior energy. This can include a sword or dagger, a shield, red or gold candles, and warrior-related imagery.
- ✧ Cleanse the space and yourself using sacred smoke, such as burning herbs or incense.

Step 2: Setting Intentions

- ✧ Stand at the center of the sacred space and ground yourself. Take deep breaths and center your focus.
- ✧ Set your intention clearly and strongly. Visualize the deceased as a divine warrior, filled with strength, courage, and protective energy.
- ✧ Speak your intention out loud, declaring the transfiguration of the deceased into a divine warrior.

Step 3: Invocation

- ✧ Light the red or gold candles, representing the warrior energy and divine power.
- ✧ Invoke the presence of warrior deities or guardians, such as Mars, Athena, or Sekhmet. Call upon their strength, protection, and guidance.
- ✧ Offer prayers or invocations specific to the warrior deity you are invoking, requesting their assistance in the transfiguration process.

Step 4: Symbolic Actions

- ✧ Hold the sword or dagger in your hand, symbolizing the divine weapon of the warrior.
- ✧ Gently touch the deceased's image or a representation of them with the sword or dagger, transferring the energy of the divine warrior.
- ✧ Visualize the deceased's spirit being enveloped by a golden or radiant light, transforming them into a powerful and protective warrior.

Step 5: Affirmations and Blessings

✧ Speak affirmations and blessings for the deceased's transfiguration into a divine warrior. This can include statements of courage, strength, protection, and victory over obstacles.
✧ Repeat these affirmations and blessings several times, infusing them with belief and intention.

Step 6: Gratitude and Closure

✧ Express gratitude to the warrior deities or guardians for their presence and assistance in the ritual.
✧ Thank the deceased for their willingness to undergo this transformation and for embracing their divine warrior essence.
✧ Close the ritual by extinguishing the candles and offering a final prayer or blessing.

Note: The Ritual for the Transfiguration of the Deceased into a Divine Warrior is a ceremonial practice that aims to invoke the warrior energy and transform the deceased into a powerful and protective force. The ritual emphasizes strength, courage, and the ability to overcome challenges. It involves setting clear intentions, invoking warrior deities or guardians, and symbolically transferring the energy of a divine weapon to the deceased's spirit. Affirmations and blessings are spoken to reinforce the qualities of a warrior, and gratitude is expressed to the spiritual forces involved. This ritual is performed with respect and reverence, honoring the deceased's journey towards embracing their innate warrior nature in the divine realms.

99. Spell for the reunion of the deceased's soul with their divine companions

In the sacred space where realms unite,
I call upon the stars shining bright.
Let the veil between worlds gently part,
As I summon the presence of the divine heart.

O spirits of love, companions divine,
Guides and allies throughout all time,
Hear my plea, with open ears,
Bring comfort and solace, dry all tears.

By the power of cosmic love's embrace,
Reunite the deceased with their divine grace.
May their souls be wrapped in warm embrace,
With their companions, in celestial space.

Across the realms, let connections ignite,
Binding spirits together, day and night.
Through dimensions, let love transcend,
And unite the departed with cherished friends.

Soul to soul, spirit to spirit,
Let this reunion be sacred and exquisite.
In divine harmony, they shall merge,
Across realms and time, their bond will surge.

Companions of light, gather near,
Guide the deceased with love sincere.
Illuminate their path, offer your support,
As they navigate the celestial courts.

Through this spell, let their union be blessed,
With divine presence, may they be caressed.
Reunited and whole, in love's eternal sway,
May the deceased and their companions forever stay.

As above, so below, let it be done,
The reunion of souls, bound as one.

With gratitude and trust, this spell is cast,
May the deceased's reunion be steadfast.

Note: The provided spell is a poetic invocation to the spirits and divine companions of the deceased. It seeks to reunite the departed with their loved ones, guides, and allies from the realm of the divine. The spell emphasizes the power of love, connection, and the transcendent nature of their bond. It is meant to be spoken with reverence, focus, and the intention of facilitating a sacred reunion.

100.   Invocation of the god Osiris for resurrection and eternal life in the afterlife.

Oh mighty Osiris, Lord of the Dead,
I call upon you with reverence and dread.
You who have traversed the realm of the deceased,
Guide me on the path to eternal peace.

With your divine wisdom and unwavering might,
Grant me resurrection in the realm of eternal light.
From the ashes of mortality, let me rise,
Transcending earthly bounds, reaching the skies.

Oh Osiris, keeper of the sacred scales,
Judge my heart, free me from earthly trails.
In your compassionate embrace, I find solace,
Grant me a place in the realm of eternal grace.

With your sacred breath, infuse me with life,
From death's grip, release me from strife.
Grant me passage to the blessed fields beyond,
Where eternal life and joy abound.

Oh Osiris, grant me the key to the afterlife's gate,
Guide me through the trials, help me navigate.
With your loving guidance, let me ascend,
To the realm where divine souls transcend.

In your name, I invoke your power divine,
Grant me resurrection, let my soul shine.
Eternally united with the divine cosmic flow,
With gratitude, I honor you, Osiris, and bestow.

Note: The above invocation is a reverent call to the god Osiris, seeking his assistance in attaining resurrection and eternal life in the afterlife. It acknowledges Osiris as the Lord of the Dead and emphasizes his role in judging the heart and granting passage to the realm of eternal peace and joy. The invocation is meant to be spoken with deep reverence and belief, with the intention of establishing a connection with Osiris and invoking his transformative powers.

101. Spell for the awakening of the deceased's spiritual sight

By the power of the sacred light,
I call upon the realms beyond sight.
Awaken now, oh dormant sight within,
Grant the deceased the vision to begin.

Open the eyes that see beyond the veil,
Reveal the mysteries that words can't unveil.
From the depths of darkness, emerge into light,
Let the deceased perceive with second sight.

Oh ancient ones, guardians of the unseen,
Grant the gift of vision, pure and keen.
Remove the veils that cloud the sight,
Illuminate the path with divine insight.

Awaken the spiritual eyes within the soul,
Unveil the truths that make us whole.
Through the dimensions, let them travel,
Gaining wisdom and unraveling the marvel.

Grant clarity to perceive the hidden signs,
The language of spirits, the celestial designs.
With each breath, let their sight expand,
Connecting to realms far beyond this land.

Oh spirits of wisdom, grace this rite,
Awaken the spiritual sight this night.
Guide the deceased on the path they tread,
As they journey with eyes newly fed.

With gratitude and reverence, this plea is made,
For the awakening of sight, not to fade.
Bless the deceased with visions bright,
In the realms of spirit, to shine their light.

Note: The above spell is a invocation that calls upon the power of the sacred light
and the ancient ones to awaken the spiritual sight of the deceased. It seeks to remove

the veils that cloud perception and open the spiritual eyes to perceive the unseen realms and gain divine insight. The spell acknowledges the guidance and assistance of the spirits of wisdom and emphasizes the importance of clarity and expansion of sight. It is spoken with reverence and intention, with the aim of facilitating the awakening of spiritual vision for the deceased.

102.   Invocation of the goddess Ma'at for balance and harmony in the afterlife

O Ma'at, Goddess of truth and justice,
Bearer of the feather of divine balance,
I call upon you in this sacred rite,
To bring harmony to the realms of the afterlife.

You who hold the scales of cosmic order,
Guide the deceased on their eternal journey,
Grant them the wisdom to navigate the paths,
And uphold the principles of truth and righteousness.

Ma'at, your presence brings equilibrium,
Your touch restores balance to the soul,
May your wings of truth encompass the departed,
And align their essence with the cosmic whole.

In the realm of the Duat, where judgment awaits,
May the heart of the deceased be light as the feather,
May their deeds and intentions be in harmony,
As they stand before the divine tribunal.

Goddess of Ma'at, I beseech you,
Bring your divine presence to the afterlife,
Let the scales tip in favor of justice,
And let balance be restored for eternity.

With reverence and gratitude, I offer this invocation,
To the goddess of truth and cosmic order.
May the deceased find solace in your embrace,
And may balance prevail in the afterlife's embrace.

Note: The above invocation calls upon the goddess Ma'at, who represents truth, justice, and cosmic balance. It seeks her guidance and intervention to bring harmony and balance to the afterlife. The invocation acknowledges Ma'at's role as the bearer of the feather of divine balance and asks for her assistance in guiding the departed on their eternal journey. It emphasizes the importance of upholding truth and righteousness and invokes Ma'at's presence to ensure fairness in the judgment of the deceased's actions and intentions. The invocation is spoken with reverence and gratitude, acknowledging Ma'at's significance in maintaining cosmic order.

103.   Ritual of purification through the sacred flames of the eternal pyre

In the embrace of the eternal fire's glow,
I stand before its radiance, ready to let go.
Ignite within me your purifying might,
Consume all darkness, restore my inner light.

Sacred flames, dance with fervor and grace,
Cleanse my spirit, my soul embrace.
Burn away impurities, release all strife,
Restore balance and harmony in my life.

As I move around your sacred pyre's light,
I surrender to your transformative might.
Purify my being, body, heart, and mind,
In your divine flames, may clarity I find.

With every step I take, with every chant I sing,
Let your flames purify me, my spirit take wing.
Release the burdens that no longer serve,
In your fiery embrace, may I fully observe.

Sacred fire, I offer my gratitude and praise,
For your purifying blessings that fill my days.
May your eternal flame forever burn bright,
Guiding me on my path, with purest light.

So mote it be!

Step 1: Preparation

✧   Gather in a sacred space, adorned with symbols of fire and purification. Create an altar at the center, adorned with candles, incense, and offerings. Place a sacred fire pit or hearth in the center of the altar.

Step 2: Invocation

✧ Stand before the sacred fire pit and invoke the presence of the divine fire. Offer a prayer or invocation to the fire element, calling upon its purifying and transformative energies. Express your intention for purification and release of negative energies.

Step 3: Offering

✧ Place sacred herbs, resins, or offerings onto the fire, symbolizing the release of impurities and negativity. As the flames consume the offerings, visualize the fire purifying your body, mind, and spirit. Feel its transformative power washing away any negative energy or attachments.

Step 4: Purification Dance

✧ Begin a ritual dance around the fire, moving in a circular motion. Let the flames mesmerize you as you surrender to the purifying energy of the fire. Dance with intention, allowing the flames to cleanse your energy field and purify your being.

Step 5: Chanting and Incantation

✧ As you dance, chant sacred mantras or incantations related to purification and release. Allow the vibrations of your voice to resonate with the sacred flames, amplifying their purifying energy. Let the words flow from your heart and connect you to the divine fire.

Step 6: Personal Release

Take a moment to reflect on any negative emotions, thoughts, or attachments that you wish to release. Visualize them being consumed by the flames, transforming into ash and smoke. Offer them to the fire, surrendering them to the divine purification.

Step 7: Blessing and Gratitude

✧ As the ritual comes to a close, extend your gratitude to the sacred fire for its cleansing and transformative power. Express your thanks for the purification it has bestowed upon you. Offer a final prayer or blessing, acknowledging the sacredness of the ritual and the healing it has brought.

Step 8: Closing

✧ Slowly bring your dance to a halt, feeling the energy of purification and renewal coursing through your being. Take a moment to ground yourself and integrate the experience. Offer any remaining offerings to the fire, giving thanks for its presence and blessings.

Note: The above ritual involves the use of a sacred fire, which represents purification and transformation. The ritual begins with invoking the presence of the fire and offering prayers and intentions for purification. Offerings are placed into the fire as symbolic representations of negativity and impurities being released. A purification dance is performed around the fire, accompanied by chanting and incantations related to purification and release. Participants visualize and feel the flames purifying their energy and releasing any negative attachments. The ritual concludes with expressing gratitude to the fire and offering blessings. It is important to ensure safety during the ritual by following proper fire safety protocols and conducting the ritual in a suitable space.

104. Spell for the transfiguration of the deceased into a celestial guide

By the celestial realms and starry skies,
I call upon the spirits, ancient and wise.
Grant me transformation, oh divine decree,
As I transcend the earthly, set my spirit free.

From mortal form to ethereal grace,
I shed my earthly bindings, embrace the cosmic space.
Guide me, celestial spirits, with radiant light,
As I become a guide, shining through the darkest night.

With each breath, my essence unfolds,
I merge with the cosmos, as the story is told.
Grant me wings of luminous flight,
To navigate realms, both day and night.

From earthly realms to celestial plane,
I become a beacon, a guide without a chain.
Illuminate paths for those who seek,
A celestial guide, both humble and meek.

Oh, celestial guide, I embrace your call,
Grant me wisdom and love, to share with all.
May my presence bring comfort and peace,
As I guide souls on their journey's release.

Transfiguration complete, I am reborn,
A celestial guide, forever sworn.
To guide with compassion, light, and grace,
In the realms of celestial embrace.

So mote it be!

105.   Incantation to awaken the divine purpose within the deceased's soul

From the depths of time, where destinies lie,
I call upon the ancient forces high.
Awaken, O soul, to your purpose divine,
Let your sacred mission brightly shine.

In realms unseen, where truths reside,
Ignite the flame, let it burn inside.
Awaken the purpose, long forgotten, yet true,
Unveil the path, reveal what you must do.

With divine guidance, let your spirit soar,
Embrace the calling that lies at your core.
Unveil the gifts that lie dormant within,
Let your purpose unfold, let the journey begin.

O soul, remember your purpose and might,
Embrace the mission with all your light.
Awaken the passion, the drive, and the zest,
For in fulfilling your purpose, you are truly blessed.

May the divine purpose within you ignite,
Guiding your steps with wisdom and insight.
Awaken, O soul, to your sacred role,
Fulfilling your purpose, making you whole.

So mote it be!

106. Spell for the transformation of the deceased into a vessel of divine love and compassion

Inscribe upon the sacred tablet of your heart,
The spell of transformation, a divine work of art.
To become a vessel of love and compassion pure,
Embrace this incantation, let your spirit soar.

By the power of the cosmic forces above,
I call upon the gods of compassion and love.
With open heart and pure intention,
I seek divine transformation and ascension.

Let love flow through me like a gentle stream,
Filling every corner, a radiant beam.
May compassion guide my every deed,
A vessel of love, in word and creed.

Release the chains that bind me to ego's sway,
Embrace the path of love, both night and day.
Transform my essence, make me anew,
A beacon of love, shining through.

As I journey through realms beyond,
May love radiate from me, ever fond.
Grant me the wisdom to heal and inspire,
A vessel of love, never to tire.

So mote it be, let the spell take flight,
Transform me into a vessel of love and light.
With gratitude and devotion, I now embrace,
The transformation, divine love's grace.

Perform this spell with pure intentions and an open heart, focusing your energy and intent on becoming a vessel of divine love and compassion. Allow the spell to infuse your being, guiding your thoughts, words, and actions. Embrace the transformation with humility and dedication, allowing the divine love to flow through you, radiating outwards to touch the lives of others.

107.   Ritual for the communion with the spirits of the sacred animals

The Ritual for Communion with the Spirits of the Sacred Animals is a sacred practice that allows one to connect with and seek guidance from the spiritual essence of the animal kingdom. It is a way to honor and tap into the wisdom, power, and unique qualities of these revered creatures. Here is an outline of the ritual and an accompanying invocation:

Materials needed:

A sacred space or altar adorned with natural elements such as plants, flowers, and crystals.
Representations or images of the sacred animals you wish to commune with.
Incense or herbs associated with purification and spiritual connection.
Offerings such as food, water, or items symbolizing the animals' significance.
Ritual Steps:

Prepare the sacred space: Cleanse and purify the space using the incense or herbs. Arrange the representations or images of the sacred animals on the altar, creating a focal point for your connection.

Ground and center yourself: Take a few moments to breathe deeply and connect with your inner self. Feel your energy aligning with the earth and the spiritual realm.

Invocation:
"O majestic spirits of the animal realm,
Guides and teachers, wise and unbound,
I call upon you with reverence and respect,
To commune with me in this sacred connect.

Lion, symbol of courage and strength,
Grant me bravery to face life's length.
Eagle, soaring high in the sky,
Share your vision and clarity, drawing nigh.

Bear, embodiment of power and healing,
Grant me strength, inner balance, and feeling.
Dolphin, playful and wise in the sea,
Guide me with your joy and intuition, be with me.

Wolf, guardian of the sacred wild,
Teach me loyalty, unity, and a fearless stride.
Butterfly, symbol of transformation and grace,
Inspire me to embrace life's changes with a peaceful pace.

And to all the creatures, big and small,
Whose essence and wisdom I humbly call,
I open my heart to receive your insight,
In this communion, may our spirits unite.

With offerings of gratitude and reverence,
I seek your guidance, your benevolence.
May this communion be pure and divine,
With spirits of the sacred animals, I align."

Connection and Communion: As you recite the invocation, feel a deep connection with each animal spirit. Open yourself to receiving their messages, guidance, and blessings. You may choose to meditate, visualize, or simply be present in the moment, allowing their energies to surround and permeate your being.

Offerings: Present your offerings to the sacred animals as a symbol of gratitude and honor. Speak your intentions and wishes, expressing your willingness to learn and grow from their wisdom.

Closing: Express your gratitude to the animal spirits for their presence and guidance. Affirm your commitment to carrying their teachings and lessons in your daily life.

Perform this ritual with sincerity, respect, and an open heart, and be receptive to the messages and insights that come your way. Remember to adapt and personalize the ritual according to your beliefs and cultural practices.

108.   Spell for the liberation of the deceased's soul from karmic ties

The Spell for the Liberation of the Deceased's Soul from Karmic Ties is a powerful invocation aimed at releasing the soul from the burden of past karmic debts and facilitating its journey towards freedom and spiritual growth. Here is a spell that can be used for this purpose:

Materials needed:

A quiet and sacred space for performing the spell.
A white candle representing purity and divine light.
An incense or herb associated with purification and release.
A small piece of paper and a pen.
Spell Steps:

Preparation: Find a peaceful space where you can focus without distractions. Light the incense or herb, filling the space with its purifying aroma. Sit comfortably and center yourself through deep breathing.

Candle Dedication: Take the white candle in your hands and visualize it as a conduit for divine light and energy. Envision the candle as a symbol of purity and liberation. Hold it up to your heart and say:

"By the power of divine light, I dedicate this candle
To the liberation of the deceased's soul from karmic ties.
May its flame guide the way to freedom and spiritual growth."

Intention Setting: Write the name of the deceased or a specific affirmation related to their liberation on the piece of paper. Hold the paper in your hands and infuse it with your intention. Visualize the karmic ties being dissolved and the soul being set free. Feel a sense of compassion and forgiveness as you focus on the desired outcome.

Incantation:
"O benevolent forces of the universe,
I call upon you to assist and intervene.
In the name of divine love and compassion,
I release the deceased's soul from karmic chains.

May all past debts and attachments be dissolved,
And their soul be liberated and refreshed.
By the power of forgiveness and divine grace,
I declare their freedom in this sacred space.

Let the karmic ties be severed and undone,
As the soul journeys towards the divine sun.
With love and light, may they ascend and transcend,
A new chapter of spiritual growth to commence.

So mote it be."

Burning the Paper: Light the paper with the candle flame and place it safely in a fireproof dish or container. As it burns, visualize the release of karmic ties and the soul's liberation. Witness the paper transforming into ashes, symbolizing the dissolution of past burdens.

Closing: Allow the candle to burn for a few more moments, expressing gratitude for the assistance and support of the divine forces. Blow out the candle, signaling the completion of the spell. Reflect on the intention and visualize the deceased's soul embarking on a new journey of spiritual freedom.

Remember, spells are a form of focused intention and energy work. Perform this spell with respect, love, and genuine intentions. It is recommended to adapt and personalize the spell according to your spiritual beliefs and practices.

109. Invocation of the god Thoth for wisdom and knowledge in the afterlife

The Invocation of the God Thoth for Wisdom and Knowledge in the Afterlife is a powerful prayer and calling upon the deity Thoth to bestow wisdom and guidance upon the deceased in their journey beyond life. Here is an invocation that can be used for this purpose:

"O Thoth, wise and mighty,
God of knowledge and divine words,
I beseech your presence and guidance.
In this sacred moment of transition,
I call upon your wisdom to illuminate the path.

Lord of scribes and keeper of records,
Your knowledge spans the ages,
From the beginning to the end of time.
Grant me, [name of the deceased], your divine favor,
As I traverse the realms of the afterlife.

Thoth, I seek your insight and understanding,
To unravel the mysteries that lie ahead.
May your words be my guiding light,
Leading me to profound wisdom and enlightenment.

With your ibis-headed form and mighty wings,
You soar above the earthly realms,
Witnessing the secrets of the universe.
I implore you, Thoth, to share your wisdom,
That I may grow in knowledge and truth.

Guide me through the halls of the afterlife,
Wherein lies the hidden wisdom of the ages.
Open the gates of divine understanding,
That I may comprehend the cosmic mysteries.

Oh Thoth, I offer my devotion and reverence,
For your wisdom is boundless and divine.
In this sacred union of mortal and divine,
May my soul be nourished by your knowledge.

I invoke your presence, Thoth, in this moment,
To bestow upon me the gifts of wisdom and insight.
Grant me clarity of thought and understanding,
As I embark on this journey into the afterlife.

By the power of your sacred name and essence,
I seek your blessings and divine favor.
Oh Thoth, hear my plea and heed my call,
Guide me with your wisdom through eternity.

Dua, Thoth! Hail and praise to you,
God of wisdom and keeper of the cosmic order.
May your knowledge flow through my being,
Now and forevermore."

Perform this invocation with utmost reverence and sincerity, focusing your intention
on connecting with the wisdom and knowledge of Thoth. Visualize his presence
surrounding you, imparting profound insights and understanding.

110. Ritual of anointing with sacred oils for spiritual enlightenment

The Ritual of Anointing with Sacred Oils for Spiritual Enlightenment is a sacred practice to enhance one's spiritual connection, clarity, and enlightenment. This ritual involves the use of consecrated oils to anoint oneself or others. Here is a suggested ritual and an accompanying incantation:

Ingredients:

Sacred oils of your choice (such as frankincense, myrrh, sandalwood, or lavender)
A small, clean bowl or dish
A small brush or your fingertips for application
Steps:

Find a quiet and sacred space where you can perform the ritual without interruption. Create an atmosphere of tranquility and reverence by lighting candles, burning incense, or playing soft instrumental music if desired.

Begin by centering yourself through deep, intentional breaths. Allow yourself to enter a state of relaxation and receptivity.

Take the small bowl or dish and pour a small amount of the sacred oil into it. Hold the bowl with both hands and visualize divine light and energy infusing the oil. Envision it becoming a vessel of spiritual enlightenment and divine connection.

Dip your fingertips or the brush into the oil, and gently anoint your forehead with a small dot or an upward stroke. As you do so, recite the following incantation or adapt it to your personal beliefs:

"In this sacred anointing, I seek enlightenment,
Divine light and wisdom, to be granted.
With each touch, may my spirit awaken,
And the veils of illusion be lifted.

Sacred oil, blessed by the divine,
I invite your wisdom to flow through me.
Illuminate my path, expand my consciousness,
Guide me to the realms of spiritual clarity.

As I anoint this sacred vessel,
May my senses be awakened to the divine.
Let the oil's fragrance and touch uplift my soul,
Open the gates of wisdom, pure and sublime.

By the power of the sacred oil and my intention,
I embrace spiritual enlightenment and insight.
As above, so below, as within, so without,
I am a vessel of divine light."

Take a moment to absorb the energy and intention of the ritual. Allow the oil to soak into your skin and aura, visualizing it spreading throughout your being, bringing forth spiritual enlightenment and clarity.

After the ritual, you may choose to meditate, pray, or engage in any spiritual practice that resonates with you. Embrace the moments of stillness and connection, allowing the sacred oil to further deepen your spiritual experience.

Remember, the ritual can be personalized to align with your beliefs and intentions. Use oils that resonate with you and adapt the incantation to suit your own words and desires. Perform this ritual with reverence and a genuine intention to invite spiritual enlightenment into your life.

111. Spell for the transformation of the deceased into a vessel of divine protection

The Spell for the Transformation of the Deceased into a Vessel of Divine Protection is a powerful incantation to invoke and embody the qualities of divine protection. This spell serves to empower the deceased and ensure their safety and guardianship in the afterlife. Here is a suggested spell:

"From realms unseen, I call upon the divine,
Grant me protection, a shield so fine.
Transform my essence, oh sacred powers,
Into a vessel of safety, both day and hours.

May I be cloaked in divine light,
Shielded from darkness, from any plight.
Let the energies around me be deflected,
No harm shall touch me, as I'm protected.

I am a vessel of divine protection,
An embodiment of strength, without exception.
I draw upon the powers of the sacred divine,
To guard and guide me, throughout all time.

By the grace of the gods and goddesses above,
I am shielded, surrounded by their love.
May their presence and power be within,
Keeping me safe, free from any sin.

I am a vessel, strong and secure,
Protected and guarded, forever pure.
In this transformation, I find solace and peace,
As divine protection around me shall increase.

So mote it be, with the blessings divine,
I am transformed, a vessel of protection, mine.
In the afterlife, I walk with courage and might,
Embracing divine protection, day and night."

As you recite this spell, visualize a divine shield forming around you or the deceased, radiating a brilliant and protective light. Feel the presence of the gods and goddesses surrounding and enveloping you, imbuing you with their divine protection. Carry the energy of this spell with you, knowing that you are a vessel of divine protection in the afterlife.

Note: It is important to remember that rituals, spells, and incantations are deeply personal and can be adapted to suit individual beliefs and preferences. Feel free to modify the spell and incantation as needed to align with your own spiritual practices and intentions.

112. Incantation to invoke the blessings of the celestial constellations

The Incantation to Invoke the Blessings of the Celestial Constellations is a powerful invocation that calls upon the energies and blessings of the stars and constellations. It is a way to connect with the cosmic forces and draw their guidance and blessings into your life. Here is a suggested incantation:

"O celestial constellations, shining bright,
Guiding lights in the vast expanse of night.
I call upon your powers, so divine,
Illuminate my path, let your blessings be mine.

From Orion's belt to the Great Bear's might,
From the Pleiades to the starry Lyra's flight,
Each constellation holds its sacred sway,
Ancient wisdom and blessings on display.

I invoke the energy of Orion's might,
Strength and courage, shining with celestial light.
From the Pleiades, I seek wisdom and grace,
Illuminate my mind, reveal secrets of time and space.

Great Bear, I call upon your steadfast ways,
Grant me resilience and fortitude all my days.
Lyra, guide my voice, let my words ring true,
Harmony and creativity in all that I do.

O celestial constellations, I honor your might,
Unveil your blessings, in this sacred rite.
May your energies flow, through the cosmic veil,
Bringing alignment and harmony, without fail.

As above, so below, in sacred harmony,
The blessings of the constellations, now bestowed on me.
I am connected to the cosmic tapestry,
Guided and blessed by celestial majesty.

So mote it be, in alignment and grace,
I carry the blessings of the celestial space.

With gratitude, I honor the stars above,
Their wisdom and blessings, forever I love."

As you recite this incantation, visualize the constellations sparkling in the night sky, their energy flowing down and surrounding you with their blessings. Feel their guidance and wisdom infusing your being, aligning you with the cosmic forces. Embrace the connection with the celestial constellations and carry their blessings with you in your journey.

Remember, the incantation can be adjusted and personalized to suit your own spiritual practices and beliefs. Adapt it as needed to align with your intentions and connection with the celestial constellations.

113.   Ritual for the transfiguration of the deceased into a guardian of the cosmic order

The Ritual for the Transfiguration of the Deceased into a Guardian of the Cosmic Order is a sacred ceremony that invokes the transformation of the departed soul into a powerful guardian and protector of the cosmic order. This ritual serves to honor the eternal connection between the deceased and the divine forces that govern the universe. Here is a suggested ritual for this purpose:

Materials needed:

A sacred space adorned with cosmic symbols and representations of the celestial bodies.
An altar with offerings such as candles, incense, flowers, and symbolic items associated with the cosmos.
A picture or representation of the deceased.
Procedure:

Prepare the sacred space by clearing any negative energies and creating a serene atmosphere. Light the candles and the incense, symbolizing the presence of the divine.

Place the picture or representation of the deceased on the altar, facing towards the cosmic symbols. This serves as a focal point for connecting with their spirit.

Stand before the altar and take a few moments to center yourself. Close your eyes and visualize the cosmic forces surrounding you, filling the space with their energy and wisdom.

Begin by reciting the following invocation:
"Oh divine cosmic forces, hear my plea,
I stand before you with reverence and sincerity.
I invoke your power, celestial and grand,
Transform the departed into a guardian of the cosmic strand."

Call upon the specific cosmic energies and deities associated with the cosmic order and protection. For example, you may invoke the names of celestial beings such as Isis, Osiris, Ma'at, and Thoth, or any other deities that resonate with your beliefs.

Express your heartfelt intentions for the deceased's transfiguration into a guardian of the cosmic order. Speak of their noble qualities, their devotion to the cosmic principles, and their commitment to upholding balance and harmony in the universe.

Offer the sacred items on the altar as a symbol of gratitude and reverence. Place them before the picture or representation of the deceased, infusing them with your intentions and blessings.

Engage in a moment of silence, allowing the energy to build and the connection between the divine forces and the departed soul to strengthen. Visualize the deceased being embraced by the cosmic energies, transforming into a radiant and powerful guardian.

Conclude the ritual by expressing your gratitude to the cosmic forces for their presence and assistance. Offer a closing prayer or affirmation, affirming your trust in the transformation taking place.

Leave the altar undisturbed for a period of time, allowing the energies to settle and the connection to strengthen. You may choose to visit the altar regularly to offer prayers and intentions for the departed guardian's ongoing role in protecting the cosmic order.

Remember, this ritual can be adapted and personalized to align with your spiritual beliefs and practices. Feel free to modify the steps, invocations, and offerings to suit your specific intentions and connection with the cosmic forces.

114. Spell for the reunion of the deceased's soul with their divine counterparts

The Spell for the Reunion of the Deceased's Soul with Their Divine Counterparts is a sacred incantation that seeks to bring together the departed soul with their divine counterparts, those beings who share a deep spiritual connection and journey. This spell acknowledges the eternal bond between the departed and their divine counterparts, facilitating their reunion in the afterlife. Here is a suggested spell for this purpose:

Procedure:

Find a quiet and sacred space where you can perform the spell without any distractions. Light a candle and some incense to create an atmosphere of spiritual energy.

Take a moment to ground yourself and center your focus on the intention of reuniting the deceased's soul with their divine counterparts. Visualize the departed soul surrounded by a warm and comforting light.

Recite the following spell, or feel free to adapt it to your personal beliefs and spiritual practices:
"Divine spirits of love and unity,
I call upon you with utmost sincerity.
Bridge the gap between realms above,
Reunite this soul with its divine love."

Close your eyes and visualize the departed soul standing in a beautiful, ethereal realm, surrounded by a shimmering light. See their divine counterparts approaching, radiating love and recognition.

Speak the name of the departed soul, invoking their presence and calling upon their divine counterparts. State their names or simply address them as "Beloved divine counterparts, come forth and reunite."

Open your heart and mind to receive any messages, signs, or feelings that may indicate the presence of the divine counterparts. Trust in your intuition and the spiritual connection you have established.

Allow the energy to flow freely and create a bridge of love and reunion between the departed soul and their divine counterparts. Envision the divine counterparts embracing the departed soul, bringing comfort, healing, and a sense of wholeness.

Express your gratitude and appreciation for the reunion, acknowledging the blessings of divine love and connection. Offer a heartfelt thank you to the divine spirits for facilitating this sacred reunion.

Sit in quiet reflection for a few moments, feeling the energy of love and unity surrounding you. Know that the departed soul is now in the loving embrace of their divine counterparts, continuing their spiritual journey together.

When you are ready, extinguish the candle and take a few deep breaths, grounding yourself in the present moment. Trust that the reunion has taken place and that the departed soul is now in the loving care of their divine counterparts.

Remember, this spell is meant to honor and facilitate the reunion between the departed soul and their divine counterparts. It is important to approach this spell with respect, love, and a genuine intention to bring healing and harmony to the departed's spiritual journey. Feel free to modify the spell as needed to align with your personal beliefs and practices.

115. Invocation of the goddess Nut for nourishment and sustenance in the afterlife

The Invocation of the Goddess Nut is a sacred incantation that calls upon the goddess Nut, the Egyptian deity associated with the sky and the nourishment of the afterlife. This invocation seeks her blessings for the departed soul, requesting nourishment and sustenance in their journey beyond life. Here is a suggested invocation for this purpose:

Procedure:

Find a serene and quiet space where you can connect with the divine energy. Light a candle or some incense to create a sacred atmosphere.

Take a moment to center yourself and open your heart to the presence of the goddess Nut. Feel her energy surrounding you, embracing you with love and compassion.

Recite the following invocation, or adapt it to your personal beliefs and spiritual practices:
"Oh, Nut, goddess of the sky,
I invoke your presence with a heartfelt cry.
Nourish and sustain the departed's soul,
Provide them with your divine role."

Visualize the radiant figure of the goddess Nut, stretching her starry body across the heavens, spreading her cosmic energy and blessings. Imagine her celestial canopy enveloping the departed soul, providing nourishment and sustenance.

Speak the name of the departed soul, calling upon the goddess Nut to bestow her blessings upon them. Say their name or simply address them as "Beloved departed, receive the nourishment of Nut."

Express your heartfelt intentions for the departed soul, requesting that Nut's divine nourishment and sustenance be bestowed upon them. Ask for her guidance and support throughout their journey in the afterlife.

Open your heart and mind to receive any messages, signs, or feelings that may indicate the presence of the goddess Nut. Allow her energy to fill your being, bringing comfort and reassurance.

Offer your gratitude and appreciation to the goddess Nut for her loving presence and blessings. Thank her for her nourishment and sustenance that she provides to the departed soul on their spiritual journey.

Take a moment to sit in silence and allow the energy to integrate. Feel the comforting embrace of Nut's divine nourishment and sustenance surrounding you and the departed soul.

When you are ready, extinguish the candle or incense, symbolizing the completion of the invocation. Take a few deep breaths, grounding yourself in the present moment, and carry the energy of Nut's nourishment and sustenance with you.

Remember, this invocation is a sacred practice intended to honor and seek the blessings of the goddess Nut for the departed soul. Approach it with reverence, love, and a genuine intention to seek nourishment and sustenance for the departed on their spiritual journey. Feel free to adapt the invocation to align with your personal beliefs and practices.

116.   Ritual of purification through the sacred waters of the eternal river

The Ritual of Purification through the Sacred Waters of the Eternal River is a ceremonial practice aimed at cleansing the body, mind, and spirit of the individual. The sacred waters symbolize purity, renewal, and the flow of life. Here is a suggested description of the ritual:

Preparation:

Choose a serene and secluded location near a natural water source, such as a river or a waterfall.
Set up a small altar or sacred space with offerings of flowers, incense, and candles.
Take a few moments to center yourself and set your intentions for the ritual.
Invocation:

Stand at the edge of the water, facing the flowing stream.
Close your eyes and take several deep breaths to calm your mind and connect with the energy of the surroundings.
Begin with an invocation to the divine or the deity associated with water, such as the goddess Hapi or the river god, Hapi.
Call upon their presence and ask for their blessings in purifying and renewing your being.
Sacred Bathing:

Undress and enter the water slowly, feeling its coolness against your skin.
As you immerse yourself, visualize the water washing away any impurities or negative energies, cleansing you on all levels.
Allow yourself to surrender to the flow of the water, feeling its gentle caress and purifying essence.
Mantras or Affirmations:

While bathing, recite mantras or affirmations that resonate with the intention of purification and renewal.
For example, you can repeat phrases such as "I release all that no longer serves me" or "I am cleansed and renewed by the sacred waters."
Intentional Release:

As you submerge yourself in the water, imagine any stagnant or negative energy being released and carried away by the current.

Visualize yourself being cleansed, purified, and rejuvenated with each moment in the water.

Let go of any burdens, worries, or attachments, allowing the river to carry them away.

Gratitude and Blessings:

When you feel ready, step out of the water and return to the edge of the river.

Express gratitude to the divine and the water element for their cleansing and purifying energies.

Offer prayers or blessings to the water, acknowledging its sacredness and its role in your spiritual journey.

Closing:

Take a moment to reflect on the experience and the symbolism of the sacred waters.

Offer any additional prayers or intentions for continued purification and renewal.

Thank the divine, the water, and the natural surroundings for their presence and blessings.

Remember, this ritual is a deeply personal practice, and you can modify it according to your beliefs and preferences. The key is to approach the ritual with reverence and mindfulness, allowing the sacred waters to cleanse and purify your being on all levels.

117.   Spell for the liberation of the deceased's soul from the illusions of mortality

In the realm of transcending mortal illusions and liberating the soul from the limitations of mortality, one can recite the following spell:

"Glorious spirits, hear my plea,
From illusions, set me free.
Unbind my soul from earthly ties,
Grant me vision, make me wise.

I cast aside the veils of time,
To reach the truth, sublime.
Illusions fade, illusions fall,
Reveal the essence, above all.

I transcend the bounds of mortal strife,
To embrace the eternal, divine life.
Illusions crumble, illusions cease,
I soar in realms of boundless peace.

With clarity, I see the grand design,
Beyond the illusions that confine.
Awakened now, my spirit roams,
Free from mortal chains, I've flown.

Grant me liberation, O sacred powers,
From transient forms and fleeting hours.
In truth and wisdom, let me dwell,
Beyond the illusions, where all is well.

As I speak these words with intent and might,
May my soul ascend to eternal light.
Liberated from the illusions of mortality,
I embrace the divine with profound reality."

Perform this spell with a focused and open heart, preferably in a sacred space where you can meditate and connect with the spiritual realm. Light candles and burn incense to create an atmosphere conducive to transcending illusions. Recite the incantation with conviction and visualize the release of earthly illusions, allowing your spirit to soar into the realm of eternal truth and wisdom. Embrace the sense of freedom and clarity that comes with the liberation of the soul from mortal illusions.

118. Incantation to awaken the dormant potential within the deceased's spirit

In the realm of awakening dormant potential within the spirit of the deceased, one can recite the following incantation:

"Spirits of ancient power and might,
Awaken the dormant within this night.
From depths unseen, arise and shine,
Ignite the embers of potential divine.

By the sacred flame, I now decree,
Unlock the hidden gifts within me.
Awaken the powers that lie asleep,
From slumber deep, their secrets keep.

Potential dormant, now come alive,
Ignite the spark, let it thrive.
Unleash the talents, the gifts untold,
As the ancient wisdom unfolds.

Through realms unseen, let knowledge flow,
As the dormant potential starts to grow.
Awaken the spirit, unleash the fire,
To fulfill the purpose, to reach higher.

With every word and every breath,
I awaken the potential, defeating death.
From beyond the veil, the power is drawn,
As the dormant spirit is reborn.

Awaken, awaken, dormant spirit arise,
Unleash the potential that within you lies.
Let the energy surge, let it unfurl,
As I embrace the power of this sacred swirl.

By the divine light, this incantation I sow,
Awakening the dormant, letting it glow.
From this moment on, I am set free,
To embody my potential, eternally."

Perform this incantation with reverence and belief in the awakening of the dormant potential within the spirit. Create a sacred space by lighting candles and burning incense. Focus your intent and recite the incantation with clarity and passion, visualizing the dormant potential within the deceased's spirit awakening and unfolding. Feel the energy building and flowing through you, empowering the spirit to rise and fulfill its true potential. Embrace the transformation and the limitless possibilities that come with the awakening of dormant powers.

119. Ritual for the communion with the spirits of the celestial gateways

Preparation:

❖ Find a quiet and secluded space where you can perform the ritual undisturbed.
❖ Set up an altar or sacred space adorned with celestial symbols such as stars, moons, or representations of the zodiac.
❖ Place candles, incense, and any other offerings that resonate with the celestial realms.
❖ Take a few moments to ground yourself and clear your mind, focusing on your intention to connect with the spirits of the celestial gateways.

Invocation:

❖ Light the candles and the incense, symbolizing the illumination and purification of the ritual space.
❖ Stand or sit before the altar, facing the celestial symbols.
❖ Close your eyes and take several deep breaths to center yourself.
❖ Begin the invocation by speaking the following words or a variation that resonates with you:
"O spirits of the celestial gateways,
Guardians of the cosmic realms,
I call upon you with reverence and respect.
Open the portals that bridge the worlds,
And grant me communion with your wisdom.
Guide me through the celestial currents,
That I may glimpse the mysteries beyond.
I seek your presence and guidance,
As I tread the path of the celestial gateways."

Communion:

❖ With your eyes closed, visualize a radiant gateway opening before you, revealing a pathway leading to the celestial realms.
❖ Imagine yourself stepping through the gateway, feeling a sense of awe and wonder as you enter the celestial realms.
❖ Allow yourself to connect with the spirits that dwell within these realms. Listen for their whispers, feel their presence, and be open to receiving their messages and guidance.

✧ Take your time in this communion, allowing the energy and wisdom of the spirits to flow through you. You may ask questions, seek guidance, or simply absorb the celestial energies.

Gratitude and Closing:

Express gratitude to the spirits of the celestial gateways for their presence and guidance.
Offer thanks for the insights and blessings you have received during the communion.
Slowly bring your awareness back to the physical world, gently grounding yourself in the present moment.
Extinguish the candles and offer any remaining offerings as a token of gratitude.
Reflect on your experiences and insights, and journal any messages or impressions that came through during the communion.
Remember, the ritual is a sacred act of connection and should be performed with sincerity and respect. Trust your intuition and the guidance you receive from the spirits of the celestial gateways, and integrate their wisdom into your life's journey.

120.   Spell for the transmigration of the deceased's soul into higher realms of existence

Preparation:

✧ Find a quiet and serene space where you can perform the spell without distractions.
✧ Create an altar or a sacred space with meaningful objects that symbolize spiritual ascent, such as feathers, crystals, or images of celestial beings.
✧ Light candles and incense to create a sacred ambiance and to invoke a connection with the divine.

Centering and Intention:

✧ Sit or stand before the altar, close your eyes, and take several deep breaths to center yourself.
✧ Focus your mind and heart on the intention of facilitating the transmigration of the deceased's soul into higher realms of existence.
✧ Repeat the following words or adapt them to resonate with your personal beliefs and practices:
"By the power of the divine within me,
I call forth the transmigration of [name of the deceased].
May their soul ascend to higher realms,
Where enlightenment and liberation await.
I invoke the aid of the celestial guides,
To guide and protect [name of the deceased] on their journey.
May their spirit transcend earthly limitations,
And embrace the boundless expanse of the cosmic realms.
As I speak, so mote it be."

Visualization and Intent:

✧ Visualize the soul of the deceased as a radiant light, untethered from the earthly realm.
✧ Imagine this light gradually ascending, moving through layers of higher dimensions and realms.
✧ Envision celestial beings or guides appearing, extending their hands to assist the soul on its journey.

✧ Hold the intention that the soul is gracefully and effortlessly transitioning into higher realms, shedding any attachments or burdens that may hinder its ascension.

Gratitude and Closure:

Express gratitude to the divine forces, celestial beings, and guides for their assistance in the transmigration process.

Offer thanks for the soul's safe passage and for the blessings of spiritual elevation.

Slowly release the visualization and bring your awareness back to the present moment.

Conclude the spell with words of closure and affirmation, such as "So be it" or "Amen."

It's important to perform this spell with reverence, love, and respect for the deceased and their journey. Trust in the power of your intentions and the support of the divine forces as you facilitate the transmigration of the soul into higher realms of existence.

121. Invocation of the god Anubis for guidance and protection in the journey of the afterlife

Preparation:

✧ Find a quiet and sacred space where you can focus without distractions.
✧ Create an altar or a dedicated space with symbols or representations of Anubis, such as statues, images, or symbols associated with the deity.
✧ Light candles and incense to create a reverent atmosphere.

Centering and Connection:

✧ Stand or sit before the altar, take a few deep breaths, and close your eyes.
✧ Visualize a connection forming between you and Anubis, envisioning a pathway of divine light or a bridge between your heart and the realm of the deity.
✧ Feel a sense of reverence and respect for Anubis as you call upon his presence.

Invocation:

Open your eyes and speak the following invocation, or adapt it to resonate with your personal beliefs and practices:
"Mighty Anubis, guardian of the afterlife,
I call upon your divine presence and guidance.
With reverence and respect, I seek your protection and wisdom.
As the scales of Ma'at weigh the heart against the feather,
May you guide me through the realms of the beyond.
Grant me clarity of mind and purity of spirit,
That I may navigate the journey with grace and purpose.
I invoke your presence, O Anubis,
To watch over me and safeguard my path.
May your wisdom illuminate the way,
And your strength shield me from any harm.
In your name, I seek your guidance and protection.
Anubis, I honor you and welcome your presence."

Connection and Meditation:

Close your eyes again and envision Anubis standing before you or by your side, emanating a comforting and protective energy.
Feel the presence of Anubis enveloping you, offering guidance, protection, and a sense of reassurance.
Take a few moments to silently communicate any specific requests or intentions for guidance in your personal journey of the afterlife.
Listen inwardly for any messages or insights that may come forth.

Gratitude and Closure:

Express gratitude to Anubis for his presence and assistance.
Offer thanks for his guidance, protection, and support throughout your journey.
Slowly bring your awareness back to the present moment, feeling grounded and connected.
Close the invocation with words of gratitude and affirmation, such as "Thank you, Anubis, for your guidance and protection. So be it."
Perform this invocation with sincerity, reverence, and an open heart, acknowledging Anubis as a powerful and benevolent guide in the afterlife journey. Trust in the connection you have established and the assistance Anubis provides as you navigate the realms of the beyond.

122. Ritual of anointing with sacred incense for spiritual elevation

Preparation:

✧ Choose a quiet and sacred space where you can perform the ritual without distractions.

✧ Set up an altar or a dedicated space with symbols or representations of the divine or your spiritual practice.

✧ Select a high-quality sacred incense that resonates with your spiritual intentions. Some commonly used incenses for spiritual elevation include frankincense, myrrh, sandalwood, or palo santo.

✧ Have a charcoal disc or an incense holder ready to burn the incense.

Cleansing and Grounding:

✧ Begin by taking a few deep breaths to center yourself and create a calm and focused state of mind.

✧ Light a charcoal disc and let it burn until it is glowing and covered in a thin layer of white ash.

✧ Hold the incense over the glowing charcoal, allowing the smoke to rise and fill the air.

✧ Stand or sit in front of the smoke and visualize it purifying your energy field, clearing away any negative or stagnant energies.

Anointing with Sacred Incense:

✧ Hold the incense in your dominant hand, and with your other hand, dip your fingers into the smoke and then touch them to your forehead, heart, and solar plexus.

✧ As you anoint these areas, silently or aloud, express your intentions for spiritual elevation, such as seeking higher knowledge, spiritual growth, or a deeper connection with the divine.

✧ Visualize the smoke infusing your being with divine energy, lifting your spirit, and expanding your consciousness.

Affirmations and Prayers:

Speak affirmations or prayers that align with your intentions for spiritual elevation. You can use existing prayers or create your own, expressing your gratitude, devotion, and desire for spiritual growth.

Repeat these affirmations or prayers as many times as you feel necessary, allowing the words to resonate within you and guide your thoughts and intentions towards spiritual elevation.

Contemplation and Meditation:

✦ After the anointing and affirmations, sit or stand in the presence of the incense smoke and allow yourself to enter a state of contemplation or meditation.
✦ Close your eyes and focus on your breath, letting go of any thoughts or distractions.
✦ Allow the scent of the incense and the intention behind the ritual to deepen your connection to the divine and elevate your spiritual awareness.
✦ Spend as much time as you desire in this state of contemplation, embracing the spiritual elevation and insights that may arise.

Closing the Ritual:

Once you feel complete with your contemplation or meditation, offer gratitude to the divine or the specific deity you invoked during the ritual.
Extinguish the charcoal or let it burn out completely in a safe and fireproof container.
Cleanse the space by wafting the smoke of the incense throughout the area, visualizing it clearing away any residual energies.
Remember, rituals are deeply personal, and you can adapt and customize this ritual according to your beliefs and preferences. The key is to approach it with reverence, intention, and an open heart, allowing the sacred incense to elevate your spirit and deepen your connection to the divine.

123.   Spell for the transformation of the deceased into a vessel of divine love and compassion

Inscribe upon the sacred tablet of your heart,
The spell of transformation, a divine work of art.
To become a vessel of love and compassion pure,
Embrace this incantation, let your spirit soar.

By the power of the cosmic forces above,
I call upon the gods of compassion and love.
With open heart and pure intention,
I seek divine transformation and ascension.

Let love flow through me like a gentle stream,
Filling every corner, a radiant beam.
May compassion guide my every deed,
A vessel of love, in word and creed.

Release the chains that bind me to ego's sway,
Embrace the path of love, both night and day.
Transform my essence, make me anew,
A beacon of love, shining through.

As I journey through realms beyond,
May love radiate from me, ever fond.
Grant me the wisdom to heal and inspire,
A vessel of love, never to tire.

So mote it be, let the spell take flight,
Transform me into a vessel of love and light.
With gratitude and devotion, I now embrace,
The transformation, divine love's grace.

Perform this spell with pure intentions and an open heart, focusing your energy and intent on becoming a vessel of divine love and compassion. Allow the spell to infuse your being, guiding your thoughts, words, and actions. Embrace the transformation with humility and dedication, allowing the divine love to flow through you, radiating outwards to touch the lives of others.

124. Incantation to invoke the blessings of the celestial mountains and deserts

By the power of the celestial realms above,
I invoke the blessings of mountains high and deserts vast.
From peaks that touch the heavens to sands that stretch afar,
I call upon their wisdom and blessings to be cast.

Oh mighty mountains, pillars of strength and might,
With your majestic presence, reach towards the sky.
Infuse me with your stability and resilience,
Grant me strength to overcome, and never to shy.

Oh ancient deserts, realms of solitude and time,
With your timeless sands, reveal the secrets you hold.
Bestow upon me endurance and adaptability,
As I navigate life's challenges, brave and bold.

I call upon the spirits that dwell within these lands,
Guardians of wisdom, protectors of ancient lore.
Wrap me in your embrace, with your sacred hands,
Guide me through life's journeys, forevermore.

From mountain peaks to desert dunes,
I seek the blessings of these sacred terrains.
Grant me their steadfastness and serenity,
As I walk my path, where destiny reigns.

By the power of the celestial mountains and deserts,
I am blessed with their grace, their essence divine.
May their blessings illuminate my every step,
As I traverse this earthly realm, with purpose and design.

So mote it be, let the incantation resound,
Invoking the blessings of mountains and deserts profound.
May their wisdom and strength forever be mine,
As I journey through life, guided by their divine.

Recite this incantation with reverence and gratitude, visualizing the majestic mountains and expansive deserts. Allow their energies to merge with your own, invoking their blessings of stability, resilience, endurance, adaptability, wisdom, and serenity. Embrace their guidance as you navigate through life's challenges and adventures, always remembering the connection between the earthly and celestial realms.

125.   Ritual for the transfiguration of the deceased into a divine seeker of truth

The Ritual for the Transfiguration into a Divine Seeker of Truth

Materials:

A sacred space adorned with symbols of wisdom and knowledge
A ritual altar with candles, incense, and a representation of the deceased
A journal or parchment and writing utensils
Optional: crystals or gemstones associated with clarity and insight
Preparation:

Find a quiet and sacred space where you can perform the ritual undisturbed.
Cleanse the space by smudging with sacred herbs or purifying incense.
Set up your ritual altar with the candles, incense, and representation of the deceased.
Take a moment to ground yourself and enter a state of calm and focus.
Ritual Steps:

Light the candles on the altar, representing the illumination of truth and wisdom.

Light the incense, allowing its fragrance to permeate the space and enhance your connection to the divine.

Stand before the altar and take a few deep breaths, centering yourself in the present moment.

Speak the following invocation aloud or silently, with sincere intent:

"Oh divine forces of truth and wisdom,
I call upon your sacred presence.
Guide me on this journey of seeking,
Illuminate the path before me with clarity.

In honor of [Name of the deceased],
I seek to transfigure their spirit,
Into a divine seeker of truth and knowledge.
Grant them the wisdom they yearn for,
So they may find the answers they seek.

As I perform this sacred ritual,
May their soul be awakened and transformed,
Embracing the pursuit of truth with fervor.
Grant them the sight to perceive the hidden,
And the courage to unravel life's mysteries.

By the power of the divine, so mote it be."

Take a moment to visualize the deceased surrounded by a brilliant light, their spirit awakening and radiating with a thirst for truth.

If you have chosen to include crystals or gemstones, hold them in your hands and infuse them with your intention for clarity and insight.

Open your journal or parchment and begin to write, allowing the words to flow freely. Write down any questions, thoughts, or insights that come to you. Let your words be a channel for the divine wisdom to flow through you.

Spend as much time as you need, engaging in this sacred act of seeking truth through writing and reflection.

Once you feel complete, offer gratitude to the divine forces and to the spirit of the deceased for their presence and guidance.

Extinguish the candles, knowing that the light of truth and wisdom remains within you.

Close the ritual by offering a final prayer or affirmation, expressing your intention for the deceased to find enlightenment and truth in their spiritual journey.

Take a moment to ground yourself once again, feeling the connection between the earthly and divine realms.

Keep the journal or parchment as a sacred artifact, a tangible representation of the seeker of truth that the deceased has become.

Perform this ritual with reverence and respect, honoring the deceased and their desire for truth. Allow the process of seeking and uncovering wisdom to be a transformative and enlightening experience, both for the deceased and for yourself as the practitioner. May the divine forces guide you on your respective journeys of truth and understanding.

126.   Spell for the reunion of the deceased's soul with their ancestral lineage

Materials:

A sacred space adorned with symbols of ancestry and connection to the past
A ritual altar with candles, photographs or representations of ancestors, and personal mementos
An offering such as food, drink, or incense
Optional: a family tree or genealogy chart
Preparation:

Find a quiet and sacred space where you can perform the ritual without interruptions.
Cleanse the space by smudging with sacred herbs or purifying incense.
Set up your ritual altar with the candles, photographs or representations of ancestors, and personal mementos.
Arrange the offering in a respectful manner.
Take a few moments to ground yourself and enter a state of reverence and connection.
Ritual Steps:

Light the candles on the altar, symbolizing the presence and guidance of the ancestral spirits.

Take a moment to breathe deeply and focus your intention on the reunion of the deceased's soul with their ancestral lineage.

Call upon the presence of the deceased and their ancestors with the following invocation, speaking it aloud or silently:

"Oh, ancestors of [Name of the deceased],
Hear my heartfelt call.
I seek to reunite their departed soul
With the lineage from which they came.

By the sacred bond of blood and kin,
I summon forth the wisdom and strength
Of all those who have gone before.
Let their love and guidance be felt
As [Name of the deceased] journeys onward.

Ancestral spirits, I honor your presence,
With respect and gratitude in my heart.
I ask for your assistance and blessings
In reuniting their soul with the past.

By the power of our shared lineage,
Let the bond be restored and strengthened.
May [Name of the deceased] find solace and connection
In the loving embrace of our ancestral line.

As it was, as it is, as it shall be,
Let the reunion begin. So mote it be."

Take a moment to visualize the deceased's soul surrounded by a warm and gentle light, embraced by the presence of their ancestors.

Extend your gratitude and appreciation to the ancestral spirits for their guidance and support.

Light the offering, whether it be incense, a candle, or a food or drink item, as a symbol of your respect and connection with the ancestors.

Spend some time in quiet reflection, feeling the presence of the ancestral lineage and allowing any messages or insights to come to you.

If you have a family tree or genealogy chart, you may choose to meditate upon it, tracing the connections and deepening your sense of belonging to the lineage.

Express any thoughts or feelings you wish to share with the ancestors or the deceased, speaking from your heart.

When you feel complete, offer a final prayer or affirmation, expressing your intention for the deceased to find solace and connection in their reunion with the ancestral lineage.

Extinguish the candles, knowing that the flame of the ancestral connection continues to burn within your heart.

Close the ritual with a gesture of gratitude, bowing or offering a final word of appreciation to the ancestral spirits.

Take a moment to ground yourself, feeling the connection between the earthly and ancestral realms.

Leave the offering on the altar or in a place of honor for a period of time, allowing the energies to infuse and mingle.

When you are ready, respectfully dispose of the offering, whether by burying it in the earth or by returning it to nature.

127.   Invocation of the goddess Hathor for joy and beauty in the afterlife

Goddess Hathor, embodiment of joy,
Radiant and beautiful, your presence brings delight.
I call upon you now, O divine Hathor,
To grace this sacred space with your light.

With golden wings, you soar through the heavens,
Spreading your love and blessings to all.
Your laughter fills the air with sweet melodies,
And your beauty captivates both great and small.

Goddess Hathor, lady of the celestial realm,
I beseech you to join us in this solemn rite.
Guide us through the mysteries of the afterlife,
And fill our souls with your eternal light.

In the realm beyond, where spirits reside,
May your presence bring joy and boundless cheer.
Grant us the gift of eternal happiness,
And let our hearts be free from all fear.

Goddess Hathor, protector of life's pleasures,
We seek your guidance and your gentle touch.
Shower us with your blessings of joy and beauty,
And let our spirits soar, never to be crushed.

As we journey through the realms unseen,
May your radiant smile light our way.
May your love and laughter surround us,
And bring us comfort both night and day.

O Hathor, goddess of joy and celebration,
Grant us the strength to face the unknown.
In the afterlife's embrace, let us find joy,
And bask in the beauty that you have shown.

Hear our invocation, O gracious Hathor,
And bless us with your presence divine.

With hearts filled with joy, we honor you,
And in your loving embrace, may our souls intertwine.

So mote it be.

Note: This invocation can be spoken aloud or recited silently, depending on your preference and the setting in which it is performed.

128.   Ritual of purification through the sacred dance of the eternal flame

Step 1: Preparation
Create a sacred space where the ritual will take place. Clear the area of any distractions and ensure a safe environment. Set up an altar at the center of the space, adorned with symbols of fire and purification.

Step 2: Invocation
Light the sacred flame on the altar, representing the eternal fire of transformation and purification. Stand before the flame, grounding yourself and centering your energy. Close your eyes and take a few deep breaths to calm the mind and connect with your inner self.

Step 3: Sacred Dance
Begin the ritual by moving gracefully around the sacred flame, allowing the rhythm of the fire to guide your movements. Let the dance be an expression of your intention for purification and transformation. As you dance, visualize the flames engulfing you, burning away any impurities or negative energies.

Step 4: Affirmation
While dancing, recite the following affirmation or create your own words of intent: "By the sacred flame, I release all that no longer serves me. I purify my body, mind, and spirit. As the fire dances, so do I, embracing transformation and emerging purified and renewed."

Step 5: Visualize and Release
As you continue to dance, visualize the flames of the sacred fire purifying every aspect of your being. Imagine any stagnant or negative energies being consumed by the fire and transformed into pure light. With each movement, release and let go of any attachments or burdens weighing you down.

Step 6: Gratitude and Closing
After completing the dance, come to a still position before the sacred flame. Express your gratitude to the divine forces, the sacred flame, and the element of fire for their transformative power. Reflect on the purification you have undergone and the potential for growth and renewal.

Step 7: Extinguish the Flame

Thank the sacred flame for its presence and extinguish it safely, offering gratitude for its energy and power. Take a moment to ground yourself and allow the energy of the ritual to integrate within you.

Note: The movements and duration of the dance can vary based on personal preference and comfort. It is important to listen to your body and dance with intention, allowing the flame to guide your movements. If desired, you can accompany the ritual with music or chants that resonate with the energy of purification and fire.

129.   Spell for the liberation of the deceased's soul from the limitations of the physical body

(To be spoken with intention and focus)

By the power of the sacred realms,
I call upon the forces divine.
In this sacred moment, I invoke,
The liberation of the soul from mortal bind.

From the limitations of the physical form,
I release the spirit that yearns to be free.
Unshackle the soul from earthly chains,
Let it soar and embrace its destiny.

With every word and every breath,
I dissolve the illusion of flesh and bone.
I open the gates to boundless existence,
Where the soul's true essence is known.

No longer confined to the earthly realm,
The spirit transcends all boundaries.
It traverses the realms of timeless space,
Unfolding its divine destinies.

From the cage of mortality, it breaks free,
Embracing the vastness of cosmic design.
The soul soars with ethereal wings,
Infinite possibilities now align.

Oh, liberate the spirit from mortal coil,
Let it dance among stars and celestial spheres.
In the realm of eternal light and truth,
The essence of the soul forever appears.

By the power of divine transformation,
By the sacred laws of cosmic decree,
I set free the deceased's immortal soul,

To explore the realms of eternity.

As I speak these words with love and might,
So shall it be, in the cosmic divine flight.

Take a moment to embrace the energy of liberation and visualize the soul breaking free from the physical body, ascending into the boundless realms of the divine. Feel a sense of freedom, lightness, and expansion as you release the limitations of the mortal existence.

Note: This spell is meant to be spoken with reverence and respect. It is essential to approach it with pure intentions and a deep understanding of the profound nature of the liberation of the soul.

130.   Incantation to awaken the dormant memories within the deceased's mind

(To be spoken with reverence and clarity)

Ancient spirits of time and space,
I call upon your timeless grace.
Awaken now the dormant mind,
Memories hidden, seek and find.

From the depths of forgotten years,
Unveil the past, dissolve all fears.
Reveal the secrets, stories untold,
Let the memories unfold.

Through the veil of time's embrace,
Illuminate the hidden trace.
Awaken the mind's forgotten store,
Unveil the treasures held in core.

Whispered echoes of ancient days,
Resurface now, in sacred ways.
Unleash the power, break the seal,
Let memories flow, with clarity and zeal.

Through the whispers of ancient lore,
Unlock the mind's mysterious door.
Let the past unravel and unfurl,
Rekindling memories, like a precious pearl.

With reverence and respect, I call,
To awaken memories, one and all.
May the deceased's mind now reclaim,
The wisdom of ages, without refrain.

As I speak these words, the spell is cast,
Awakened memories, hold steadfast.
May the mind remember what was once concealed,
With clarity and understanding, revealed.

Take a moment to visualize the awakening of dormant memories within the deceased's mind. See the veil of forgetfulness lifting, and the memories surfacing, bringing clarity and understanding. Allow the ancient wisdom to flow and guide the soul on its journey of remembrance.

Note: This incantation is intended to invoke the awakening of memories in a respectful and compassionate manner. It is essential to approach this practice with pure intentions and a deep understanding of the profound impact it may have on the deceased's soul.

131. Ritual for the communion with the spirits of the celestial realms

Preparation:

✧ Find a quiet and serene location, preferably outdoors under the open sky, where you can feel connected to the celestial realms.

✧ Create a sacred space by placing candles or lanterns in a circle around you, symbolizing the guiding light of the celestial beings.

✧ Gather symbols or representations of celestial bodies such as stars, moons, and suns, to enhance the connection.

Procedure:

✧ Begin by grounding yourself and centering your energy. Take a few deep breaths, allowing your body and mind to relax.

✧ Light the candles or lanterns, one by one, as you invoke the presence of the celestial spirits. Speak the following words or adapt them to resonate with your beliefs:

"Divine beings of the celestial realms,
I call upon your presence and wisdom.
Open the gates between the earthly and the celestial,
As I seek communion with your sacred essence."

✧ Hold the symbols or representations of celestial bodies in your hands and raise them towards the sky, as if offering them to the heavens.

✧ Close your eyes and visualize a radiant beam of light descending from the celestial realms, enveloping you in its divine energy. Feel yourself merging with the celestial energies, becoming one with the vastness of the cosmos.

✧ As you bask in the celestial light, speak your intentions and desires for communion with the spirits of the celestial realms. Share your gratitude, seek guidance, or request their presence and blessings in your life's journey.

✧ Allow yourself to be still and receptive, listening for any messages or signs from the celestial spirits. Trust in the divine guidance that may come in the form of feelings, visions, or intuitive insights.

✧ Spend as much time as you need in this sacred communion, feeling the connection and exchanging energy with the celestial beings.

✧ When you feel ready to conclude the ritual, express your gratitude to the celestial spirits for their presence and guidance. Lower your hands, bringing the symbols or representations of celestial bodies back to your heart, acknowledging the connection that remains within you.

✧ Extinguish the candles or lanterns, one by one, thanking the celestial spirits as you do so.

✧ Take a few deep breaths and slowly return to your awareness of the physical world, carrying the blessings and insights of the celestial realms with you.

Note: This ritual is a sacred act of communion with the celestial realms. It is essential to approach it with reverence and respect, maintaining a pure intention of connection and seeking divine wisdom.

132.   Spell for the transmigration of the deceased's soul into the realm of eternal light

Gathered here, in sacred space,
I call upon the realm of grace.
By the power of celestial might,
Guide the soul to eternal light.

Oh, departed one, set free thy ties,
Soar beyond earthly veils and skies.
Transcend the realms of mortal strife,
Embrace the boundless cosmic life.

With words of power, I now invoke,
The sacred realms where spirits cloak.
Let the gates of light swing open wide,
As the soul embarks on this cosmic ride.

Through the depths of darkness, now ascend,
To the realm where all illusions end.
Unbind the chains that hold you tight,
Embrace the brilliance of eternal light.

With each breath, release the earthly binds,
Awaken to the cosmic winds.
Soar on the wings of celestial fire,
To realms where love and truth inspire.

By the sacred flame, I now ignite,
The spark within to burn so bright.
Let the soul transcend, elevate, and rise,
In the realm of eternal light, it lies.

By the power of divine decree,
Let the soul be forever free.
Transmigrate to the celestial sphere,
Where love and bliss will draw you near.

As I speak these words with sacred intent,

May the soul's journey be divinely sent.
Into the realm of eternal light,
Embrace the gift of infinite sight.

So mote it be, let it be done,
As I will, it is now begun.
May the soul find peace and liberation,
In the realm of eternal illumination.

Note: This spell is intended to facilitate the transmigration of the deceased's soul into the realm of eternal light. It should be performed with reverence, focused intention, and respect for the spiritual journey of the departed soul. Adapt and modify the spell as needed to align with your beliefs and practices.

133. Invocation of the god Ra for illumination and enlightenment in the afterlife

Hail, Ra, radiant Sun, majestic and divine,
I call upon your sacred light to shine.
In the realm beyond, where spirits dwell,
Guide the departed soul, as I now tell.

Ra, the bringer of illumination and truth,
Grant your blessings to the departed's sooth.
With your fiery rays, illuminate their way,
In the afterlife's realm where they may stay.

Oh, Ra, mighty sun, source of all life,
Bestow upon the departed soul, free from strife.
Grant them wisdom, knowledge, and insight,
As they traverse the realms, day and night.

In the afterlife's realm, let their path be clear,
Enlighten their journey, dispel any fear.
Illuminate their mind, their heart, and soul,
With your divine light, make them whole.

Oh, Ra, glorious deity, I call upon your name,
To bring forth illumination, like a sacred flame.
Guide the departed soul with your radiant grace,
In the afterlife's realm, a sacred space.

Through the veils of time and space they'll roam,
In your divine presence, they'll find their home.
Grant them enlightenment, pure and profound,
As they traverse the afterlife's hallowed ground.

Hail, Ra, god of illumination and might,
Bless the departed soul with your divine light.
Illuminate their path with your celestial glow,
In the afterlife's realm, may they eternally know.

As I speak these words with reverence and devotion,
May Ra's guidance shine upon the soul's ocean.
In the afterlife's realm, may they find their way,
Enlightened and blessed by Ra's eternal ray.

Note: This invocation is intended to seek the guidance and blessings of the Egyptian god Ra for illumination and enlightenment in the afterlife. Adapt and modify the invocation as needed to align with your beliefs and practices.

134. Ritual of anointing with sacred resins for spiritual transformation

Gather the sacred resins, fragrant and pure,
Aromatic gifts that will help ensure,
The spiritual transformation of the soul,
As we embark on this sacred goal.

Prepare the space, serene and still,
A sanctum where divine energies will fill.
Light the incense, let its smoke arise,
As we enter into a sacred guise.

Hold the resins in your hands with care,
Feel their essence, potent and rare.
Invoke the divine, the higher power,
To bless this ritual, this sacred hour.

With reverence and intention, anoint your brow,
Symbolizing the awakening of the sacred now.
Feel the resin's fragrance infuse your being,
As you enter a state of divine seeing.

Anoint your throat, your heart, and hands,
Symbolizing the alignment of divine plans.
Feel the resin's energy flow through your veins,
Awakening your spirit, releasing any chains.

Anoint your feet, symbolizing the path,
The journey of the soul, beyond life's wraths.
Feel the resin's essence ground your being,
As you walk the path of spiritual freeing.

As the resin's fragrance fills the air,
Let go of all worries, all burdens to bear.
Embrace the transformation, the spiritual fire,
Ignite the soul's desires, reaching higher.

In this sacred ritual of anointing and grace,
May the resins bring forth divine embrace.

May they elevate your spirit, awaken your soul,
And guide you on a journey towards wholeness and whole.

Note: This ritual is designed to incorporate the use of sacred resins for anointing purposes. Adapt and modify the ritual as needed to align with your beliefs and practices. Choose resins that resonate with your intentions for spiritual transformation and ensure that you use them in a well-ventilated space and with caution.

135.   Spell for the transformation of the deceased into a vessel of divine power

By the sacred veil of time and space,
I call upon the powers of ancient grace.
From realms unseen and mysteries untold,
Let divine power now unfold.

Through the realms of life and death,
I invoke the forces with every breath.
May the deceased be reborn anew,
As a vessel of power, strong and true.

Let the essence of divine energy flow,
Into the soul of the deceased, bestow.
Awaken within them the dormant might,
To radiate brilliance, shining bright.

By the elements of earth, water, air, and fire,
Ignite the spark of divine power's desire.
Infuse the spirit with strength and might,
To manifest miracles and bring forth light.

With each word spoken, each verse recited,
The transformation is being ignited.
As the deceased's essence merges with the divine,
Let them become a channel of power sublime.

Grant them wisdom, courage, and insight,
To navigate realms both day and night.
Let their presence radiate divine grace,
As they embody the power of a sacred space.

May this transformation be swift and true,
As the deceased embraces their power anew.
With the blessings of the gods and goddesses above,
Let divine power flow through them with love.

136.   Incantation to invoke the blessings of the celestial rivers and lakes

By the sacred words I speak, I call upon the powers deep,
Of celestial rivers and lakes, their blessings I now seek.
From distant realms they flow, in cosmic currents wide,
Their waters pure and divine, in them I shall abide.

Oh, mighty rivers, coursing through the heavens above,
Your gentle ripples and cascades, symbols of endless love.
Your waters carry wisdom, from ancient times untold,
With every drop that falls, secrets of the universe unfold.

Oh, tranquil lakes, serene and still, mirrors of the divine,
Reflecting the celestial realm, where mystic energies align.
In your depths, the mysteries lie, waiting to be explored,
A gateway to other realms, where divine knowledge is stored.

I invoke your sacred essence, flowing with celestial grace,
Pour your blessings upon me, in this sacred time and space.
Grant me serenity and tranquility, as calm as your gentle flow,
In your embrace, let divine energies and wisdom grow.

Oh, celestial rivers and lakes, your power I now embrace,
I immerse myself in your currents, feeling your sacred embrace.
Guide me on this journey, as I navigate the cosmic tides,
With your blessings, I shall find peace, where the divine resides.

With gratitude and reverence, I honor your eternal flow,
May your blessings wash over me, wherever I may go.
In harmony with your essence, I find my inner peace,
Forever connected to your sacred waters, may my soul find release.

Note: This incantation is meant to invoke the blessings and energies associated with celestial rivers and lakes. Adapt and modify the incantation as needed to align with your own beliefs and practices. Remember to approach this invocation with respect and reverence for the cosmic forces invoked.

137. Ritual for the transfiguration of the deceased into a divine guardian of sacred knowledge

Step 1: Preparation
✧ Gather in a sacred space adorned with symbols of wisdom and knowledge. Create an altar at the center, featuring books, scrolls, and symbols representing the pursuit of enlightenment. Light candles and incense to purify the space.

Step 2: Invocation
✧ Stand before the altar and enter a state of reverence and focus. Close your eyes and take deep breaths, grounding yourself in the present moment. Recite the following invocation:

"Divine guardians of sacred knowledge,
I call upon your wisdom and grace.
Guide us through this sacred rite,
As we seek the transfiguration of the deceased.

Grant us access to the hidden realms,
Where profound truths and secrets dwell.
Empower us to become guardians of wisdom,
Protectors of the sacred knowledge's well.

May the deceased be transformed,
Into a beacon of enlightenment and truth.
Let their spirit shine with divine brilliance,
As they guard the sacred knowledge, eternal and uncouth."

Step 3: Anointing
✧ Take a vial of sacred oil, infused with herbs and essences representing knowledge and wisdom. Dip your fingers into the oil and anoint the forehead of the deceased, symbolizing the awakening of their divine purpose as a guardian of sacred knowledge.

Step 4: Communion
✧ Light a candle on the altar and hold it before the deceased. Gently wave the flame over the body, symbolizing the transfer of spiritual energy and illumination. Imagine the deceased's spirit embracing the flame, absorbing its divine essence.

Step 5: Affirmation
✧ Speak words of affirmation and intention, directing them towards the deceased:

"By the power of this sacred rite,
I affirm your transformation into a guardian of sacred knowledge.
May your spirit rise to higher realms,
Guided by the light of divine wisdom.

Protect the ancient teachings,
Preserve the wisdom of ages past.
Through you, may enlightenment be nurtured,
And the sacred knowledge forever last."

Step 6: Closing
✧ Thank the divine guardians for their presence and guidance throughout the ritual. Extinguish the candles and incense, symbolizing the completion of the sacred act. Leave the space with a sense of reverence and gratitude for the transfiguration of the deceased into a divine guardian of sacred knowledge.

Note: This ritual is a symbolic representation and should be adapted to align with your personal beliefs and practices. It is important to approach such rituals with respect and sincerity.

138.   Spell for the reunion of the deceased's soul with their spiritual guides and teachers

Gathered in a quiet and sacred space,
I call upon the unseen realms of grace.
With love and reverence, I speak this spell,
To reunite the deceased with their guides so well.

By the power of the ancient divine,
Let the veil between worlds gently unwind.
Bring forth the spirits, guides, and teachers true,
To guide and support the deceased anew.

Oh, spirits of wisdom and infinite light,
Hear my plea on this sacred night.
Gather around and form a guiding band,
To lead the deceased to the promised land.

Spirit guides, with your loving embrace,
Guide the departed to a higher place.
With your wisdom, light, and gentle touch,
Help them reunite, oh, spirits, as such.

Open the doors to the realms unseen,
Let the deceased's soul find peace serene.
Together with guides and teachers divine,
May they find solace and purpose align.

Through the veils of time and space,
Bridge the gap with divine grace.
Lead the departed on their destined path,
In the company of teachers, free from wrath.

May the reunion be filled with love and light,
Guided by wisdom, shining ever bright.
Blessed be this sacred union made,
As the deceased's soul finds solace in the shade.

With gratitude and reverence deep,
I release this spell and let it seep,
Into the realms where spirits reside,
Guiding the deceased with love as their guide.

As it is spoken, so shall it be,
The reunion of souls, blessed and free.
In the embrace of spiritual guides and teachers,
May the departed find eternal peace and features.

Note: This spell is intended to facilitate a connection between the deceased and their spiritual guides and teachers. It is important to approach such rituals with respect and sincerity. Adapt the spell to align with your personal beliefs and practices, and always remember to work with positive intentions and for the highest good of all involved.

139.   Invocation of the goddess Isis for healing and protection in the afterlife

Hail, mighty Isis, goddess of love and light,
I call upon you on this sacred night.
With reverence and devotion, I open my heart,
To seek your guidance and blessings to impart.

Isis, great healer, with your wings spread wide,
Wrap your loving embrace around the one who died.
In the realm of the afterlife, guide them with care,
Provide healing and protection beyond compare.

Goddess of magic, with your powerful charm,
Shield the departed soul from all harm.
Banish the shadows that may seek to oppress,
And bring forth your divine light to impress.

Isis, mother goddess, with your nurturing grace,
Restore the soul's essence in its rightful place.
With your wings of protection, encompass the soul,
Healing any wounds and making it whole.

In the afterlife's realm, where energies flow,
I beseech you, Isis, to let your healing glow.
Bless the departed with your divine touch,
And grant them strength and healing as such.

May your sacred presence bring solace and peace,
To the departed soul, may all troubles cease.
In the afterlife's embrace, let them find rest,
Protected and healed, by your love, blessed.

Oh, Isis, goddess of healing and protection,
I offer my gratitude for your divine connection.
Thank you for your presence in this sacred rite,
May your blessings guide the departed in their flight.

140.   Ritual of purification through the sacred breath of the divine wind

In this sacred space, where spirits intertwine,
I invoke the power of the divine wind sublime.
With every breath, I cleanse and purify,
To release all impurities that within me lie.

I stand with arms open, facing the sky above,
Connecting with the winds that carry divine love.
I inhale deeply, drawing in the sacred air,
Feeling its purity cleanse my spirit with care.

As the wind whispers secrets of the ancient trees,
I exhale, releasing what no longer serves me.
With each breath, I let go of doubts and fears,
Allowing the divine wind to wipe away all tears.

The breeze caresses my skin, revitalizing my soul,
I feel its gentle touch making me whole.
As I breathe in the essence of the celestial air,
I am filled with light, free from all despair.

In this sacred ritual of purification and release,
I surrender to the wind's cleansing peace.
With gratitude and reverence, I embrace its flow,
Allowing the divine breath to heal and bestow.

May the sacred wind carry away all that's impure,
Leaving behind a soul that is radiant and pure.
As I exhale, I release what no longer serves,
Welcoming the divine wind's blessings and reserves.

In the sacred breath of the divine wind's embrace,
I find solace, renewal, and a sense of grace.
I am purified, revitalized, and truly free,
Connected to the divine in eternal harmony.

Note: This ritual is intended to purify and release negative energies through the symbolic use of the divine wind.
Adapt the ritual to suit your personal beliefs and practices, and always approach it with respect and intention.
Remember to work with positive intentions and focus on the purification and renewal of your spirit.

141. Spell for the liberation of the deceased's soul from the burdens of past lives

In this sacred moment, where time meets eternity,
I call upon the cosmic forces for soul's liberty.
With words of power and intention profound,
I release the burdens of past lives, unbound.

By the ancient forces that govern the divine,
I sever the ties that bind the soul's lifeline.
Through this incantation, let the past dissolve,
Freeing the deceased's spirit, evolving and resolve.

I summon the energy of renewal and transformation,
To break the chains of karmic limitation.
With every word spoken, I break the cycle's hold,
Releasing the soul's journey, untold.

From this moment forward, let the past unwind,
As the deceased's soul is liberated, unconfined.
I speak these words with reverence and might,
Releasing all burdens, embracing the light.

May the weight of past lives be lifted away,
As the soul finds freedom, embracing a new day.
Let go of regrets, traumas, and strife,
Embracing the infinite possibilities of a new life.

With the power of this spell, I set the spirit free,
From the shackles of past lives, it shall be.
Let the soul soar and reclaim its true essence,
Embracing its purpose, transcending past lessons.

As I speak these words with love and care,
I send forth the energy for the soul to repair.
In the realm of liberation, the spirit will dwell,
Free from the burdens of past lives, fare thee well.

Note: This spell is intended to aid in the liberation of the deceased's soul from the burdens of past lives. Adapt the spell to align with your personal beliefs and practices, and approach it with reverence and respect. Remember to work with positive intentions and focus on the liberation and healing of the soul.

142.   Incantation to awaken the dormant gifts within the deceased's spirit

By the power of the sacred flame's light,
I call upon the energies of day and night.
In this sacred space, where spirits reside,
I invoke the dormant gifts deep inside.

With reverence and respect, I speak these words,
To awaken the talents, once silent and unheard.
From the depths of the soul, they shall arise,
Unveiling the gifts hidden beneath the guise.

Ancient forces and cosmic energies near,
Hear my plea, lend your divine ear.
Let the dormant gifts now come alive,
As the deceased's spirit begins to thrive.

Awaken, awaken, from slumber deep,
Unleash the gifts that the soul shall keep.
Let creativity flow, like a river's embrace,
Empowering the spirit, full of grace.

From within the spirit's core they emerge,
Gifts unique and sacred, a celestial surge.
With every word spoken, their power is gained,
Unleashing the dormant gifts, unchained.

I call upon the universe's infinite might,
To ignite the dormant gifts, shining bright.
May they blossom and flourish, strong and true,
In the afterlife's realm, renewed.

Let the gifts flow forth, like a gentle breeze,
Enriching the soul, bringing it ease.
With gratitude and joy, I embrace this sight,
As the deceased's spirit awakens in its light.

Note: This incantation is intended to awaken the dormant gifts within the deceased's spirit. Adapt the incantation to align with your personal beliefs and practices, and approach it with reverence and respect. Remember to work with positive intentions and focus on the awakening and empowerment of the spirit.

143.   Ritual for the communion with the spirits of the celestial stars and planets

Prepare a sacred space under the open sky,
Where the celestial wonders catch the eye.
With reverence and awe, stand in this place,
To commune with the spirits of cosmic grace.

Light candles and incense, symbols of connection,
Creating a bridge to celestial realms of perfection.
Arrange crystals and gems, shimmering and bright,
As conduits for the energies of celestial light.

Stand with arms outstretched, palms open wide,
Feeling the cosmic energies flow inside.
Close your eyes and breathe in deeply,
Entering a state of meditation, calm and serenely.

Visualize the stars and planets above,
Their radiant energies shining with love.
See the constellations forming intricate patterns,
Guiding you on this celestial communion.

Raise your voice to the heavens high,
Reciting sacred words that amplify.
Call upon the spirits of stars and planets near,
To grace you with their wisdom, loud and clear.

"Glorious stars and planets of the cosmic expanse,
I seek your presence in this sacred dance.
Come forth, celestial beings of divine might,
Illuminate my path with your celestial light.

Grant me knowledge of the mysteries untold,
Wisdom and insights that the heavens hold.
As above, so below, in perfect harmony,
May our communion be filled with celestial unity.

Stars and planets, guardians of the night,
Bless me with your presence, shining bright.

Guide me on my journey with your cosmic fire,
Ignite my spirit's desire to reach higher.

In this sacred space, we join as one,
Merging our energies under the celestial sun.
I give gratitude for this communion divine,
For the celestial wisdom that is now mine."

Stay in this sacred space as long as you need,
Feeling the cosmic energies gently recede.
Express gratitude to the celestial spirits above,
For their presence and guidance, their divine love.

When you are ready, slowly open your eyes,
Knowing that the celestial connection never dies.
Carry the wisdom and insights gained with you,
As you walk your path, celestial and true.

Note: This ritual is intended to establish a communion with the spirits of the celestial stars and planets. Adapt the ritual to align with your personal beliefs and practices. Remember to approach it with reverence and respect, and be open to the energies and wisdom that the celestial spirits may share with you.

144. Spell for the transmigration of the deceased's soul into the realm of divine mysteries

In the stillness of the sacred night,
Where darkness and light intertwine,
I call upon the forces unseen,
To guide the soul, transcending time.

By the power of the ancient ones,
Who dwell in realms beyond our sight,
I seek to journey to the depths,
Where mysteries reside, veiled in light.

O spirits of the cosmic plane,
With wisdom vast and secrets profound,
Hear my plea and grant me passage,
To the realm where mysteries abound.

I release the earthly binds that tie,
And open my spirit to the unknown,
With pure intention and open heart,
I venture where the divine is shown.

Through realms unseen and astral gates,
I traverse the thresholds of existence,
In pursuit of knowledge and revelation,
Embracing the divine with persistence.

Grant me passage, celestial guides,
To the realm of ancient truths untold,
Where symbols dance and wisdom flows,
In a tapestry of mysteries to behold.

May my spirit soar and transcend,
The limitations of this mortal plane,
In the realm of the divine mysteries,
Let my consciousness eternally remain.

By the power of intention and divine will,
I invoke the transmigration sublime,
To journey through the sacred veil,
And explore the realm where mysteries chime.

As I venture forth into the unknown,
Guide me with your celestial light,
Reveal the secrets of the cosmic web,
And bestow upon me profound insight.

With gratitude and reverence, I embrace,
The journey that lies ahead of me,
Transcending the boundaries of mortality,
To dwell in the realm of the divine, set free.

So mote it be.

145. Invocation of the god Ptah for creation and manifestation in the afterlife

Oh Ptah, the Great Craftsman divine,
Master of creation, architect of time,
I call upon your ancient name,
To bring forth the power of your sacred flame.

You who shaped the world with your hands,
Breathing life into the barren lands,
Guide me now in this afterlife quest,
To manifest my desires and manifest my best.

Ptah, the weaver of dreams and design,
With your wisdom and skill, align,
Grant me the ability to create and mold,
A reality of beauty, as my story unfolds.

In this realm beyond the mortal veil,
Where the limits of imagination fail,
I seek your guidance, O Ptah, my guide,
To harness the forces and dreams coincide.

With your divine touch and creative might,
Let my intentions take shape in this new light,
From thought to form, from idea to being,
I invoke your presence, Ptah, in this sacred seeing.

By the power of your sacred name,
I draw upon your essence, vibrant and untamed,
Infuse my spirit with your creative fire,
Ignite the spark within, soaring higher and higher.

Ptah, the master of craftsmanship true,
In this afterlife realm, I turn to you,
Unleash the powers of creation's embrace,
And guide me in shaping my soul's new space.

With each thought, each word, each action I take,
May I weave a tapestry, with beauty at stake,

Manifesting my desires with divine precision,
Aligned with the cosmic plan, in perfect collision.

Oh Ptah, I call upon your name,
In this afterlife realm, where dreams remain,
Guide me, inspire me, and show me the way,
To create a reality where I eternally stay.

In your presence, Ptah, I find solace and might,
I honor your wisdom, your creative insight,
With gratitude, I embrace your divine flame,
And weave the tapestry of my afterlife's name.

So be it, in accordance with divine will,
Ptah, I thank you for your presence still,
May your creative energies forever shine,
As I navigate this afterlife realm, divine.

Note: This invocation is a tribute to Ptah and can be adapted to fit your personal beliefs and practices. Approach it with reverence and sincerity, allowing your intention to align with the creative forces of the universe.

146.   Ritual of anointing with sacred herbs for spiritual renewal

Gather now, seekers of renewal and light,
As we embark on this sacred rite,
In the realm of spirit, we gather near,
To anoint ourselves, embracing what's dear.

Prepare the space, adorned with care,
A sanctuary where intentions we share,
Let the smoke of sacred herbs arise,
Cleansing the space, opening our eyes.

The scent of sage, a cleansing force,
Releasing stagnant energies, setting a new course,
Purify our spirits, let negativity dissolve,
As we prepare for the mysteries to unfold.

Next, the fragrant lavender, soothing and calm,
Infuse our being with tranquility's balm,
Easing the mind, relaxing the soul,
As we surrender to the divine's gentle control.

Rosemary, the herb of remembrance and grace,
Awaken our senses, bring clarity to our space,
Strengthen our connection to the realms unseen,
As we seek spiritual renewal, pure and pristine.

Now, the invigorating scent of peppermint,
Revitalizing our spirits, removing impediment,
Stimulate our senses, awaken our inner fire,
As we embark on this journey, reaching higher.

Finally, the mystical aroma of frankincense,
Elevate our consciousness, bring forth the immense,
Unveil the mysteries, connect us to the divine,
As we anoint ourselves, in sacredness we align.

Take a moment now, hold the sacred oils near,
Invoke your intentions, without hesitation or fear,

Anoint your forehead, your heart, and your hands,
Symbolic gestures, where spirit forever stands.

As the sacred oils touch your being,
Feel the energy, the vibrancy freeing,
Open yourself to the wisdom they contain,
A gateway to spiritual growth, a transformative domain.

In this sacred act of anointing, we find,
Renewal of spirit, a transcendent state of mind,
Embrace the blessings, let your soul unfold,
As you journey on the path of spiritual gold.

Note: This ritual of anointing with sacred herbs can be customized to your own preferences and beliefs. Choose herbs that resonate with you and create a space that feels sacred and serene. Allow yourself to fully immerse in the experience and set clear intentions for spiritual renewal and growth.

147.   Spell for the transformation of the deceased into a vessel of divine wisdom

By the power of the ancient ones, I stand,
Seeking transformation, guided by hand.
In this sacred space, I call upon the divine,
To awaken wisdom, a radiant light to shine.

From the depths of the universe, I draw,
The essence of wisdom, ancient and raw.
Let it flow through me, as a timeless stream,
Transforming the deceased into a vessel of gleam.

With reverence and respect, I now decree,
That wisdom shall blossom, for all to see.
Release the veils that shroud mortal mind,
Awaken the wisdom that's been left behind.

From the realms beyond, the ancient sages,
Unveil the wisdom of the eternal ages.
Infuse the deceased with knowledge profound,
Divine wisdom to be forever renowned.

Oh, spirits of wisdom, hear my call,
Descend upon us, upon one and all.
Fill the deceased with your sacred lore,
A vessel of wisdom, forevermore.

Let ignorance be banished, let insight be gained,
In the journey beyond, wisdom unchained.
Grant clarity of thought, discernment of truth,
As the deceased becomes a vessel of wisdom, sooth.

With every breath, let wisdom arise,
Guiding the deceased to infinite skies.
In the realm of eternity, may they be wise and keen,
A vessel of divine wisdom, a radiant sheen.

As I speak these words, so mote it be,
The transformation unfolds, for all to see.

The deceased shall rise, enlightened and free,
A vessel of divine wisdom, eternally.

Note: This spell can be performed with utmost respect and reverence for the deceased and the divine forces invoked. It is important to adapt and personalize the spell according to your own beliefs and practices. Remember to approach such rituals with sincerity, love, and a deep understanding of the profound transformation sought.

148.   Incantation to invoke the blessings of the celestial forests and gardens

Ancient spirits of the sacred groves,
Whisper your secrets, as nature behoves.
With reverence and awe, I call upon thee,
To bless me with the wisdom of the celestial tree.

From the depths of the celestial forests so grand,
Where magic and wonder forever expand,
I seek your guidance, O spirits divine,
In this incantation, may your blessings shine.

Oh, guardians of the mystical woods,
With wisdom ancient, your presence intrudes.
Grant me the essence of your vibrant life,
Fill my spirit with harmony, free from strife.

Beneath the canopy of the celestial trees,
Let their whispers of wisdom put my heart at ease.
May their branches reach towards the stars above,
And their roots anchor me in unconditional love.

In the celestial gardens where beauty thrives,
I seek your blessings to nurture and revive.
Let the fragrant blossoms intoxicate my soul,
And the vibrant colors make me whole.

With each step I take upon the sacred ground,
May the energy of the celestial gardens surround.
May the flowers bloom, and the leaves dance,
As I invoke the blessings of this enchanting trance.

Oh, spirits of the celestial forests and gardens fair,
With gratitude, I offer my heartfelt prayer.
Guide me with your ancient wisdom and grace,
As I walk this earthly path with an enchanted pace.

As I speak these words, I call upon your might,
To bless my journey, both day and night.

With your wisdom and love, my spirit aligns,
In harmony with the celestial forests and gardens divine.

Note: This incantation is a way to invoke the blessings and guidance of the celestial forests and gardens. Feel free to adapt and modify it according to your own beliefs and connection with nature. It is important to approach such invocations with respect, love, and a deep reverence for the natural world.

149. Ritual for the transfiguration of the deceased into a divine protector of sacred rituals

Gather, O spirits of the ancient ones,
In this sacred space where darkness shuns.
With reverence and intent, I summon thee,
To witness the transformation of what used to be.

In this ritual, we honor the departed soul,
Whose spirit seeks purpose, to make it whole.
Grant them the transfiguration they desire,
To become a guardian of rituals that inspire.

O sacred flame, burn bright and true,
Illuminate this path, both old and new.
As the fire dances with ethereal grace,
Let it cleanse and transform, leaving no trace.

In the circle of power, let the elements converge,
Air, fire, water, and earth, their forces surge.
May the deceased's spirit awaken and rise,
Claiming their role as a guardian in the skies.

With symbols of power, I anoint their soul,
To guide and protect, their sacred role.
Let their presence be felt in every sacred rite,
A guardian of rituals, shining with divine light.

As the incense swirls and the candles glow,
Let the energy shift, let the transformation show.
Through the sacred words spoken and chanted,
Let the deceased's purpose be firmly implanted.

In this ritual of transfiguration, we invoke,
The blessings of the divine, the sacred cloak.
Grant the deceased the wisdom and insight,
To safeguard rituals, day and night.

By the power of the ancient ones we call,
Let the transformation be complete, one and all.
From this moment forward, their purpose clear,
A divine protector of rituals, forever near.

Note: This ritual is meant to facilitate the transfiguration of the deceased into a guardian of sacred rituals. Adapt and modify it according to your specific beliefs and practices. Always approach such rituals with respect, reverence, and a deep understanding of the spiritual realm.

150.   Spell for the reunion of the deceased's soul with their soulmates and kindred spirits

By the power of love, both earthly and divine,
I call upon the spirits to intertwine,
With this sacred spell, I seek to unite,
The souls of the departed, in love's pure light.

In this sacred space, where spirits reside,
I invoke the presence of those who've died,
To guide and connect with their beloved kin,
Soulmates and kindred spirits, let the reunion begin.

I call upon the spirits of the departed,
Across the realms, let their connections be charted,
Through time and space, their souls shall align,
In the realm of love, where destinies intertwine.

By the threads of fate, woven strong and true,
I beckon the souls to find their way through,
Across the veil, from the realms unseen,
Let them be drawn to their beloved, serene.

May the bonds of love be strong and clear,
Guiding the departed, drawing them near,
To their soulmates and kindred spirits so dear,
Let them reunite, casting away all fear.

With love as the beacon, shining bright,
I ask the universe to bring them in sight,
The souls once separated, now reunited,
In love's embrace, forever ignited.

By the power of love, this spell is sealed,
May the reunion be blessed and revealed,
In the afterlife's realm, where spirits roam,
Let the souls find solace and forever call it home.

151.   Invocation of the goddess Bastet for strength and courage in the afterlife

Mighty Bastet, lioness of the divine,
Goddess of protection, strength that shines,
I call upon your sacred presence near,
To grant me strength and courage, without fear.

In the realm of the afterlife, I seek your aid,
As I journey through the paths that are laid,
Guide me, oh Bastet, with your fierce grace,
Empower me in this sacred space.

Goddess of the sun, with radiant light,
Unleash your power, fierce and bright,
Bestow upon me your courage and might,
To face the challenges of the afterlife's night.

Bastet, protector of souls departed,
Grant me the strength to be strong-hearted,
To overcome obstacles that may arise,
With your guidance, I shall be wise.

In the afterlife's realm, where spirits dwell,
I invoke your presence, oh Bastet, to quell,
Any fears or doubts that may arise,
Fill me with courage, strong and wise.

With your divine essence, I am shielded,
Protected from darkness, safely guided,
Grant me strength to face what lies ahead,
In the afterlife's realm, where I am led.

Bastet, lioness goddess, fierce and true,
In your presence, I find strength anew,
Empower me now, in this sacred rite,
To navigate the afterlife with courage and light.

With gratitude and reverence, I call your name,
Bastet, may your blessings forever remain,

In the afterlife's realm, guide and protect me,
Grant me strength and courage, eternally.

Note: This invocation is intended to seek the presence and assistance of the goddess Bastet for strength and courage in the afterlife. Modify and adapt it according to your personal beliefs and practices. Approach the invocation with respect and a sincere heart, inviting Bastet's divine energy to empower you and guide you through the challenges of the afterlife. Trust in her protection and draw upon her strength as you navigate the realms beyond.

152. Ritual of purification through the sacred chants of the eternal hymns

Gather in the sacred space, seekers of light,
Where purity reigns and darkness takes flight.
With hearts open wide and intentions pure,
We embark on a journey of spiritual cure.

Let the sacred chants resonate in the air,
As we invoke the divine presence with care.
With each melodic note and harmonious tone,
We cleanse our beings and make our spirits known.

In the stillness of this sacred moment,
We release all negativity, let it be sent.
Through the power of sound and sacred hymns,
We purify our souls and release all sins.

Hear the rhythm of the universe's heartbeat,
As we chant the ancient words, so sweet.
Let the vibrations cleanse our every cell,
As divine energy within us powerfully dwells.

With each chant, we shed layers of illusion,
Revealing our true selves in perfect fusion.
We align with the cosmic currents of grace,
Transcending limitations, finding our rightful place.

The sacred chants carry us to higher realms,
Where divine wisdom and serenity overwhelm.
We are purified, reborn, and made anew,
In this moment of unity, our spirits renew.

As the chants fade and the echoes subside,
We stand in the purity of our soul's stride.
Grateful for this ritual of cleansing and healing,
With love and light, our spirits are sealing.

May the sacred chants continue to guide,
As we walk the path of truth with pride.

In this ritual of purification, we find our way,
Connected to the divine, each and every day.

153. Spell for the liberation of the deceased's soul from the cycle of birth and death

By the power of the eternal realms,
Where time and space intertwine,
I call upon the forces unseen,
To release the soul, divine.

From the cycle of birth and death,
Let the spirit soar free,
No longer bound by earthly ties,
But united with eternity.

I summon the cosmic energies,
To break the chains that bind,
To transcend the mortal realm,
And leave all suffering behind.

Oh, great universe, hear my plea,
Grant liberation to the departed soul,
Guide it through the realms unknown,
To reach its ultimate goal.

Let the soul find eternal peace,
In realms beyond this earthly plane,
Where there is no more pain or strife,
Only love and light remain.

As I speak these words with reverence,
May the divine forces intervene,
Liberating the departed soul,
From the cycle of birth and death, serene.

With pure intentions and heartfelt prayer,
I send forth this spell, strong and true,
May the soul be freed from the cycle,
And embrace its destiny anew.

So mote it be.

Note: This spell is intended to be performed with utmost respect and reverence for the departed soul. Adapt and modify the spell to align with your own beliefs and practices. Create a sacred space, light candles or incense, and focus your energy and intention on releasing the soul from the cycle of birth and death. Speak the words with clarity and conviction, allowing your intention to be carried by the power of your voice. Visualize the soul being liberated and guided to a realm of eternal peace and bliss. Trust in the divine forces to work in alignment with your intentions and the highest good of the departed soul.

154. Incantation to awaken the dormant creativity within the deceased's spirit

By the cosmic forces that govern all creation,
I invoke the dormant powers of inspiration,
From the realms unseen, I call upon the divine,
To awaken the creativity that lies dormant in time.

Within the spirit of the departed soul so dear,
Lies a wellspring of creativity waiting to appear,
Through the veils of the eternal, I reach out my hand,
To ignite the spark of artistic brilliance, grand.

Arise, O spirit, from the depths of slumber deep,
Let your creative essence awaken from its silent keep,
Unleash the floodgates of imagination and art,
Let your spirit soar and express its divine part.

I call upon the muses, the guardians of inspiration,
To infuse the deceased's spirit with creative elation,
Let the brush stroke the canvas with colors so bold,
Or the pen dance upon the paper, stories to be told.

May melodies flow from the spirit's deepest core,
Harmonies of the soul, resounding evermore,
Sculptures and creations, born from the heart,
Unveil the beauty of the deceased's creative art.

Awaken, O spirit, let your creativity be unfurled,
Manifest your visions, let them transform the world,
Break free from the shackles of time and space,
Let your artistic expression find its rightful place.

As I speak these words with reverence and might,
I call forth the creative energy, pure and bright,
May the dormant creativity within the deceased's soul,
Awaken and flourish, making the spirit whole.

So mote it be.

Note: This incantation is meant to be spoken with respect and intention to awaken the dormant creativity within the deceased's spirit. Modify and adapt the incantation as needed to align with your beliefs and practices. Create a sacred space, light candles or incense, and focus your energy and intention on awakening the creative essence of the departed soul. Visualize the spirit becoming infused with inspiration, imagination, and artistic expression. Trust in the power of the words and the divine forces to ignite the creative spark within the soul.

155. Ritual for the communion with the spirits of the celestial elements

Gather in a sacred space, where earth meets sky,
In the presence of the stars, where celestial spirits fly,
With open hearts and minds, let us now begin,
A ritual of communion, a sacred dance with the elements within.

Light a candle, representing the eternal flame,
A beacon of guidance in this mystical game,
Feel its warmth and glow, connecting to the divine,
As we invite the spirits of the elements to intertwine.

Call upon the spirit of Earth, stable and strong,
The foundation beneath us, where we belong,
Feel the grounding energy, solid and secure,
As we commune with Earth, let its essence endure.

Next, we invoke the spirit of Air, gentle and free,
The breath of life, carrying messages to see,
Inhale deeply, feel the air fill your lungs,
As we commune with Air, let its wisdom be sung.

Now, we invite the spirit of Fire, fierce and bright,
The flame that ignites our passions, burning with might,
Light the incense, let the smoke rise to the skies,
As we commune with Fire, let its transformative energy arise.

Next, we call upon the spirit of Water, flowing and pure,
The source of life, cleansing and healing for sure,
Pour water into a sacred vessel, feel its cool embrace,
As we commune with Water, let its flow bring solace.

Lastly, we invoke the spirit of Spirit, divine and divine,
The essence of all elements, intertwining in this shrine,
Stand in awe of the cosmic dance, the unity we find,
As we commune with Spirit, let our souls be aligned.

In this sacred space, let us commune with the celestial,
Connecting with the elements, embracing the ethereal,

Feel the presence of the spirits, their wisdom and grace,
As we commune with the celestial elements, embodying their embrace.

Take a moment to reflect, to offer gratitude and thanks,
To the spirits of the elements, for their sacred ranks,
Release any intentions or desires into the cosmic flow,
Knowing that the spirits of the elements will guide us as we grow.

Close the ritual with reverence and love,
Thanking the spirits of the celestial above,
May their presence and wisdom continue to be,
Guiding us on our spiritual journey, eternally.

So mote it be.

Note: This ritual is meant to honor and commune with the spirits of the celestial elements (Earth, Air, Fire, Water, and Spirit). Modify and adapt the ritual as needed to align with your beliefs and practices. Create a sacred space, set up representations of the elements (such as candles, incense, water, and symbols), and engage in meditative and reflective practices to connect with the spirits of the elements. Offer gratitude, intentions, and prayers during the ritual, and trust in the presence and guidance of the celestial spirits.

156. Spell for the transmigration of the deceased's soul into the realm of eternal peace

By the power of the sacred realms and divine grace,
I call upon the forces that transcend time and space.
With utmost reverence and love, I cast this spell,
To guide the departed soul where serenity does dwell.

From this mortal plane to the realm unseen,
Let the soul traverse, on wings pristine.
Release the ties that bind to earthly strife,
Embrace the tranquility of the eternal life.

With focused intention and words sincere,
I invoke the spirits of peace to draw near.
May the soul find solace, free from pain and sorrow,
In the realm where tranquility flows like a gentle stream's flow.

O spirits of peace, guardians of serenity divine,
Wrap the departed soul in your embrace benign.
Guide them through the veils of existence and time,
To the realm of eternal peace, sublime.

Let the burdens of earthly life dissolve away,
As the soul transcends to a blissful bay.
In this sacred journey, may they find release,
And dwell in the serenity that grants eternal peace.

With gratitude and trust, I release this plea,
Knowing the divine forces guide the soul to be free.
May the transmigration be gentle and light,
As the soul finds its place in eternal delight.

As it is spoken, so mote it be,
By the powers of the unseen, may it be decree.
In harmony and love, let the spell take flight,
Guiding the soul to the realm of eternal peace, shining bright.

Note: This spell is intended to be used with respect and love, aiming to assist the deceased's soul in finding peace and serenity in the afterlife. Modify and adapt the spell as necessary to align with your beliefs and practices. Create a sacred space, focus your intention, and speak the spell with heartfelt sincerity. Trust in the guidance of the divine forces and the spirits of peace as you cast the spell.

157.   Invocation of the god Sobek for protection and abundance in the afterlife

Mighty Sobek, fierce and wise,
I call upon you, God of the Nile's rise.
With your powerful jaws and scales adorned,
Protect and bless the departed soul reborn.

Oh, Sobek, Lord of the fertile lands,
Grant your divine presence and guiding hands.
In the afterlife's realm, be their guardian strong,
Defending them against any harm or wrong.

You, who rule over waters vast and wide,
Bring forth abundance, a bountiful tide.
Let the soul be nourished, sustained and fed,
With blessings and prosperity on which they tread.

Sobek, mighty crocodile deity,
Your strength and power bring tranquility.
Wrap the departed soul in your protective embrace,
Shielding them from any darkness they may face.

In the afterlife's journey, let them thrive,
With your guidance, may their spirits revive.
Grant them courage, resilience, and might,
As they navigate the realms of eternal light.

Oh, Sobek, I offer my heartfelt plea,
That you may hear and answer me.
With gratitude and reverence, I invoke your name,
For protection and abundance, I humbly claim.

So be it, as I speak these words aloud,
May your blessings be received, strong and proud.
In the afterlife's realm, may the departed soul find,
Protection and abundance, eternally intertwined.

Note: This invocation is intended to seek the protection and abundance of the god
Sobek for the deceased in the afterlife. Modify and adapt the invocation as necessary

to align with your beliefs and practices. Create a sacred space, focus your intention, and speak the invocation with reverence and sincerity. Trust in the presence and guidance of Sobek as you invoke his name.

158. Ritual of anointing with sacred crystals for spiritual clarity

Gather before you a selection of sacred crystals,
Each imbued with unique energies and spiritual miracles.
Crystals of clear quartz, amethyst, and selenite,
Radiating purity, insight, and divine light.

Prepare a sacred space, cleansed and pure,
Where the energies can flow and endure.
Place the crystals before you in a sacred arrangement,
With reverence and intention, a symbol of engagement.

Close your eyes and breathe deeply, finding calm,
As you enter a state of meditation, a healing balm.
Feel the energy of the crystals resonating within,
Awakening your senses, where clarity begins.

Take the first crystal, smooth and pure,
Anoint it with sacred oils, a gentle lure.
Hold it to your third eye, the center of insight,
Invoking clarity and vision, day or night.

Repeat this process with each crystal in turn,
Anointing them with love, respect, and concern.
Place them gently upon your body's energy points,
Allowing their vibrations to heal and anoint.

Visualize the crystals' energy merging with your own,
Clearing away confusion, doubts, and the unknown.
Feel their power spreading through your being,
Awakening clarity and insight, freeing and freeing.

With gratitude, thank the crystals for their aid,
For the clarity and wisdom they have conveyed.
Leave them upon your altar, a symbol of connection,
To be cleansed and recharged for future introspection.

As you go forth, carry the energy of clarity within,
With a heart open to guidance, where truth begins.

Embrace the spiritual clarity the crystals provide,
Walking your path with purpose, side by side.

Note: This ritual is intended to harness the energy of sacred crystals for spiritual clarity. Adapt the ritual as needed, incorporating crystals that resonate with your intention and practice. Create a sacred space and a meditative atmosphere. Use high-quality oils and handle the crystals with care and respect. Visualize the energy of the crystals merging with your own, infusing you with clarity and insight. Express gratitude for the assistance received and honor the crystals in your ongoing spiritual journey.

159. Spell for the transformation of the deceased into a vessel of divine guidance

With reverence and intention, I call upon the sacred powers,
To transform the departed soul into a vessel of guidance that empowers.
I summon the energies of divine wisdom and light,
To guide the departed soul through eternal night.

By the ancient forces that shape the cosmos above,
I invoke the divine presence and their boundless love.
May the soul be transformed, reborn, and renewed,
Into a beacon of guidance, strong and true.

In this sacred space, I speak the words with care,
Infusing them with love, faith, and the utmost prayer.
From the depths of my being, this spell I cast,
To guide the departed soul, from present to past.

By the divine wisdom of the cosmic realms,
May the departed soul awaken and overwhelm,
With knowledge and insight, let them shine,
As a vessel of guidance, eternally divine.

Grant them the ability to see beyond the veil,
To guide those in need with compassion and prevail.
Let their words be a beacon, their touch a healing balm,
As they navigate the realms, a divine calm.

May their guidance be a light in the darkest night,
Bringing clarity, wisdom, and spiritual sight.
With each step they take in the celestial sphere,
May they inspire and guide, forever near.

By the power of this spell, so mote it be,
As I will it, so shall it be, for all eternity.
In harmony with the cosmic flow, this transformation unfolds,
The deceased soul now a vessel of guidance, as this spell holds.

Note: This spell is intended to transform the deceased into a vessel of divine
guidance. It is important to perform this spell with respect, love, and a pure intention

to assist the departed soul in their journey. Adapt the spell as needed to align with your personal beliefs and practices. Create a sacred space, invoke the divine powers, and infuse your words with intention and energy. Visualize the departed soul transformed into a vessel of guidance, radiating wisdom and light. Release the spell with faith and trust in the divine plan.

160. Incantation to invoke the blessings of the celestial temples and shrines

By the celestial temples and shrines so grand,
I call upon their blessings from across the land.
With reverence and respect, I open the gateway,
To receive their divine blessings without delay.

O celestial temples and shrines of ancient grace,
Beacons of light in the celestial space.
From the realms above, where mysteries unfold,
I seek your blessings, radiant and bold.

With every step I take on this sacred ground,
May your blessings shower and surround.
Infuse me with your wisdom and sacred power,
In your presence, may my spirit flower.

Let the celestial temples and shrines align,
To grant me guidance, protection divine.
From the highest heavens to the depths below,
Your blessings upon me, forever flow.

Grant me clarity of mind and purity of heart,
As I walk this path, may I never depart.
Bless my intentions, actions, and deeds,
In alignment with the highest cosmic needs.

By the sacred energy that flows within,
I invoke your blessings, let the journey begin.
May the celestial temples and shrines bestow,
Their blessings upon me, as above, so below.

With gratitude and reverence, I give my thanks,
For the blessings received, along life's banks.
As I walk this path, guided by your light,
I honor the celestial temples, day and night.

This incantation I speak with love and respect,
For the celestial temples and shrines, I connect.

May their blessings guide me on my way,
As I navigate the realms, day after day.

So mote it be, in harmony and grace,
I am blessed by the celestial temples' embrace.
With their blessings, I move forward with might,
In harmony with the celestial realms' divine light.

Note: This incantation is meant to invoke the blessings of the celestial temples and shrines. Adapt the incantation to align with your personal beliefs and practices. Create a sacred space, open yourself to the energy of the celestial temples and shrines, and speak the words with reverence and intention. Visualize their blessings showering upon you and guiding your path. Offer gratitude for their presence and the blessings they bestow upon you. Trust in the divine connection and allow their guidance to unfold in your life.

161. Ritual for the transfiguration of the deceased into a divine embodiment of sacred rituals

Before embarking on this sacred rite,
Prepare yourself for the transformational flight.
Create a space that is pure and serene,
A sanctuary where divine energies convene.

Light the candles, their flames ablaze,
Setting the stage for mystical ways.
Anoint yourself with oils, fragrant and sweet,
To elevate your spirit and make the ritual complete.

As you stand in the sacred space you've made,
Call upon the spirits, ancient and forbade.
Invoke the presence of the divine,
To guide you through this transformative shrine.

With focused intent and deep respect,
Open your heart and soul, fully expect,
To be a vessel of sacred rituals divine,
To channel their wisdom, a divine lifeline.

Raise your voice in incantation and prayer,
To the gods and goddesses, beyond compare.
Call upon their presence, their ancient might,
To bless and empower you with their sacred light.

Now, embody the rituals, one by one,
Dance the dances, chant the ancient hymns, let them be done.
Feel the energy flow through your veins,
Transforming you into a vessel that contains,
The essence of the sacred, the wisdom of old,
An embodiment of rituals, majestic and bold.

As you perform each act with reverence and grace,
Embrace the divine energy in this sacred space.
Let it flow through you, intertwine with your being,

Awakening the dormant powers, forever freeing.

Embrace the wisdom of the ages untold,
A conduit of rituals, sacred and bold.
Transfigured now, a divine embodiment,
Walking the path of rituals, heaven-sent.

When the ritual is complete, offer your gratitude,
To the spirits, gods, and goddesses, who imbued,
Their essence upon you, transforming your soul,
Into a vessel of rituals, pure and whole.

Remember, dear seeker, this transformation profound,
To honor the rituals, in all that you do, let it resound.
Embody their essence, carry their flame,
And in the sacred rituals, forever remain.

Note: This ritual is a symbolic representation of the transformation into a divine embodiment of sacred rituals. Adapt the ritual to align with your personal beliefs and practices. Create a sacred space, set the atmosphere with candles and anointing oils, and call upon the presence of divine energies. Perform the rituals and ceremonies with reverence and intention, embracing the wisdom and power they hold. After completing the ritual, express gratitude to the spiritual forces involved and commit to honoring and embodying sacred rituals in your daily life.

162. Spell for the reunion of the deceased's soul with their spiritual allies and companions

In the realm between worlds, where spirits reside,
I call upon the forces, both near and wide.
Bring forth the allies and companions dear,
To reunite with the departed soul, now clear.

With utmost reverence and respect, I say,
Guide the departed soul on its destined way.
Bring forth the spirits, united in kin,
To aid the departed soul's journey to begin.

I summon the spirits, steadfast and true,
Those who walked with the departed, through and through.
Let their presence be felt, let their voices be heard,
As they gather around, like a comforting herd.

Spirits of love, compassion, and strength,
Join us now in this sacred length.
Bridge the gap between realms, interlace,
And lead the departed soul to its rightful place.

Spirits of wisdom, guidance, and light,
Illuminate the path through the darkest night.
Guide the departed soul with your celestial might,
As it reunites with allies in realms of infinite height.

Let the veil between worlds become thin,
As spirits gather, united, the reunion begins.
In the embrace of love and kinship, let it be,
The departed soul and its allies, eternally free.

By the power of the cosmos, I make this plea,
May the reunion of souls happen harmoniously.
With gratitude and reverence, I bid you all,
Thank you, spirits, for heeding the call.

Note: This spell is intended to facilitate the reunion of the deceased's soul with its spiritual allies and companions. Adapt the spell to align with your personal beliefs and practices. Create a sacred space, where you can focus and connect with the spiritual realm. Call upon the spirits, specifically those who were close to the departed, to join in the reunion. Ask for their guidance and support in leading the departed soul to its destined place among its allies. Express gratitude for their assistance and trust in the power of the spiritual realm to bring about a harmonious reunion.

163. Invocation of the goddess Sekhmet for courage and healing in the afterlife

Oh mighty Sekhmet, fierce and powerful,
Goddess of courage and healing, I call upon thee.
In the realms of the afterlife, where spirits reside,
I seek your presence, O Goddess, to be my guide.

With your fiery strength and protective might,
Wrap your wings around the departed's soul tonight.
Banish fear and uncertainty, instill courage and resolve,
As the journey through the afterlife begins to evolve.

Great Sekhmet, with your fierce lioness roar,
Unleash your healing power, I implore.
Cleanse the wounds of the departed soul's past,
With your sacred flames, let healing be cast.

In the realm beyond time, where spirits dwell,
Let Sekhmet's presence be felt, a story to tell.
Grant the departed soul strength to face each trial,
And with your divine touch, let healing defile.

Through the challenges and tests that lie ahead,
May Sekhmet's courage guide the soul that has fled.
Protect from harm, heal all wounds and pain,
So the departed's spirit can rise and regain.

Goddess Sekhmet, with your fiery embrace,
Grant the departed soul solace and grace.
Infuse their being with your divine light,
In the afterlife's journey, make their path bright.

Oh, fierce and compassionate Sekhmet, I pray,
Extend your protection in the afterlife's way.
Bring courage and healing, strength and might,
To the departed soul, as it takes flight.

As above, so below, may it be done,
In Sekhmet's name, this invocation is spun.

Guide the departed soul with your divine care,
In the afterlife's realm, let them thrive and fare.

Note: This invocation is a representation of calling upon the goddess Sekhmet for courage and healing in the afterlife. Adapt it to suit your beliefs and practices. Create a sacred space where you can focus and connect with the divine energy of Sekhmet. Call upon her presence, invoking her fiery strength, courage, and healing power. Request her guidance and protection for the departed soul as it embarks on its journey in the afterlife. Trust in Sekhmet's power and express gratitude for her presence and assistance.

164. Ritual of purification through the sacred gestures of the eternal dance

Step 1: Preparation
✧ Create a sacred space for the ritual, adorned with symbols of the divine and elements of nature. Light candles and incense to purify the atmosphere and set the mood. Wear loose, comfortable clothing suitable for dancing.

Step 2: Centering
✧ Stand at the center of the sacred space, close your eyes, and take deep breaths. Allow your body to relax and your mind to clear. Focus your energy on the intention of purification and connection with the divine.

Step 3: Invocation
✧ Open your eyes and raise your hands above your head in a gesture of invocation. Call upon the energies of the divine and the spirits of the elements to guide and bless your dance. Speak your intention aloud, expressing your desire for purification and spiritual renewal.

Step 4: Sacred Gestures
✧ Begin moving your body in a slow, flowing motion. Let the rhythm guide you as you perform sacred gestures, each one representing a purification of different aspects of your being. Move with grace and intention, allowing the dance to express your innermost desires for release and transformation.

✧ Gesture of Release: Extend your arms out to the sides and then bring them together, symbolizing the release of negative energies and attachments.
✧ Gesture of Cleansing: Bring your hands to your heart, then sweep them down and away from your body, symbolizing the cleansing of impurities and the removal of stagnant energy.
✧ Gesture of Renewal: Lift your arms overhead and slowly lower them, envisioning a shower of divine light washing over you, renewing your spirit and purifying your soul.
✧ Gesture of Transcendence: Extend one arm upwards while the other arm reaches towards the ground, symbolizing the connection between heaven and earth, transcending earthly limitations.

Step 5: Sacred Music

✧   Play music that resonates with your intention and enhances the energy of the ritual. Allow the rhythm and melody to guide your movements, surrendering to the flow of the music and the energy it evokes within you.

Step 6: Expression and Release

✧   As you dance, allow any emotions, thoughts, or burdens to surface and be released. Express them through your movements, letting them flow out of your body and dissipate into the space around you. Surrender to the transformative power of the dance and trust in the process of purification.

Step 7: Gratitude and Closure

✧   When you feel a sense of completion, gradually slow down your movements and come to a still position. Place your hands on your heart and express gratitude for the purification and spiritual renewal you have experienced. Offer thanks to the divine and the spirits of the elements for their presence and guidance.

Step 8: Grounding

✧   Stand with your feet firmly on the ground, feeling the stability and grounding energy beneath you. Take a few deep breaths, connecting with the earth's energy and anchoring yourself in the present moment.

Step 9: Integration

✧   Take a few moments to reflect on the ritual and its significance for your spiritual journey. Embrace the renewed sense of purity and connection with the divine that you have cultivated through the sacred dance.

Step 10: Closing

✧   Offer a closing prayer or affirmation, expressing your intention to carry the energy of purification and spiritual renewal with you in your daily life. Blow out the candles and extinguish the incense, symbolizing the end of the ritual.

Note: Adapt this ritual to suit your personal beliefs and practices. Feel free to incorporate additional gestures, chants, or sacred objects that resonate with your spiritual path. The key is to approach the ritual with reverence, intention, and an open heart.

165. Spell for the liberation of the deceased's soul from the illusions of the material world

Gather the following items:

A white candle
A piece of paper
A pen or marker
A small container
A handful of salt or sand

Step 1: Preparation
✧ Find a quiet and peaceful space where you can perform the spell without any interruptions. Light the white candle and place it in front of you.

Step 2: Clearing the Mind
✧ Close your eyes, take a few deep breaths, and clear your mind of any distractions. Focus your intention on the liberation of the deceased's soul from the illusions of the material world.

Step 3: Writing the Illusions
✧ Take the piece of paper and write down any illusions or attachments related to the material world that you wish to release on behalf of the deceased. These may include desires for wealth, possessions, status, or ego-driven ambitions. Write them down with clarity and honesty.

Step 4: Burning the Illusions
✧ Hold the paper over the flame of the candle, allowing it to catch fire. As the paper burns, visualize the illusions and attachments being consumed by the flames, releasing their hold on the deceased's soul. Repeat the following incantation:

"By the power of fire's light,
I release these illusions tonight.
May the soul be liberated, free,
From the binds of materiality."

Step 5: Collecting the Ashes

✧ Once the paper has burned completely, let the ashes fall into the small container. Sprinkle a pinch of salt or sand on top of the ashes, symbolizing purification and grounding.

Step 6: Setting the Soul Free

✧ Hold the container with the ashes and imagine the deceased's soul being freed from the illusions of the material world. Visualize the soul ascending to higher realms of spiritual awareness and enlightenment. Speak the following words:

"With this spell and sacred rite,
I set the soul free from worldly plight.
Released from illusions that hold it back,
It transcends the material, on a divine track."

Step 7: Release and Gratitude

✧ Open your hand and release the ashes into the wind, or bury them in the earth, as a symbolic act of releasing the illusions and allowing the soul to move forward. Express gratitude to the divine for guiding the liberation process.

Step 8: Closing

✧ Extinguish the candle, acknowledging the completion of the spell. Reflect on the significance of the liberation and affirm your commitment to spiritual growth and the pursuit of truth beyond the material realm.

Note: This spell is intended as a symbolic ritual and should be performed with respect and reverence.

166.   Incantation to awaken the dormant intuition within the deceased's spirit

Stand in a quiet and sacred space, centering yourself and connecting with the energy of the deceased. Take a deep breath and recite the following incantation:

"Spirit of the departed, hear my call,
Awaken from slumber, intuition enthrall.
From the depths of the soul, arise and ignite,
Unleash the wisdom, intuition's light.

Through the realms of the unseen and unknown,
Guide the spirit, let intuition be shown.
Unleash the knowing, buried deep inside,
Open the pathways, let intuition be my guide.

Break the barriers, dissolve the veil,
Awaken the senses, let intuition prevail.
Unfold the truths, hidden and untold,
Empower the spirit, intuition unfold.

With the divine guidance, let intuition bloom,
Navigate the realms beyond the earthly tomb.
Intuition's flame, burning bright and true,
I call upon you now, awakening anew.

By the power of ancient wisdom and grace,
I invoke the intuition, time and space.
Spirit of the departed, embrace this call,
Awaken the dormant intuition, one and all."

As you recite the incantation, envision a radiant light enveloping the deceased's spirit, awakening and stirring their intuition from its dormant state. Feel the energy of intuition flowing and expanding within the spirit.

After the incantation, take a moment of silence to allow the energy to settle and integrate. Express gratitude to the divine and the spirit of the departed for their presence and willingness to awaken intuition.

Note: This incantation is intended as a spiritual practice and should be performed with respect and reverence. Adjust the words and actions as needed to align with your personal beliefs and intentions.

167. Ritual for the communion with the spirits of the celestial music and melodies

Prepare a sacred space where you can be undisturbed. Light candles and incense to create an atmosphere of tranquility. Gather musical instruments or recordings of ethereal and uplifting music.

Grounding and Centering:
✧ Sit or stand comfortably in the center of the sacred space. Close your eyes and take a few deep breaths, allowing your body and mind to relax. Visualize roots extending from your feet, connecting you to the earth, grounding and centering your energy.

Invocation:
✧ Open the ritual by invoking the spirits of celestial music and melodies. You can use the following invocation or create your own:

"Spirits of celestial music, I call upon you,
Harbingers of harmony, melodies so true.
Guide me through realms of enchantment and light,
With your ethereal sounds, lift my spirit to new heights.

In this sacred space, I invite your presence near,
To commune with me, let our souls intertwine and adhere.
With every note and rhythm, may our connection be strong,
Divine music of the heavens, join us in this sacred song."

Musical Offering:
✧ Begin playing or listening to the chosen music, allowing the celestial melodies to resonate within your being. Let the music flow through you, igniting your senses and opening your heart to the realm of the spirits.

Communion and Meditation:
✧ As you immerse yourself in the music, envision a bridge forming between you and the spirits of celestial music. Feel their presence, their energy, and their guidance. Allow yourself to enter a meditative state, where you can experience a deep connection with the celestial realms.

Communication and Revelations:

✧ During this communion, be open to receiving messages, insights, and inspirations from the spirits of celestial music. Listen to the melodies and harmonies, as they may carry hidden meanings and guidance for your spiritual journey. Trust your intuition and let the music lead you to profound revelations.

Gratitude and Closure:

✧ When you feel the communion is complete, express your gratitude to the spirits of celestial music for their presence and guidance. Offer a sincere thank you for the wisdom and inspiration received. Close the ritual with a final affirmation or prayer, acknowledging the beauty and power of celestial music.

Remember to take some time to reflect and integrate the experience before returning to your everyday activities. The insights and connections made during this ritual can continue to resonate and guide you in your spiritual journey.

168.   Spell for the transmigration of the deceased's soul into the realm of eternal bliss

This spell is designed to guide the soul of the deceased into the realm of eternal bliss and peace. Perform this spell with a clear intention and a compassionate heart.

You will need:

A white candle
Frankincense or sandalwood incense
A small bowl of purified water
A clear quartz crystal
Preparation:
Create a sacred space where you can perform the spell without interruption. Light the white candle and the incense to cleanse and purify the energy in the space.

Invocation:
✧   Stand or sit in front of the candle and take a few deep breaths to center yourself. Hold the clear quartz crystal in your hands and say the following invocation:

"O divine spirits of light and love,
I call upon you from realms above.
Guide the soul of (name of the deceased) on their way,
To the realm of eternal bliss where they shall stay.

With this clear quartz crystal as a guide,
May their journey be peaceful, smooth, and wide.
I ask for your divine assistance and care,
To help (name of the deceased) find solace there."

Symbolic Gesture:
✧   Hold the clear quartz crystal in one hand and dip your other hand into the bowl of purified water. Visualize the water as a conduit for the soul's transition into the realm of eternal bliss. Gently sprinkle a few drops of water on the crystal, representing the cleansing and purification of the soul.

Affirmation:
- ✧ Hold the crystal up to the candle's flame, allowing the light to shine through it. As the light passes through the crystal, envision it illuminating the path to the realm of eternal bliss. Repeat the following affirmation:

"By the light of this flame and the power of this crystal,
I guide (name of the deceased) to a realm ethereal.
May their soul be bathed in joy and serenity,
In the realm of eternal bliss, their new reality."

Release and Gratitude:
- ✧ Place the crystal next to the candle and allow it to absorb the energy of the flame. Express your gratitude to the divine spirits for their guidance and assistance in the transmigration of the soul. Thank them for their love and support in this sacred journey.

Closure:
- ✧ When you feel complete, extinguish the candle and the incense, symbolizing the end of the ritual. Leave the crystal on an altar or sacred space as a reminder of the spell's intention and as a token of connection with the deceased.

Remember to send love and blessings to the departed soul, knowing that they are guided to the realm of eternal bliss. Trust that the divine spirits will continue to watch over and care for them on their spiritual journey.

169.   Invocation of the god Horus for protection and divine vision in the afterlife

This invocation is intended to call upon the deity Horus for protection and divine vision in the afterlife. Horus is associated with protection, royalty, and the sun. Perform this invocation with reverence and a sincere heart.

You will need:

A quiet and sacred space
A representation or image of Horus (such as a statue or picture)
Incense (sandalwood or frankincense)
A white candle
Preparation:
Create a sacred space where you can perform the invocation without interruption.
Light the white candle and the incense to cleanse and purify the energy in the space.

Centering:
✧   Take a few deep breaths to center yourself and focus your attention on the representation or image of Horus. Clear your mind of any distractions and allow yourself to enter a state of calm and receptivity.

Opening Prayer:
✧   Begin by reciting an opening prayer to set the intention and invite the presence of Horus.:

"Great Horus, falcon-headed god,
Protector and guide in the realms of the divine,
I call upon you with reverence and respect,
To grant me your protection and divine vision.

In the afterlife's embrace, I seek your presence,
To navigate the celestial realms with grace.
With unwavering strength and wisdom, I aspire,
To walk the path of illumination and aspire.

Horus, mighty guardian of the skies,
I humbly invoke your sacred essence,
Grant me protection and insight profound,

As I journey in the realms beyond earthly bound."

Invocation:
- ✧ Gaze at the representation or image of Horus, connecting with his energy and symbolism. Visualize his majestic form and powerful presence. Feel his protective wings encompassing you, surrounding you with divine light and shielding you from any negative influences.
- ✧ Speak from your heart and call upon Horus by saying:

"O Horus, the divine protector,
Mighty falcon of the sky,
I call upon you in this sacred space,
To grant me your watchful eye.

Wrap me in your wings of light,
Shield me from all harm and strife.
Grant me divine vision and clarity,
To navigate the afterlife's vast sea.

Guide me through the realms unseen,
With your strength and wisdom keen.
As I seek knowledge and enlightenment,
Keep me safe, secure, and content."

Gratitude and Closing:
- ✧ Express your gratitude to Horus for his presence and protection. Offer thanks for his guidance and support on your spiritual journey. Convey your respect and appreciation, knowing that his energy will be with you in the afterlife.
- ✧ Take a moment to bask in the energy of Horus and feel his divine presence surrounding you. When you feel complete, offer a final prayer of gratitude, extinguish the candle, and let the incense burn out. Reflect on the connection you have made with Horus and carry his protective energy with you as you continue your spiritual path.

170. Ritual of anointing with sacred symbols for spiritual empowerment

This ritual is designed to empower and activate your spiritual energy through the anointing of sacred symbols. Symbols have long been used as powerful tools for manifestation, protection, and spiritual connection. The anointing process enhances the symbolism and infuses it with your intention, creating a potent tool for spiritual empowerment.

You will need:

Sacred symbols (such as a pentagram, ankh, Om symbol, or any symbol that resonates with your spirituality)
Essential oils or sacred oils of your choice
A small dish or container to hold the oil
A quiet and sacred space

Preparation:
✧   Select the sacred symbols that hold significance to you and resonate with your spiritual path. Cleanse the symbols by gently wiping them with a soft cloth or consecrate them using your preferred method of purification, such as passing them through incense smoke or holding them under running water.

Setting Intentions:
✧   Sit in your sacred space and take a few moments to ground yourself. Close your eyes, take deep breaths, and allow yourself to enter a state of calm and focused awareness. Reflect on your spiritual journey and the specific areas in which you seek empowerment and growth. Clarify your intentions and visualize yourself embodying the qualities and energies represented by the sacred symbols.

Anointing:
✧   Pour a small amount of the chosen essential or sacred oil into the dish or container. With reverence and mindfulness, dip your finger into the oil and lightly touch the sacred symbols. As you anoint each symbol, focus your intention on infusing them with the energy and power to manifest your desired spiritual empowerment.

✧   While anointing each symbol, you can recite the following:

"With this sacred oil, I anoint this symbol,
Infusing it with divine energy and power.
May it be a conduit for spiritual empowerment,
Guiding me on my path every hour.

By the touch of my finger, I activate its might,
Enhancing its symbolism, radiant and bright.
As I embrace its energy, I am filled with grace,
Empowered to manifest my spiritual embrace."

Connection and Activation:
✧ Hold each anointed symbol in your hands, one at a time, and connect with its energy. Visualize the symbol radiating with light and its associated qualities becoming infused within you. Feel the energy of empowerment flowing through your entire being, strengthening your connection to your spirituality and purpose.
✧ Take a moment to reflect on the significance of each symbol and its role in your spiritual journey. Express gratitude for the empowerment and support they bring to your life.

Sacred Space Closing:
✧ Once you have anointed and connected with all the symbols, place them in a sacred space that holds spiritual significance to you. This can be an altar, a special shelf, or any place where you can regularly see and interact with them. As you do, remember the intentions you set and the empowerment you seek.
✧ Close the ritual by offering a prayer, affirmation, or moment of silence to honor the connection you have made and to express your gratitude to the divine energies and forces that support and guide you on your spiritual path.

Remember to regularly connect with the anointed symbols, meditate upon them, or incorporate them into your spiritual practices to enhance your spiritual empowerment and growth.

171. Spell for the transformation of the deceased into a vessel of divine grace and beauty

This spell is intended to facilitate the transformation of the deceased into a vessel of divine grace and beauty, allowing their spirit to radiate with the qualities of elegance, harmony, and inner beauty in the afterlife. By invoking the divine energies and setting the intention for transformation, this spell aims to elevate the spirit and enhance its connection with the divine essence.

You will need:

A quiet and sacred space
A white candle
A small mirror
Fresh flowers or petals
A photo or representation of the deceased (optional)
Your focused intention and belief in the power of transformation

Preparation:
✦ Set up your sacred space in a quiet area where you can perform the spell without interruptions. Place the white candle in a candle holder and light it, creating a calm and serene atmosphere. Arrange the fresh flowers or petals around the candle, creating a beautiful and sacred space.

Invocation:
✦ Close your eyes, take several deep breaths, and enter a state of centeredness and inner focus. Visualize the divine presence surrounding you, filling the space with loving and compassionate energy. Begin by invoking the divine forces of grace and beauty that resonate with your spiritual beliefs. You may call upon deities or energies such as Aphrodite, Venus, or any other divine presence associated with beauty and grace. Speak or chant an invocation to invite their presence and assistance. :

"Divine forces of grace and beauty,
I call upon you in this sacred space.
Unfold your divine essence and power,
Transform the deceased with your gentle embrace.

With love and compassion, I ask for your aid,
In this spell of transformation I have made.
Infuse the spirit with elegance and inner light,
Radiating grace and beauty, shining ever bright."

Mirror Reflection:
- ✧ Hold the mirror in your hands and gaze into it. Visualize the deceased's spirit reflected in the mirror, bathed in divine light and radiating grace and beauty. See their essence transforming and becoming an embodiment of divine elegance. Feel a deep sense of love and compassion for the deceased, and affirm their innate beauty and grace.

Offering:
- ✧ If you have a photo or representation of the deceased, place it in front of the mirror, facing it. Offer a few heartfelt words or thoughts expressing your love, gratitude, and intention for their transformation into a vessel of divine grace and beauty.

Candle Dedication:
- ✧ Hold your hands over the candle flame, feeling its warmth and energy. Speak or mentally affirm your intention for the deceased's transformation, infusing it with your love and belief in their divine essence. :

"By this candle's sacred flame, I dedicate
The transformation of the deceased's fate.
May divine grace and beauty forever shine,
Elevating their spirit, a presence so fine."

Closing:
- ✧ Express gratitude to the divine forces you invoked, thanking them for their presence, assistance, and the transformation you seek. Allow the candle to burn for a while as a symbol of the ongoing transformation and connection with the divine. If necessary, extinguish the candle in a safe manner.
- ✧ Remember to honor the memory of the deceased and their innate beauty throughout your spiritual practices and daily life. Offer prayers, meditations, or moments of remembrance to honor their transformation into a vessel of divine grace and beauty.

172.   Incantation to invoke the blessings of the celestial rainbows and auroras

This incantation is designed to connect with the celestial energies of rainbows and auroras, drawing their blessings and illuminating your spirit with their vibrant and ethereal qualities. By reciting this incantation with focused intention and an open heart, you can invoke the beauty, harmony, and magical essence of these celestial phenomena.

Stand or sit in a comfortable position, preferably outdoors where you can observe the sky. Take a few moments to center yourself and connect with the natural world around you. Feel the energy of the earth beneath your feet and the expansive sky above you. Take a deep breath and allow yourself to enter a state of calm and receptivity.

Raise your arms to the sky, palms facing upward, as if you are embracing the celestial energies. Close your eyes and visualize a magnificent rainbow arching across the sky or vibrant auroras dancing across the night sky. See their radiant colors and ethereal glow, filling the atmosphere with enchantment and wonder.

Recite the following incantation with conviction and belief:

"From celestial realms, where wonders unfold,
I call upon the rainbows and auroras bold.
With vibrant hues and shimmering light,
Bless me with their beauty, shining so bright.

Rainbow's arc, in colors divine,
Bring harmony and joy, make my spirit shine.
Auroras dancing, with mystical grace,
Illuminate my path, reveal the sacred space.

Blessings of rainbows and auroras rare,
Fill me with wonder, in awe I share.
With open heart, I embrace their might,
Infuse my being with celestial light.

By the power of celestial wonders above,
I invoke the blessings, in truth and love.
Rainbows and auroras, your magic I seek,

Grant me your gifts, divine and unique."

Visualize the rainbows and auroras growing brighter and more vibrant in response to your invocation. Feel their energy flowing into your being, filling you with their blessings and illuminating your spirit with their enchanting qualities.

Take a few moments to bask in the energy and embrace the essence of the rainbows and auroras. Express your gratitude for their presence and the blessings they bestow upon you. Lower your arms and offer a moment of silence or meditation to integrate the energies.

Whenever you seek the guidance, beauty, and enchantment of the rainbows and auroras, you can recite this incantation and connect with their celestial energies. Embrace their gifts and allow them to inspire and uplift your spirit in your journey of life.

173.   Ritual for the transfiguration of the deceased into a divine weaver of cosmic tapestries

This ritual is intended to honor and guide the deceased on their journey towards becoming a divine weaver of cosmic tapestries, symbolizing the weaving and creation of the interconnectedness of the universe. By performing this ritual, we seek to invoke the energies of creation, harmony, and unity to assist the deceased in their spiritual transformation.

Materials needed:

A sacred space or altar
A representation of a loom (can be a small decorative loom or a symbolic representation)
Different colored threads or yarns representing the cosmic energies and interconnectedness
Incense or candles for purification and ambiance
Any personal items or symbols associated with the deceased

Instructions:

✧   Set up your sacred space or altar in a quiet and serene area. Place the representation of the loom at the center, surrounded by the threads or yarns of different colors. Light the incense or candles to purify the space and create a sacred ambiance.

✧   Take a moment to ground yourself and connect with the energy of the ritual. Take a few deep breaths and center your focus.

✧   Begin by holding the representation of the loom in your hands. Close your eyes and envision the deceased standing beside you, ready for their transfiguration. Feel their presence and the love that connects you.

✧   Speak the following words or create your own heartfelt invocation:

"O divine weavers of the cosmic tapestries,
I call upon your sacred presence and guidance.
With reverence, I gather here today

To honor and support [Name of the deceased] on their journey.

May the threads of their existence intertwine
With the cosmic energies, vast and divine.
Through the loom of creation, we seek to weave
A tapestry of unity, love, and harmony.

[Name of the deceased], in your spirit's flight,
Embrace the role of the cosmic weaver, shining bright.
With each thread you lay upon this cosmic loom,
Unfold the mysteries, weave a celestial bloom.

Guide them, O divine weavers, with your gentle touch,
Illuminate their path, bless them so much.
Grant them wisdom, creativity, and grace,
As they weave the tapestry of the cosmic embrace.

May their threads connect all beings, near and far,
Creating a tapestry woven with love, without a scar.
In unity, harmony, and cosmic light,
[Name of the deceased] transcends the earthly night.

By the power of the cosmic tapestry, divine and true,
I honor [Name of the deceased], as they journey anew.
Bless them with the transformation they seek,
As they weave the cosmic tapestry, unique."

As you recite the invocation, imagine the threads or yarns intertwining and weaving together, symbolizing the interconnectedness of all things. Visualize the deceased embracing their role as a divine weaver, skillfully crafting the cosmic tapestry with love, wisdom, and creativity.

After the invocation, invite any participants to share their blessings, memories, or messages for the deceased. Encourage them to express their love, support, and well-wishes for the deceased's spiritual journey.

When ready, allow a moment of silence for reflection and integration of the energies invoked. Feel the presence of the divine weavers and the energy of the cosmic tapestry surrounding you.

Conclude the ritual by expressing gratitude to the divine weavers and to the deceased for their presence. You may choose to leave the representation of the loom and the threads as a symbol of ongoing connection and support.

Remember to honor the deceased's journey and the sacredness of their transformation as they embrace the role of a divine weaver of cosmic tapestries. This ritual can be performed with love and intention to assist them in their spiritual evolution.

174.   Spell for the reunion of the deceased's soul with their divine purpose and destiny

This spell is intended to assist the deceased in reuniting with their divine purpose and destiny, helping them align with their higher calling and find fulfillment in the afterlife. By performing this spell, we seek to invoke the guidance and support of divine forces to assist the departed soul in rediscovering their true path.

Materials needed:

A quiet and sacred space
A representation or image of the deceased
A white candle
Incense (such as sandalwood or frankincense)
A small piece of paper and a pen

Instructions:

✧   Prepare your sacred space by lighting the incense and placing it in a holder. Clear your mind and create a peaceful atmosphere.

✧   Take the representation or image of the deceased and place it in the center of the space. Light the white candle next to it as a symbol of divine presence and illumination.

✧   Sit comfortably in front of the representation and close your eyes. Take a few deep breaths to center yourself and connect with the energy of the ritual.

✧   Visualize the deceased standing before you, surrounded by a warm and loving light. Feel their presence and imagine them open and receptive to divine guidance.

✧   Take the small piece of paper and the pen. Write down the following affirmation:

"With love and reverence, I call upon the divine,
To guide [Name of the deceased] on their sacred path.
In this realm beyond, may they be aligned,

With their purpose and destiny, a reunion of divine math.

Let the light of truth and clarity shine bright,
Reveal their path, their calling, with heavenly might.
Ignite their passion, their gifts, their unique flame,
As they fulfill their purpose, let destiny reclaim.

O divine forces, hear my plea,
Guide [Name of the deceased] towards their destiny.
Unite them with their purpose and divine design,
In the afterlife, may their true path shine.

As this candle burns and the incense wafts high,
Let [Name of the deceased] reunite with purpose, soaring in the sky.
Aligned with their calling, fulfilling their soul's quest,
In harmony with divine will, they are eternally blessed."

✧　Hold the piece of paper with the affirmation close to your heart. Visualize the words on the paper infused with divine light, carrying your intention for the deceased's reunion with their divine purpose.

✧　Open your eyes and gently fold the piece of paper. Place it near the representation or image of the deceased, allowing their energy to be infused with the intention and affirmation.

✧　Take a moment to express gratitude to the divine forces and to the deceased for their presence and guidance. Offer any additional prayers or blessings from your heart.

✧　Allow the candle to burn completely or extinguish it safely if you need to leave the space. Leave the piece of paper near the representation as a reminder of the intention set.

✧　In the days following the spell, you can continue to hold the intention for the deceased's reunion with their divine purpose. Offer them love, support, and encouragement as they navigate their spiritual journey.

Remember, this spell is performed with love and reverence for the deceased. It is a way to honor their soul's journey and assist them in finding fulfillment in alignment with their divine purpose and destiny.

175.   Invocation of the goddess Nephthys for comfort and solace in the afterlife

Goddess Nephthys, compassionate and comforting,
I invoke your presence in this sacred space.
Guide and protect the departed soul,
Offering solace and soothing grace.

With wings outstretched and heart aflame,
You embrace those who mourn and grieve.
Bring your gentle touch and healing light,
To those who in the afterlife find reprieve.

Nephthys, sister of Isis, beloved companion,
You understand the depths of sorrow and loss.
Wrap your wings around the departed one,
Let them feel your embrace, calming as moss.

In the realm beyond, where shadows dwell,
May your presence be a source of peace.
Guide the departed through the veil of transition,
Grant them solace as their earthly bonds cease.

With your wisdom and understanding,
Illuminate their path with gentle rays.
May they find comfort in your embrace,
And in your presence, find solace that stays.

Goddess Nephthys, in your caring arms,
Hold the departed close, ease their pain.
Surround them with love and understanding,
As they traverse the afterlife's terrain.

I offer my gratitude and reverence to you,
Goddess Nephthys, kind and compassionate.
Thank you for your comforting presence,
In the afterlife, your solace is anticipated.

As I conclude this invocation and prayer,
May your blessings continue to flow.

Bring comfort and solace to the departed,
In the afterlife, where their spirits grow.

So mote it be.

176.   Ritual of purification through the sacred rituals of the eternal cycle

In this sacred space, where time is but a thread,
I embark on a journey of purification ahead.
With reverence and intention, I begin this rite,
To cleanse my spirit, to banish all blight.

I call upon the elements, earth, air, fire, and water,
To guide me through this ritual, as their sacred daughter.
May the earth ground me, steady and firm,
As I release what no longer serves, let it affirm.

I invoke the cleansing power of the gentle breeze,
To sweep away negativity, to bring me ease.
Let the air purify my thoughts, my mind,
As I release all worries that I may find.

With the flicker of flames, I call upon fire's might,
To burn away impurities, to bring forth light.
May the fire cleanse my spirit, ignite my soul,
As I let go of all that hinders, I become whole.

I immerse myself in the soothing embrace of water,
Its purifying essence washes away any falter.
Let the water cleanse my emotions, my heart,
As I release all burdens, I make a fresh start.

In this sacred space, I honor the eternal cycle,
The rhythm of life, the journey so vital.
As I move through this ritual, I am reborn,
Pure and cleansed, my spirit adorned.

I offer my gratitude to the elements so grand,
For their presence and guidance, like an outstretched hand.
May their cleansing energy surround me now,
As I embrace the purity that they endow.

With each breath, I release what no longer serves,
Inviting in the light, allowing my spirit to observe.

In this sacred ritual, I find renewal and grace,
Purified and cleansed, I embrace my sacred place.

So mote it be.

177. Spell for the liberation of the deceased's soul from the chains of earthly desires

By the power of divine light and eternal grace,
I call upon the spirits of wisdom to embrace.
Release the chains that bind the departed's soul,
And free them from earthly desires taking their toll.

With words of power and intentions pure,
I sever the ties that the soul must endure.
Let the temptations of the world fade away,
As the spirit transcends, on a higher path to stray.

I invoke the sacred flame to burn away attachment,
To release the desires that cause soul's detachment.
May the fire's transformative energy ignite,
And guide the soul towards a celestial flight.

With each spoken word and every heartfelt plea,
I ask the universe to set the departed soul free.
May their spirit soar on wings of liberation,
Transcending the earthly realm, finding salvation.

Let the bonds of desire be broken and released,
As the soul journeys towards eternal peace.
May they find solace in the realm beyond,
Where earthly desires no longer correspond.

In this sacred moment, I declare their freedom,
Untethered from desires, they find wisdom.
May their soul be liberated from all earthly chains,
To ascend to higher realms where true freedom reigns.

By the power of the divine and the cosmic decree,
I release the departed's soul, forever set free.
As it is spoken, so mote it be.

Note: This spell is intended for spiritual and metaphorical purposes. It is important to remember that the journey of the soul after death is complex and unique to each individual's beliefs and experiences.

178.   Incantation to awaken the dormant resilience within the deceased's spirit

In the realm of spirits, ancient and grand,
I call upon the resilience buried deep within the sand.
Awaken, dormant spirit, rise and be seen,
Let your strength and courage shine, evergreen.

From the ashes of trials and tribulations past,
I summon your resilience, mighty and steadfast.
Unveil the dormant power within your soul,
Embrace the challenges, make them your goal.

Through the depths of darkness and despair,
May your spirit rise, unyielding and rare.
Awaken the fire within, burning bright,
Ignite the embers of resilience, day and night.

From the deepest recesses of your being,
Let resilience flow, forever foreseeing.
Through the storms of life, unbreakable you'll be,
Guided by your strength, eternally free.

Rise, spirit of resilience, with unwavering might,
Embrace life's struggles, transform the fight.
As the phoenix emerges from ashes renewed,
Let your resilience awaken, fully imbued.

By the powers of the universe, I declare,
The dormant resilience within you, now aware.
Arise, spirit, and face every trial,
With resilience awakened, you'll conquer any mile.

In this sacred invocation, I set you free,
To embody resilience in eternity.
As it is spoken, so mote it be,
Awakened resilience, now set forth and see.

Note: This incantation is intended to symbolically awaken the dormant resilience
within the deceased's spirit. Resilience is a personal quality that varies from individual

to individual. The intention behind this incantation is to invoke and enhance the spirit's inner strength and ability to overcome challenges.

179.   Ritual for the communion with the spirits of the celestial realms of dreams

Prepare yourself for the sacred journey ahead,
To commune with spirits in the realm of dreams, widespread.
In a tranquil space, create your sacred abode,
Where the celestial realms and earthly realms coincide.

Light a candle to illuminate the path,
Symbolizing the spark of consciousness, a righteous bath.
Find solace in the darkness, as the flame dances bright,
Merging with the stars, guiding your spirit's flight.

Sit in stillness, in a posture of peace,
Close your eyes, let distractions cease.
Breathe in deeply, inhale the cosmic air,
Exhale the worries, let go of every care.

Invoke the spirits of the celestial realms of dreams,
With words of reverence, let your intentions gleam.
"O spirits of dreams, guardians of the night,
I humbly seek your presence, bathed in celestial light.

Grant me passage to your ethereal domain,
Where dreams and realities intertwine, without restrain.
Open the doors to the secrets you hold,
Reveal the wisdom and visions untold.

Guide me through the realms with gentle grace,
Unveil the mysteries that time can't erase.
In this sacred communion, our spirits align,
Together we journey through the dream realms divine."

With each breath, feel the connection grow,
As the boundaries blur, let your spirit's essence flow.
Enter the realm of dreams, where the spirits reside,
With reverence and openness, let your soul confide.

Listen to the whispers of the dream spirits' call,
Witness their stories, as they rise and fall.

Embrace the symbols, the messages they impart,
Guiding you towards the awakening of your heart.

When the time is right, bid farewell to the dream realm,
Express gratitude for the guidance at the helm.
Slowly return to the present, back to earthly ground,
Carrying the essence of the celestial dreams profound.

Reflect upon the visions, the insights gained,
Let them nourish your spirit, like droplets of rain.
For in the communion with the celestial realms of dreams,
Our souls find solace, in the realm where magic gleams.

As you conclude this sacred ritual of communion,
Thank the spirits for their guidance and union.
Blow out the candle, marking the end of the rite,
Carry the wisdom of the dream realm's light.

Note: This ritual is designed to create a sacred space for communing with the spirits of the celestial realms of dreams. It is important to approach this ritual with respect and reverence. Remember that dreams can be highly personal and symbolic, so interpretations may vary. Always honor your intuition and personal experiences when engaging in dream work.

180.   Spell for the transmigration of the deceased's soul into the realm of eternal wisdom

In the sacred stillness, where realms converge,
Where the veil is thin and spirits surge,
I call upon the cosmic forces grand,
To guide the departed to wisdom's land.

By the power of the divine decree,
I invoke the path of transcendence, set them free.
From earthly ties and mortal strife,
Transmigrate their soul to the realm of eternal life.

Oh, ancient ones, guardians of the veil,
With reverence, I implore, let the soul prevail.
Grant passage through the sacred gates,
To the realm where wisdom illuminates.

By the whispers of ancient scrolls and sacred lore,
Let the deceased's spirit now soar.
Unleash the wisdom of ages untold,
Unlock the secrets that time did enfold.

Guide their journey to the realms unseen,
To the heart of knowledge, where insights convene.
Let them bathe in the fountains of eternal truth,
Absorb the wisdom that transcends mortal youth.

As they traverse the celestial sphere,
May wisdom's light dispel all fear.
Grant them clarity of thought and sight,
In the realm where knowledge takes flight.

May their soul merge with the cosmic flow,
Absorbing wisdom, like a river's gentle glow.
Embrace the teachings of the enlightened few,
Infuse their spirit with eternal wisdom true.

By the power of this sacred spell,
I call upon the cosmic forces to dispel,
The limitations of mortal mind,
And elevate the deceased to wisdom divine.

So mote it be, in alignment with the cosmic plan,
As I will it, so shall it expand.
May the transmigration of their soul be done,
Into the realm of eternal wisdom, they shall become one.

Note: This spell is intended to aid in the transmigration of the deceased's soul into the realm of eternal wisdom. It is essential to approach this spell with respect and pure intentions. Remember that the soul's journey after death is deeply personal, and each individual may experience it uniquely. Trust your intuition and honor the wisdom that arises within you.

181.   Invocation of the god Geb for grounding and stability in the afterlife

Oh, mighty Geb, embodiment of the Earth,
With reverence and gratitude, I call upon your divine worth.
In the realm beyond, where souls take flight,
I seek your presence, your grounding might.

Geb, the stable foundation beneath our feet,
In this sacred invocation, I entreat,
Guide and guard the departed's soul,
In the afterlife's vast and mysterious fold.

As the deceased embarks on their ethereal quest,
Grant them stability, as their spirit does rest.
Wrap them in the embrace of your nurturing soil,
Provide a firm anchor amidst the turmoil.

Oh, Geb, keeper of ancient wisdom and lore,
Bestow upon them strength to endure and explore.
In the shifting realms of the afterlife's domain,
Let stability and balance be their eternal terrain.

By the power of your unwavering might,
Grant them grounding through day and night.
Steady their soul in the celestial expanse,
As they journey through the eternal dance.

Guide their steps with unwavering stability,
Root their spirit in the essence of tranquility.
Amidst the cosmic wonders and ethereal plains,
Let them find solace in your steady reigns.

Geb, provider of grounding and stability true,
I invoke your presence, I call upon you.
Protect and support the departed's soul,
In the afterlife's journey, make them whole.

So mote it be, in alignment with the divine flow,

As I speak, may your energy bestow.
Grounding and stability upon their path,
In the afterlife's realm, amidst its aftermath.

Note: This invocation is intended to call upon the god Geb for grounding and stability in the afterlife. It is important to approach this invocation with respect and reverence. Remember that the journey of the deceased's soul is unique, and their experience may vary. Trust your intuition and honor the wisdom that comes forth.

182.   Ritual of anointing with sacred colors for spiritual transformation

Prepare a sacred space, a sanctuary divine,
Where colors of the spectrum beautifully shine.
Gather the hues that hold symbolic power,
To anoint the spirit in this transformative hour.

Begin with red, the color of passion and fire,
Anoint the body with its vibrant desire.
Feel the energy ignite, the will awakened,
As the flame of transformation is stoked and taken.

Next, orange, the hue of creativity and joy,
Anoint the spirit, let inspiration deploy.
Let the creative essence within arise,
Igniting the flame of limitless enterprise.

Yellow, the color of intellect and clarity,
Anoint the mind, embrace mental prosperity.
Open the channels of wisdom and insight,
As the yellow light brings clarity's delight.

Green, the color of balance and renewal,
Anoint the heart, let love and compassion fuel.
Let healing energies flow through every vein,
As the green hue washes away all pain.

Blue, the color of communication and truth,
Anoint the throat, let expression be uncouth.
Open the gates of authentic words and voice,
As the blue hue grants you the power of choice.

Indigo, the color of intuition and perception,
Anoint the third eye, invite divine connection.
Unlock the gateway to spiritual insight,
As indigo hues awaken inner sight.

Finally, purple, the color of spirituality and grace,

Anoint the crown, let divine presence embrace.
Connect with the realms beyond earthly ties,
As the purple hue reveals spiritual skies.

With each sacred color, let transformation take hold,
As you anoint body, mind, and soul untold.
Embrace the power of colors divine,
For spiritual transformation, a sacred design.

Note: This ritual of anointing with sacred colors is a symbolic and personal practice for spiritual transformation. The colors and their associations may vary depending on individual belief systems and traditions. Use your intuition and choose colors that resonate with you and hold personal significance. Create a peaceful and sacred space before performing this ritual, and approach it with reverence and intention.

183.   Spell for the transformation of the deceased into a vessel of divine protection and guidance

By the powers that be, both seen and unseen,
I call upon the divine to intervene.
In this sacred space, with love and respect,
I invoke the forces of protection and intellect.

From the realms beyond, where spirits reside,
I call upon their wisdom, so vast and wide.
Grant this departed soul transformation and grace,
A vessel of divine protection in this sacred place.

May the light of the divine surround and shield,
Guiding the departed on their spiritual field.
Banish all darkness, dispel all fear,
Let divine protection draw near.

I call upon the guardians, ancient and wise,
To watch over and guide this soul that flies.
Grant strength and courage in their eternal flight,
As they navigate realms of infinite light.

Empower this vessel with celestial might,
A beacon of guidance in the darkest night.
Let divine wisdom flow through their being,
As they embark on a journey worth seeing.

In this spell, I set the intention clear,
That divine protection and guidance appear.
For the deceased, a transformation divine,
A vessel of light, forever to shine.

So mote it be, with reverence and love,
May the deceased ascend to the realms above.
Transformed into a vessel, guided by the divine,
Protected and guided for all of time.

Note: This spell is intended to be performed with respect and reverence. It is important to create a sacred space, set clear intentions, and call upon divine energies in a manner that aligns with your personal beliefs and spiritual practices. Modify and adapt the spell as necessary to suit your specific needs and circumstances.

184.   Incantation to invoke the blessings of the celestial cycles of time

O celestial cycles, guardians of eternity,
I call upon your wisdom and divinity.
From the dawning of creation to the present day,
Unveil your blessings, illuminate the way.

By the rising sun and the setting moon,
By the turning of seasons, in harmony we swoon.
Through the ebb and flow of cosmic tides,
May your blessings descend upon our lives.

From the celestial bodies that light the sky,
To the rhythmic dance of planets passing by,
I invoke your power, your timeless grace,
Unfold the mysteries, reveal the sacred space.

As the sun ascends to its zenith high,
And shadows yield to the bright blue sky,
Bless us with strength, vitality, and might,
Empower our journey, embrace the light.

As the moon waxes and wanes in its cycle,
And stars twinkle with radiance, ever so subtle,
Bless us with intuition, insight, and dreams,
Illuminate our path with celestial beams.

By the turning of the wheel, the seasons' embrace,
Bless us with growth, change, and abundant grace.
In the cycle of birth, death, and rebirth anew,
May we find renewal, wisdom, and breakthrough.

In the celestial cycles, time's endless flow,
We honor the past, embrace the present's glow.
With gratitude, we tread upon this earthly plane,
In harmony with the cosmos, our spirits remain.

O celestial cycles, we offer our praise,
For the blessings bestowed upon our days.

Guide us with your wisdom, unfold the sublime,
As we journey through the dance of cosmic time.

By the powers of the celestial realms above,
I invoke your blessings, divine and eternal love.
May the cycles of time enrich our souls,
And align us with the universe's sacred goals.

So mote it be, in reverence we declare,
The blessings of celestial cycles we share.
May the divine energies forever intertwine,
As we honor the celestial cycles divine.

Note: This incantation is intended to honor and invoke the blessings of the celestial cycles of time. It is important to approach the incantation with respect and reverence, creating a sacred space and aligning with your personal beliefs and practices.

185.   Ritual for the transfiguration of the deceased into a divine guardian of sacred sites

Note: This ritual is intended to honor and empower the deceased as a guardian of sacred sites. It is important to approach the ritual with reverence and respect, creating a sacred space and aligning with your personal beliefs and practices. .

Materials needed:

✧ An altar or sacred space
✧ Candles (preferably white or colors associated with guardianship and protection)
✧ Incense (such as frankincense, myrrh, or sage)
✧ Crystals or gemstones (such as amethyst, clear quartz, or black tourmaline)
✧ Symbolic objects representing sacred sites (such as miniature replicas, photographs, or drawings)
✧ An offering (such as water, flowers, or food)

Preparation:

✧ Find a quiet and undisturbed space where you can set up your altar or sacred space.
✧ Cleanse the space by smudging with the incense or using any other preferred method of purification.
✧ Place the candles, incense, crystals or gemstones, and symbolic objects on the altar.
✧ Light the candles and the incense, creating an atmosphere of sacredness and reverence.

Grounding and Centering:

✧ Take a few moments to ground yourself by taking deep breaths and connecting with the energy of the Earth.
✧ Close your eyes and visualize roots growing from the soles of your feet, anchoring you to the Earth's core.
✧ Feel the stability and strength of the Earth's energy rising through your body, grounding you firmly in the present moment.

Invocation and Intent:

✧ Stand before the altar and speak the following invocation or create your own heartfelt words:
"In this sacred space, I invoke the presence of the divine.
I call upon the spirits of the deceased, guardians of sacred sites.
With reverence and honor, I seek your guidance and blessings.
May this ritual transfigure the departed into a guardian of sacred sites,
Protecting and preserving their wisdom for generations to come."

✧ Set your intention clearly in your mind, focusing on the transfiguration of the deceased into a divine guardian of sacred sites. Visualize the transformation taking place, envisioning the deceased embracing their role with grace and strength.

Symbolic Connection:

✧ Hold the symbolic objects representing sacred sites in your hands, one by one.
✧ As you hold each object, visualize the energy and essence of the sacred site merging with the deceased, empowering them with the wisdom and protection associated with that place.
✧ Speak the name of the sacred site and any prayers or blessings that resonate with its energy.

Offering and Gratitude:

✧ Place the offering of your choice on the altar, expressing gratitude to the deceased for
✧ their willingness to serve as a guardian of sacred sites.
✧ Offer words of thanks and appreciation for their dedication to preserving the sacredness of these places.

Closing:

✧ Take a moment to offer any final prayers or blessings, expressing your trust in the transfiguration process and the guidance of the deceased as guardians of sacred sites.
✧ Extinguish the candles and allow the incense to burn out naturally, releasing the energy into the space.
Note: Remember to honor the deceased's memory and the sacredness of the sites they will be guarding. You can revisit this ritual periodically to reaffirm the connection and continue strengthening the bond between the deceased and their role as a guardian.

186.   Spell for the reunion of the deceased's soul with their celestial origins

Materials needed:

✧ An altar or sacred space
✧ Candles (preferably white or colors associated with celestial energies)
✧ Incense (such as sandalwood, lavender, or frankincense)
✧ Crystals or gemstones (such as selenite, amethyst, or clear quartz)
✧ Symbolic objects representing the celestial realms (such as star symbols, representations of the sun, moon, or planets)
✧ An offering (such as water, flowers, or a personal item that represents the deceased)

Preparation:

✧ Find a quiet and undisturbed space where you can set up your altar or sacred space.
✧ Cleanse the space by smudging with the incense or using any other preferred method of purification.
✧ Place the candles, incense, crystals or gemstones, and symbolic objects on the altar.
✧ Light the candles and the incense, creating an atmosphere of sacredness and reverence.

Grounding and Centering:

✧ Take a few moments to ground yourself by taking deep breaths and connecting with the energy of the Earth.
✧ Close your eyes and visualize roots growing from the soles of your feet, anchoring you to the Earth's core.
✧ Feel the stability and strength of the Earth's energy rising through your body, grounding you firmly in the present moment.

Invocation and Intent:

✧ Stand before the altar and speak the following invocation or create your own heartfelt words:

"In this sacred space, I call upon the celestial realms.
I summon the energy and essence of the deceased's celestial origins.
May their soul be reunited with their celestial heritage.
May their journey be guided by the stars and the celestial energies that shape the universe.
Grant them reunion with their celestial origins, so they may find their place among the heavens."

✧ Set your intention clearly in your mind, focusing on the reunion of the deceased's soul with their celestial origins. Visualize their soul ascending, guided by celestial energies and reuniting with their cosmic heritage.

Symbolic Connection:

✧ Hold the symbolic objects representing the celestial realms in your hands, one by one.
✧ As you hold each object, visualize the energy and essence of the celestial realms merging with the deceased's soul, drawing them closer to their celestial origins.
✧ Speak any prayers or blessings that resonate with the energy of the celestial realms and the deceased's connection to them.
✧ Offering and Gratitude:
✧ Place the offering of your choice on the altar, expressing gratitude to the celestial realms for their assistance in the reunion of the deceased's soul with their celestial origins.
✧ Offer words of thanks and appreciation for the guidance and support received throughout the ritual.

Closing:

✧ Take a moment to offer any final prayers or blessings, expressing your trust in the reunion process and the celestial energies guiding the deceased's journey.
Extinguish the candles and allow the incense to burn out naturally, releasing the energy into the space.

Note: Remember to honor the deceased's memory and their celestial origins. This spell can be performed periodically to strengthen the connection and support the reunion of the deceased's soul with their celestial heritage.

187.   Invocation of the goddess Nut for expansiveness and freedom in the afterlife

Note: This invocation is designed to call upon the goddess Nut, who is associated with the sky and the heavens, to bring forth expansiveness and freedom to the deceased in the afterlife.

Preparation:

✧ Find a quiet and sacred space where you can focus and connect with the energy of the divine.
✧ Light a candle or incense as a symbol of divine presence.
✧ Take a few deep breaths to center yourself and enter a state of calm and receptivity.

Opening:

✧ Begin by stating your intention clearly and with reverence. You may say:

"Oh, mighty and gracious Goddess Nut,
I call upon you in this sacred moment,
To invoke your divine presence and guidance,
And ask for your assistance in granting expansiveness and freedom to the deceased in the afterlife."

Acknowledgement:
✧ Take a moment to acknowledge and honor the power and essence of the goddess Nut. You may say:

"Goddess Nut, embodiment of the vast sky,
The bringer of infinite possibilities and freedom,
I honor your divine presence and wisdom,
And I invite your blessings to flow."

Invocation:

✧ Speak the following invocation, or create your own heartfelt words to invoke the goddess Nut:
"Oh, Goddess Nut, whose body is the celestial canopy,
Whose expanse stretches above us, embracing all,

I beseech you, grant your expansive presence to [name of the deceased],
As they embark on their journey through the afterlife.
Bestow upon them the freedom to soar among the stars,
To traverse the cosmic realms without limitation or confinement.
Let them be embraced by your nurturing and boundless love,
And feel the liberation that comes with merging into the eternal sky.
Goddess Nut, in your name, I invoke the power of expansiveness and freedom,
And ask for your divine blessings upon [name of the deceased].
May their soul find solace and liberation in the afterlife,
As they become one with your celestial expanse."

Connection and Gratitude:

✧ Take a moment to visualize the deceased being embraced by the expansive energy of the goddess Nut. Feel their spirit being lifted and released from any earthly constraints, free to explore the vastness of the afterlife.
✧ Express your gratitude to the goddess Nut for her presence and assistance. You may say:
"Goddess Nut, I express my deepest gratitude for your divine presence and blessings. Thank you for bestowing expansiveness and freedom upon [name of the deceased]. May their journey in the afterlife be filled with joy, liberation, and boundless possibilities.
I offer my heartfelt thanks and appreciation."

Closing:

✧ Conclude the invocation with a final statement or prayer, expressing your trust in the goddess Nut's guidance and assistance. You may say:
"Goddess Nut, I release this invocation into the cosmic expanse,
Trusting in your divine wisdom and loving guidance.
May your expansive energy remain with [name of the deceased],
As they embark on their journey in the afterlife.
So be it, and so it is."

✧ Allow the candle or incense to burn out naturally, symbolizing the completion of the invocation and the continued presence of the goddess Nut's energy.

Note: Remember to approach this invocation with reverence and respect, and adjust the language and elements used according to your personal beliefs and practices.

188.   Ritual of purification through the sacred gestures of the eternal mudras

Note: Mudras are symbolic hand gestures that have deep spiritual significance and are believed to channel and direct energy within the body. This ritual combines the power of mudras with the intention of purification to cleanse the spiritual and energetic aspects of the self.

Preparation:

✧   Find a quiet and sacred space where you can perform the ritual without distractions.
✧   Light a candle or incense to create a sacred atmosphere.
✧   Take a few deep breaths to center yourself and enter a state of focus and presence.

Opening:

✧   Stand or sit comfortably, with your spine straight and your hands resting on your thighs or in your lap.
✧   Close your eyes and take a moment to connect with your inner self.
✧   Set the intention for the ritual by stating your desire for purification. You may say:
"In this sacred moment, I invoke the power of the eternal mudras
To purify my body, mind, and spirit.
May this ritual cleanse and release any negative or stagnant energy within me,
Bringing forth clarity, balance, and renewed vitality."

Invocation:

✧   Begin by bringing your hands together at your heart center in the Anjali Mudra (prayer pose).
✧   Take a deep breath in and as you exhale, extend your arms out to the sides and overhead, forming the Namaste Mudra (hands pressed together above the head).
✧   Visualize divine energy flowing through your fingertips and filling the space around you, creating a sacred and purifying atmosphere.
✧   Silently or aloud, recite the following invocation:
"Through the sacred gestures of the eternal mudras,
I call upon the divine forces of purification and renewal.
May the energy of these sacred hand movements

Cleanse and purify every aspect of my being.
As I perform each mudra, I release all impurities,
And I invite divine light and purity to fill me.
With each gesture, I am cleansed and renewed."

Mudra Sequence:
✧ Perform each mudra in the following sequence, holding each mudra for a few
deep breaths and focusing on the intention of purification.

a. Prana Mudra:

Join the tips of your thumb, ring finger, and little finger while keeping the other
fingers extended.
Focus on deepening your breath and visualize inhaling pure, vital energy and
exhaling any impurities or stagnant energy.

b. Vajra Mudra:

Interlace your fingers and extend your index fingers upward, touching at the tips.
Hold this mudra at your heart center and envision a powerful and pure energy
radiating from it, cleansing and purifying your heart.

c. Shunya Mudra:

Fold your middle finger and place your thumb over it, pressing gently.
Close your eyes and direct your attention inward, connecting with the silence and
stillness within. Allow any thoughts or distractions to dissolve.

d. Linga Mudra:

Interlock your fingers, with the left thumb pointing upward and encircled by the right
thumb and index finger.
Visualize a pillar of light extending from your base, passing through your center, and
reaching up to the heavens, purifying and energizing your entire being.

e. Prithvi Mudra:

✧ Touch the tips of your ring finger and thumb together, while keeping the other
fingers extended.
✧ Feel a sense of groundedness and stability, connecting with the earth's energy
and allowing it to purify and stabilize your body and mind.

Closing:

- After completing the mudra sequence, bring your hands back to the Anjali Mudra at your heart center.
- Take a few moments to observe the sensations in your body and the state of your mind.
- Express gratitude for the purification process and for the energy of the mudras. You may say:

"I offer my deep gratitude to the divine forces that guided me in this ritual.
I thank the eternal mudras for their cleansing and purifying energy,
And I carry their transformative power within me.
May I be purified and renewed on all levels of my being."

- Gently open your eyes, extinguish the candle or incense, and carry the sense of purification with you as you continue your day.

Note: This ritual is meant to be adapted and personalized according to your beliefs and preferences. You can modify the mudras or add any other elements that resonate with you. Trust your intuition and let it guide you in creating a meaningful and powerful ritual of purification.

189.   Spell for the liberation of the deceased's soul from the illusions of separation

Note: This spell is intended to help the deceased's soul release the illusions of separation and awaken to the truth of interconnectedness and unity. It is a prayer for liberation and a reminder of the eternal bond that exists between all beings.

Preparation:

✧   Find a quiet and sacred space where you can perform the spell without distractions.
✧   Light a candle or incense to create a sacred atmosphere.
✧   Take a few deep breaths to center yourself and enter a state of focus and presence.

Opening:

✧   Stand or sit comfortably, with your spine straight and your hands resting on your thighs or in your lap.
✧   Close your eyes and take a moment to connect with your inner self.
✧   Set the intention for the spell by stating your desire to assist the deceased's soul in transcending the illusion of separation. You may say:
"In this sacred moment, I invoke the power of love and unity.
I offer this spell to support the liberation of [name of the deceased]'s soul
from the illusions of separation and the realization of eternal oneness.
May this spell help [name of the deceased] awaken to the truth of interconnectedness and be freed from all perceived boundaries that hinder spiritual growth."

Invocation:

✧   Begin by visualizing the presence of the deceased's soul, surrounded by divine light and love.
✧   Speak the following invocation, directing your words towards the soul of the deceased:
"Oh, spirit of [name of the deceased], I call upon you now,
Hear my words and feel my intention.
I invoke the power of unity and interconnectedness,
To guide you on your journey of liberation.

Release the illusions of separation that bind you,
And embrace the truth of eternal oneness.
Know that you are connected to all beings,
Bound by the sacred thread of existence.
With this spell, I offer my support and love,
Helping you transcend the limitations of the physical realm
And embrace the boundless nature of your soul."

Affirmation:

✧ Take a moment to express your affirmation and belief in the liberation of the
   deceased's soul. You may say:
"I affirm that [name of the deceased]'s soul is free,
Released from the illusions of separation and duality.
They are one with the eternal essence of all beings,
Embracing the interconnectedness of existence.
As their soul soars and expands in boundless love,
They remember the truth of unity and oneness.
May [name of the deceased] find peace, freedom, and eternal joy
In the embrace of universal consciousness."

Closing:

✧ Offer your gratitude and love to the deceased's soul and to the divine forces that
   support this journey of liberation. You may say:
"With gratitude, I release this spell to the divine.
I thank [name of the deceased]'s soul for their presence and trust.
May their journey be filled with light, love, and infinite connection.
And may the illusions of separation be forever dissolved.
As I extinguish this candle [or incense], I carry the intention
of unity and interconnectedness within my own being."
✧ Gently open your eyes, extinguish the candle or incense, and allow the energy of
   the spell to radiate and manifest in the world.

Note: This spell is offered as a way to honor and support the deceased's soul. It is
important to personalize and adapt the spell according to your own beliefs and
practices. Trust your intuition and modify the words or actions as necessary to make
it meaningful and aligned with your intentions.

190.   Incantation to awaken the dormant courage within the deceased's spirit

Note: This incantation is intended to awaken the dormant courage within the deceased's spirit, empowering them to overcome fear and embrace bravery in their spiritual journey. It serves as a reminder of their inner strength and the support of divine forces.

Preparation:
✧ Find a quiet and sacred space where you can perform the incantation without distractions.
✧ Light a candle or incense to create a sacred atmosphere.
✧ Take a few deep breaths to center yourself and enter a state of focus and presence.

Opening:

✧ Stand or sit comfortably, with your spine straight and your hands resting on your thighs or in your lap.
✧ Close your eyes and take a moment to connect with your inner self.
✧ Set the intention for the incantation by stating your desire to awaken the dormant courage within the deceased's spirit. You may say:
"In this sacred moment, I call upon the courage and strength that lies dormant within [name of the deceased]'s spirit. May this incantation awaken their bravery and empower them to face challenges in the afterlife. Let the light of courage shine forth and guide their journey, supported by divine forces. May [name of the deceased] be fearless and resilient in their pursuit of spiritual growth and transformation."

Invocation:

✧ Visualize the presence of the deceased's spirit, surrounded by a radiant golden light. Feel their essence and imagine their courage awakening.
✧ Speak the following incantation, directing your words towards the spirit of the deceased:

"Oh, spirit of [name of the deceased], arise and awaken,
Within you lies the dormant courage waiting to be stirred.
I call upon the depths of your being,
To embrace bravery and face the challenges ahead.
Let fear dissipate, replaced by unwavering strength.

Rise, courageous spirit, and conquer all obstacles.
You are supported by the divine forces that guide you,
Empowered by their love and protection.
Let the fire of courage burn brightly within your soul,
Illuminating your path and inspiring others.
Be brave, [name of the deceased], and fear no more,
For you are a warrior of light, eternally courageous."

Affirmation:

✧ Take a moment to express your affirmation and belief in the awakening of
courage within the deceased's spirit. You may say:
"I affirm that [name of the deceased]'s spirit is filled with courage,
Awakened from slumber and shining with bravery.
They embrace challenges with fearlessness and determination,
Guided by the divine forces that surround them.
May their courage be a beacon of light and inspiration,
Illuminating their path and supporting their journey.
As their spirit soars in fearless pursuit,
May they find strength, resilience, and triumph."

Closing:

✧ Offer your gratitude and love to the spirit of the deceased and to the divine
forces that support their awakening of courage. You may say:
"With gratitude, I release this incantation to the divine.
I thank [name of the deceased]'s spirit for their presence and courage.
May they be blessed and guided on their path of bravery.
As I extinguish this candle [or incense], I carry the intention
of awakened courage within my own being."
✧ Gently open your eyes, extinguish the candle or incense, and allow the energy of
the incantation to resonate and manifest in the world.

Note: This incantation is offered as a way to honor and support the deceased's spirit.
It is important to personalize and adapt the incantation according to your own beliefs
and practices. Trust your intuition and modify the words or actions as necessary to
make it meaningful and aligned with your intentions.

191.   Ritual for the communion with the spirits of the celestial realms of imagination

Note: This ritual is designed to open a channel of connection and communication with the spirits of the celestial realms of imagination. It is meant to foster creativity, inspiration, and a deeper understanding of the limitless possibilities within the realm of imagination.

Preparation:

✧ Find a quiet and comfortable space where you can perform the ritual without interruptions.
✧ Set up a small altar or sacred space with objects that represent your connection to the celestial realms of imagination, such as crystals, feathers, a journal, or artwork.
✧ Light candles or incense to create a sacred atmosphere.

Centering and Grounding:

✧ Take a few moments to ground yourself by taking deep breaths and connecting with the present moment.
✧ Close your eyes and visualize roots growing from the soles of your feet, anchoring you to the Earth. Feel the stability and support of the Earth beneath you.

Opening:

✧ Stand or sit in front of your altar or sacred space, facing it with reverence.
✧ Extend your arms outward, palms facing upward, and speak the following words:
"I open myself to the celestial realms of imagination,
Where limitless creativity and inspiration reside.
I invite the spirits of these realms to join me now,
To commune and share their wisdom and insights."

Invocation:

- Lightly ring a bell or chime to signal the beginning of the invocation.
- Speak the following invocation, directing your words to the spirits of the celestial realms of imagination:

"Spirits of the celestial realms of imagination,
I call upon you with reverence and respect.
From the depths of my being, I seek communion with you,
To awaken the realms of infinite possibility within.
Guide me, inspire me, and expand my creative horizons,
That I may connect with the essence of creation itself.
I open myself to your presence and guidance,
With love, gratitude, and a pure intention."

Communion:

- Sit or stand in front of your altar and take a moment to focus your attention on the objects representing the celestial realms of imagination.
- Close your eyes and allow your mind to quiet, entering a state of receptivity.
- Visualize a gateway opening before you, revealing a realm of vibrant colors, swirling energies, and boundless imagination.
- Mentally or verbally express your invitation to the spirits of the celestial realms of imagination, inviting them to share their insights, wisdom, and creative inspiration with you.
- Take your time in this space, allowing yourself to receive any messages, ideas, or visions that come to you. Trust your intuition and embrace the flow of your imagination.

Expression:

- When you feel ready, pick up a journal or art supplies and allow the inspiration from the communion with the spirits of the celestial realms of imagination to flow through you.
- Write, draw, paint, or create in any way that feels natural to you. Let your creativity be guided by the insights and inspiration received during the communion.
- Allow yourself to explore new ideas, experiment with different techniques, and embrace the freedom of the imaginative realm.
- Gratitude and Closing:

- ✧ When you have finished expressing your creativity, take a moment to express gratitude to the spirits of the celestial realms of imagination for their presence and guidance.
- ✧ Offer thanks for the insights received and the inspiration that has flowed through you.
- ✧ Close the ritual by extinguishing the candles or incense, and by saying:

"With deep gratitude, I thank the spirits of the celestial realms of imagination for their wisdom and inspiration. I carry their guidance within me as I continue on my creative journey. May the connection and communion with these realms always be open."

- ✧ Take some time to reflect on your experiences and the messages received during the ritual. Consider how you can incorporate the insights and inspiration into your creative endeavors and daily life.

Remember, rituals are personal and can be adapted to suit your beliefs and practices. Feel free to modify the steps or words to align with your own spiritual path and intentions.

192. Spell for the transmigration of the deceased's soul into the realm of divine harmony

Note: This spell is intended to facilitate the transmigration of the deceased's soul into the realm of divine harmony, where peace, balance, and unity prevail.

Preparation:

✦ Find a quiet and peaceful space where you can perform the spell without interruptions.
✦ Set up an altar or sacred space with objects that represent the concept of harmony, such as a white candle, a quartz crystal, and symbols of peace or balance.
✦ Light the white candle to create a serene atmosphere.

Centering and Grounding:

✦ Take a few deep breaths to center yourself and bring your focus to the present moment.
✦ Close your eyes and imagine roots extending from the soles of your feet, grounding you to the Earth. Feel a sense of stability and connection.

Opening:

✦ Stand or sit in front of your altar, facing it with reverence.
✦ Hold the quartz crystal in your hands and close your eyes.
✦ Speak the following words, or adapt them to your own beliefs and intentions:
"I open the gateway to divine harmony,
Where peace and balance intertwine.
I invoke the power of unity and serenity,
To guide the soul's transmigration in this sacred time.
By the grace of the cosmic forces, I invite,
The deceased's soul to transcend and unite.
Let divine harmony be their eternal home,
Where love and tranquility forever roam."

Invocation:

- ✧ Lightly ring a bell or chime to signal the beginning of the invocation.
- ✧ Speak the following invocation, addressing the higher powers or deities you resonate with:

"I call upon [name of deity or higher power], the embodiment of harmony divine,
Grant the deceased's soul a passage to the realm sublime.
Let their spirit be enveloped in serenity's embrace,
Transmigrating to the realm where harmony finds its place.
Release them from the bonds of the mortal world's strife,
And guide them towards everlasting harmony and life."

Transmigration:

- ✧ Hold the quartz crystal in your hands, envisioning it as a conduit of energy and a symbol of divine harmony.
- ✧ Visualize a serene and radiant light surrounding the deceased's soul, gently lifting them from the earthly realm and guiding them towards the realm of divine harmony.
- ✧ Imagine the soul merging with the harmonious energies of the higher realm, finding peace, balance, and unity.

Closing:

- ✧ Express your gratitude to the higher powers or deities you invoked for their presence and assistance.
- ✧ Thank the divine forces for facilitating the transmigration of the deceased's soul into the realm of divine harmony.
- ✧ Extinguish the white candle to signify the completion of the spell.
- ✧ Take a moment to reflect on the intention of the spell and send love and blessings to the departed soul, trusting that they have found their place in the realm of divine harmony.

Remember, rituals and spells are personal and can be adapted to suit your beliefs and practices. Feel free to modify the steps or words to align with your own spiritual path and intentions.

193.   Invocation of the god Osiris for resurrection and rebirth in the afterlife

Note: This invocation is intended to call upon the divine presence of the god Osiris, who is associated with resurrection, rebirth, and the afterlife. It seeks his guidance and assistance in facilitating the process of resurrection and rebirth for the deceased.

Preparation:

✦ Find a quiet and sacred space where you can perform the invocation without distractions.
✦ Create an altar or a focal point dedicated to Osiris. You can place an image or statue of Osiris, along with offerings such as fresh flowers, incense, or symbolic representations of life and rebirth.
✦ Light a candle or lamp to symbolize the presence of divine light and wisdom.
✦ Centering and Grounding:
✦ Take a few deep breaths to center yourself and clear your mind.
✦ Focus on the intention of the invocation and the connection with Osiris.
✦ Visualize a divine light surrounding you, bringing a sense of peace and tranquility.

Opening:

✦ Stand or sit before the altar, facing the image or statue of Osiris.
✦ Place your hands together in a prayer position, or extend your arms with palms facing upward.
✦ Speak the following words, or adapt them to resonate with your beliefs and intentions:
"Oh Osiris, mighty Lord of resurrection and rebirth,
I stand before you with reverence and worth.
In this sacred space, I call upon your divine might,
To guide and bless the deceased's soul in its flight.
Grant them the gift of resurrection and new birth,
As they traverse the afterlife's infinite mirth."

Invocation:

✦ Close your eyes and take a moment to connect with the energy of Osiris.
✦ Speak the following invocation, or use your own heartfelt words:
"Osiris, the bringer of life and renewal,
I invoke your presence, strong and true.

Unite with the departed soul in this hour,
Embrace them with your divine power.
From the depths of the Duat, rise and appear,
Grant them resurrection, casting away fear.
By your wisdom and grace, may they be led,
To eternal life, where all sorrows are shed."

Connection:

✧ Visualize the divine energy of Osiris surrounding you and the departed soul.
✧ Imagine the soul being enveloped in a golden light, symbolizing the resurrection and transformation process.
✧ Feel the presence and guidance of Osiris, assuring the soul's journey to the afterlife and its subsequent rebirth.

Closing:

✧ Express your gratitude to Osiris for his presence and assistance in the invocation.
✧ Thank him for his guidance and his role in facilitating the resurrection and rebirth of the departed soul.
✧ Offer any final prayers or blessings, expressing your trust in Osiris's divine wisdom.

Remember, invocations are personal and can be adapted to align with your own beliefs and practices. Modify the words and gestures as necessary to create a meaningful connection with Osiris and to suit your spiritual path and intentions.

194. Ritual of anointing with sacred sounds for spiritual transcendence

Note: This ritual is designed to engage with the transformative power of sacred sounds to facilitate spiritual transcendence and connection with the divine. It involves anointing oneself with sacred oils while chanting or listening to sacred sounds.

Preparation:

✧ Find a quiet and comfortable space where you can perform the ritual without interruptions.
✧ Gather sacred oils that resonate with your spiritual practice. Examples include frankincense, myrrh, sandalwood, or lavender. Ensure that you have a small amount available for anointing.
✧ Prepare any sacred objects or symbols that hold significance for you and your spiritual journey.
✧ Choose sacred sounds or music that evoke a sense of peace, transcendence, or connection with the divine. This can include chants, mantras, or instrumental music.

Setting the Sacred Space:

✧ Clear the space by smudging or using any other cleansing ritual that resonates with you.
✧ Set up your sacred objects or symbols in a way that feels meaningful and sacred to you.
✧ Light candles or lamps to create an atmosphere of spiritual reverence and focus.

Anointing:

✧ Take a few deep breaths to center yourself and prepare for the ritual.
✧ Take a small amount of the sacred oil in your hands and rub them together gently to warm the oil.
✧ Close your eyes and bring your attention to your intention for spiritual transcendence and connection with the divine.
✧ Begin to anoint your body with the sacred oil, starting from the crown of your head and moving down to your feet. As you do so, silently or aloud, affirm your intention for spiritual transcendence and divine connection. For example:

"With this sacred oil, I anoint myself for spiritual transcendence. May every cell of my being be infused with divine light and love. May I transcend limitations and open myself to the realm of the sacred."

Sacred Sounds:

✧ As you continue anointing, introduce the sacred sounds or music that you have chosen.
✧ You can chant sacred mantras, sing devotional songs, or listen to instrumental music that elevates your consciousness and facilitates a sense of connection with the divine.
✧ Allow yourself to fully immerse in the sounds, feeling their vibrations resonating through your body and expanding your awareness.

Visualization and Meditation:

✧ Close your eyes and allow yourself to enter into a meditative state.
✧ Visualize yourself surrounded by a sphere of radiant light, representing divine energy and protection.
✧ As you listen to the sacred sounds, imagine that the vibrations are gently dissolving any blockages or limitations within you, allowing your spirit to expand and soar.
✧ Feel a deep sense of connection with the divine, knowing that you are transcending the ordinary and entering into a sacred realm of consciousness.

Closing:

✧ When you feel ready, gradually bring your awareness back to the present moment.
✧ Express gratitude for the divine presence and the experience of spiritual transcendence.
✧ Conclude the ritual in a way that feels appropriate for you. This may include offering a final prayer, a moment of silence, or any other closing ritual that holds meaning for you.

Remember, rituals are personal and can be adapted to align with your own spiritual beliefs and practices. Modify the steps and elements of this ritual as necessary to create a meaningful and transformative experience that resonates with your spiritual path.

195.   Spell for the transformation of the deceased into a vessel of divine illumination

Note: This spell is intended to facilitate the transformation of the deceased into a vessel of divine illumination, allowing their spirit to radiate with light and wisdom. Perform this spell with respect and reverence for the departed and their spiritual journey.

Preparation:

✦ Find a peaceful and quiet space where you can perform the spell without distractions.
✦ Set up a small altar or sacred space with candles, crystals, and any other objects that hold personal significance or represent illumination and spirituality.
✦ Light the candles to create an ambiance of sacredness and divine presence.
✦ Take a few moments to ground yourself and center your energy through deep breaths and quiet contemplation.

Invocation:

✦ Stand or sit in front of the altar and take a moment to connect with the energy of the deceased, visualizing their presence or calling upon their spirit.
✦ Speak or recite the following invocation aloud, or adapt it to fit your personal beliefs and relationship with the deceased:
"By the power of divine light and the grace of the sacred,
I invoke the transformation of [Name of the deceased] into a vessel of divine illumination.
May their spirit be filled with radiant light and wisdom,
Guiding them through the realms of the afterlife with clarity and grace.
As the physical body is released, let their essence shine forth,
A beacon of illumination for their eternal journey.
In this sacred space, I call upon the divine to bless this transformation,
Infusing their spirit with divine light and granting them profound illumination."

Visualization and Intent:

✦ Close your eyes and visualize the deceased surrounded by a radiant, golden light, symbolizing divine illumination.
✦ See this light entering their being, filling them with wisdom, clarity, and spiritual radiance.

✧ Hold the intention that the deceased is transformed into a vessel of divine illumination, allowing their spirit to shine brightly and guide them on their journey in the afterlife.

Blessing and Farewell:

✧ Extend your hands towards the altar or the representation of the deceased, as if sending your blessings and love.
✧ Offer your words of farewell, expressing gratitude for their presence in your life and wishing them a journey filled with divine light and guidance.
✧ If desired, you can say a personal prayer or blessing that resonates with your beliefs and relationship with the deceased.

Closing:

✧ Take a moment to sit in silence, acknowledging the power and significance of the spell you have performed.
✧ Express gratitude to the divine forces or spiritual entities you invoked for their presence and assistance.
✧ Gently extinguish the candles, symbolizing the completion of the ritual.

Remember, this spell is meant to honor the deceased and support their spiritual journey. Perform it with love, respect, and the genuine intention to facilitate their transformation into a vessel of divine illumination.

196.   Incantation to invoke the blessings of the celestial cycles of seasons

Note: This incantation is intended to invoke the blessings and harmonious energy of the celestial cycles of seasons, representing the natural rhythms and transformative powers of nature. Use this incantation to connect with the changing seasons and their inherent wisdom.

Preparation:

✧ Find a quiet and peaceful space where you can focus your energy and connect with the natural world.
✧ Take a few moments to ground yourself by taking deep breaths and centering your awareness in the present moment.
✧ If possible, step outside and feel the presence of the current season in the air, the temperature, and the surrounding environment.

Invocation:

✧ Stand or sit in a comfortable position, facing the direction that represents the current season (e.g., East for spring, South for summer, West for autumn, North for winter).
✧ Raise your arms slightly, palms facing upwards, as if you are embracing the energy of the season.
✧ Speak or recite the following invocation aloud, or adapt it to resonate with your personal beliefs and connection to nature:
"By the cycles of the celestial spheres and the dance of the seasons,
I invoke the blessings of [Name of the season] upon this sacred space.
May the vibrant energy of [Name of the season] flow through me,
Guiding me in harmony with the natural rhythms of life.
As the earth transforms and renews itself, so do I,
Embracing the lessons and gifts [Name of the season] bestows upon me.
In this sacred moment, I open myself to the wisdom of the seasons,
May their blessings inspire and guide me through the cycles of my own life."

Connection and Reflection:

✧ Take a moment to connect with the energy of the invoked season, visualizing its unique qualities, colors, scents, and sensations.

✧ Reflect on the lessons and symbolism associated with this season, considering how they relate to your own life journey and experiences.

✧ Open your heart and mind to receive the blessings and insights that the season offers, allowing its energy to infuse you with inspiration and guidance.

Gratitude and Integration:

✧ Offer your gratitude to the season and its blessings by expressing thanks for its presence in your life.

✧ Reflect on how you can align your actions and intentions with the energy of the season, embracing its transformative qualities and applying them to your personal growth and well-being.

✧ Close your eyes, take a deep breath, and visualize the energy of the season merging with your being, creating a harmonious connection between yourself and the natural world.

Closing:

✧ Take a moment to sit in silence, allowing the energy and intentions of the incantation to settle within you.

✧ Express gratitude to the natural world and the cycles of the seasons for their continuous presence and wisdom.

✧ If desired, you can conclude with a personal prayer, blessing, or affirmation that honors your connection to the seasons and the cyclical nature of life.

Remember, this incantation is meant to deepen your connection with the seasons and the wisdom they offer. Use it as a tool to align yourself with the transformative energies of nature and to gain insight and guidance on your spiritual journey.

197. Ritual for the transfiguration of the deceased into a divine keeper of sacred wisdom

Note: This ritual is intended to honor and facilitate the transfiguration of the deceased into a guardian and keeper of sacred wisdom. It is a ritual of transformation and empowerment, allowing the departed soul to embody and protect the wisdom they have acquired during their lifetime.

Preparation:

✧ Find a peaceful and quiet space where you can perform the ritual without interruption.
✧ Gather items that symbolize wisdom, such as books, scrolls, or sacred texts.
✧ Create a sacred space by placing these items on an altar or a special surface.
✧ Light candles or incense to create an atmosphere of reverence and spiritual connection.

Invocation:

✧ Begin by standing or sitting in front of the sacred space, focusing your attention on the items that symbolize wisdom.
✧ Take a moment to center yourself and connect with the divine presence within and around you.
✧ Speak or recite the following invocation aloud, or adapt it to resonate with your personal beliefs and connection to the divine:
"Divine spirits of wisdom and sacred knowledge,
I call upon you in this sacred space and time.
I honor the departed soul [Name of the deceased],
who has journeyed beyond the veil of mortal existence.
May their spirit be transfigured and elevated,
Becoming a guardian of sacred wisdom and divine truth.
In this ritual of transformation, I invoke their essence
To be a keeper of wisdom for eternity."

Anointing:

✧ Take a small vial of sacred oil or a natural substance, such as olive oil or frankincense oil.

- Hold the vial in your hands, infusing it with your intention for the transfiguration of the deceased into a keeper of sacred wisdom.
- Gently anoint your fingertips with the oil, symbolizing the transfer of divine energy and wisdom.

Ritual Gesture:

- With the anointed fingertips, touch the forehead of the deceased's image or a photograph, representing their spirit.
- As you make contact, visualize a radiant light filling their being, illuminating their consciousness with divine wisdom.
- Offer a few moments of silent meditation or prayer, allowing the energy of the ritual to permeate the space.

Reflection and Offering:

- Take a moment to reflect on the wisdom and knowledge that the deceased embodied during their lifetime.
- Consider the lessons they shared and the impact they had on others through their teachings and insights.
- Express gratitude for their contributions to the world of knowledge and the spiritual legacy they left behind.

Closing:

- Conclude the ritual by expressing gratitude to the divine spirits and the deceased for their presence and guidance.
- Blow out the candles or extinguish the incense, symbolizing the completion of the ritual.
- If desired, spend a few moments in silence, allowing the energy of the ritual to settle and integrate.

Remember, this ritual serves as a way to honor the deceased and facilitate their transformation into a guardian of sacred wisdom. It is a symbolic act that acknowledges the importance of wisdom and the eternal nature of knowledge. By performing this ritual, you are recognizing and celebrating the legacy of the departed soul, ensuring that their wisdom continues to inspire and guide future generations.

198.   Spell for the reunion of the deceased's soul with their cosmic heritage

Note: This spell is intended to facilitate the reunion of the deceased's soul with their cosmic heritage, connecting them to the vastness of the universe and their place within it. It is a spell of remembrance and reconnection, allowing the departed soul to embrace their cosmic origins and find solace in their eternal connection to the cosmos.

Preparation:

✧ Find a quiet and sacred space where you can perform the spell without interruption.
✧ Create a peaceful atmosphere by lighting candles or incense, and if desired, playing soft, cosmic-inspired music.
✧ Have a photograph or representation of the deceased's image present, along with any personal objects that hold cosmic significance.

Invocation:

✧ Begin by standing or sitting in front of the sacred space, holding the photograph or representation of the deceased's image.
✧ Take a few deep breaths to center yourself and open your heart to the energy of the universe.
✧ Speak or recite the following invocation aloud, or adapt it to resonate with your personal beliefs and connection to the cosmos:
"Spirit of the departed, whose essence transcends time and space,
I call upon the cosmic forces that bind us all.
In this sacred space and time, I honor your cosmic heritage,
And invoke the reunion of your soul with the cosmos.
May you remember your eternal connection,
And find solace in the embrace of the infinite.
Together, we unite in the cosmic dance of existence."

Cosmic Offering:

✧ Hold the photograph or representation of the deceased's image close to your heart, infusing it with your love and intention for the reunion of their soul with their cosmic heritage.

✧ Offer words of remembrance, expressing gratitude for their presence in your life and acknowledging their eternal connection to the universe.

Cosmic Meditation:

✧ Close your eyes and visualize the departed soul's essence expanding and merging with the cosmic energies that surround us.
✧ Imagine them reconnecting with the stars, galaxies, and cosmic realms, embracing their true cosmic heritage.
✧ Envision them surrounded by the boundless beauty and wisdom of the universe, feeling a sense of unity and belonging.

Cosmic Affirmation:

✧ Speak or recite the following affirmation aloud, allowing its words to resonate within you and ripple out into the cosmos:
"As you journey beyond the earthly realm,
May your soul find peace in the embrace of the cosmos.
May you remember your cosmic heritage,
And feel the eternal connection that binds us all.
In the cosmic tapestry of existence,
You are forever a part of the infinite whole."

Closing:

✧ Conclude the spell by expressing gratitude to the cosmic forces and the departed soul for their presence and guidance.
✧ Take a moment to offer any personal prayers, blessings, or intentions for the departed soul's journey in the cosmos.
✧ When you are ready, gently release the energy of the spell, allowing it to flow out into the universe.

Remember, this spell is a way to honor the departed soul and facilitate their reunion with their cosmic heritage. It is a symbolic act that recognizes their connection to the vastness of the universe and the eternal nature of their being. By performing this spell, you are affirming their cosmic essence and embracing the infinite beauty and wisdom that surrounds us all.

199. Invocation of the goddess Taweret for protection and fertility in the afterlife

Note: This invocation is designed to call upon the goddess Taweret, an ancient Egyptian deity associated with protection and fertility, to provide guidance, strength, and abundance to the deceased in their journey through the afterlife. Taweret is often depicted as a protective deity with the head of a hippopotamus and the body of a pregnant woman. By invoking her, you seek her blessings and assistance for the well-being of the departed soul.

Preparation:

✧ Find a quiet and sacred space where you can perform the invocation without interruption.
✧ Set up a small altar or sacred space, adorned with symbols or images associated with Taweret, such as statues, drawings, or symbols of a hippopotamus and a pregnant woman.
✧ Light candles and incense to create a serene and reverential atmosphere.
✧ You may also have offerings of food, water, or flowers to place on the altar as a gesture of respect and invitation.

Invocation:

✧ Stand or sit in front of the altar, facing the symbols or images of Taweret.
✧ Take a few deep breaths to center yourself and open your heart to the presence of the goddess.
✧ Speak or recite the following invocation aloud, or adapt it to resonate with your personal connection to Taweret:
"Great goddess Taweret, protector and nurturer,
With the strength of the hippopotamus and the fertility of the pregnant woman,
I call upon you in this sacred space and time.
In the realm of the afterlife, where the departed soul now resides,
I beseech your guidance, protection, and abundance.

Taweret, mighty guardian of the eternal waters,
Wrap your loving embrace around the departed soul,
Shielding them from harm and offering them your unwavering strength.
In this journey through the afterlife, may they find solace in your presence,
And may your protection be their constant companion.

Goddess of fertility, bring forth your bountiful blessings,
Nourish the departed soul with abundant life-force,
And grant them the vitality to transcend and flourish.
May their journey through the afterlife be filled with fertile opportunities,
And may their spirit be renewed and rejuvenated.

I offer my reverence and gratitude to you, Taweret,
For your watchful eye and caring touch.
In the realm of the afterlife, I invoke your presence,
And invite your benevolent energy to guide and bless the departed soul.

Great goddess Taweret, protector and fertility bringer,
I honor and call upon you in this sacred moment."

Connection and Offering:

✦ Take a moment to connect with the energy of Taweret, feeling her presence and the power she embodies.
✦ If you have offerings of food, water, or flowers, place them on the altar as a symbolic gesture of respect and invitation for Taweret's blessings.
✦ Spend some time in quiet contemplation or meditation, allowing the energy of the invocation to permeate your being and the sacred space.

Closing:

✦ Conclude the invocation by expressing gratitude to Taweret for her presence and blessings.
✦ Offer any personal prayers or intentions for the departed soul's protection and fertility in the afterlife.
✦ When you are ready, gently release the energy of the invocation, knowing that your words and intentions have been heard.

Remember, this invocation is a way to honor the goddess Taweret and seek her protection and fertility blessings for the departed soul. By invoking her, you establish a connection with her divine energy and invite her guidance and support in the afterlife journey. Taweret's presence brings strength, protection, and fertility, ensuring that the departed soul is nurtured and cared for as they navigate the realms of the beyond.

200. Ritual of purification through the sacred silence of the eternal void

Note: This ritual is intended to facilitate a deep sense of purification and inner stillness by embracing the power of silence and connecting with the vastness of the eternal void. It can be performed as a personal practice or incorporated into a larger spiritual ceremony.

Preparation:

✧ Find a quiet and undisturbed space where you can perform the ritual.
✧ Create a sacred atmosphere by lighting candles or incense, dimming the lights, or using any other elements that help you create a serene and contemplative environment.
✧ Sit comfortably in a meditation posture, either on a cushion or a chair, with your spine straight and your body relaxed.
✧ Take a few deep breaths to center yourself and let go of any external distractions or thoughts.

Grounding and Centering:

✧ Close your eyes and bring your awareness to your breath. Take a few moments to focus on the sensation of the breath as it enters and leaves your body.
✧ Allow your breath to become slow and steady, anchoring yourself in the present moment.
✧ Visualize roots extending from the soles of your feet, grounding you deep into the earth. Feel the stability and support of the earth beneath you.
✧ Embracing Silence:
✧ Shift your attention from external sounds to the internal sounds of your body, such as your heartbeat or the rhythm of your breath.
✧ Gradually allow the sounds to fade into silence, creating a space of stillness within you.
✧ Embrace the silence as a sacred space, free from distractions and external influences.
✧ Be fully present in the silence, observing any thoughts or emotions that arise without judgment. Allow them to pass through your awareness without attachment.

Connection with the Eternal Void:

✧ With your inner focus, bring your awareness to the concept of the eternal void, the vast emptiness from which all things arise.
✧ Visualize yourself merging with this infinite space, expanding your consciousness to encompass the boundless expanse of the void.
✧ Feel the peace, clarity, and purity that emanate from this eternal silence.
✧ Allow yourself to dissolve into the void, transcending individuality and merging with the essence of the divine.

Purification and Stillness:

✧ In this state of deep connection with the eternal void, allow any lingering attachments, worries, or disturbances to dissolve.
✧ Surrender any negative emotions or thoughts to the void, knowing that they will be transmuted and released.
✧ Bathe in the purity and stillness of the void, feeling a sense of inner purification and renewal.
✧ Rest in this state of silence and stillness for as long as feels right, allowing the healing and transformative power of the void to permeate your being.

Closing:

✧ When you are ready to conclude the ritual, slowly bring your awareness back to your physical body.
✧ Express gratitude for the experience of silence and purification, acknowledging the transformative power it holds.
✧ Take a few deep breaths and gently wiggle your fingers and toes to reawaken your physical senses.
✧ Carry the sense of inner stillness and purification with you as you continue your journey.

Remember, the ritual of purification through the sacred silence of the eternal void is a deeply personal and introspective practice. It allows you to connect with the power of silence and the vastness of the void to cleanse and renew your inner being. Embrace the silence, surrender to the stillness, and allow the transformative energy of the eternal void to bring you a sense of deep purification and clarity.

201.   Spell for the liberation of the deceased's soul from the confines of time and space

Note: This spell is intended to help release the deceased's soul from the limitations of time and space, allowing it to transcend earthly boundaries and embrace a state of limitless freedom. It can be performed during a memorial ceremony or as an individual practice to honor and support the soul's journey beyond physical existence.

Preparation:

✧ Find a quiet and sacred space where you can perform the spell without interruptions.
✧ Set up an altar or a designated area with symbolic objects that represent the deceased or their spiritual beliefs. This can include candles, flowers, photographs, or any other items that hold significance.
✧ Take a few moments to center yourself and create an intention for the spell. You may wish to focus on the liberation of the deceased's soul from the constraints of time and space, and their transition into a state of boundless existence.

Invocation:

✧ Light a candle on the altar, symbolizing the presence of divine light and guidance.
✧ Close your eyes and take a few deep breaths, allowing yourself to enter a calm and focused state.
✧ Speak the following invocation or adapt it to your own words:
"By the power of eternity, I call upon the forces beyond time and space. I invoke the divine essence that transcends all limitations. I seek liberation for the departed soul, that it may soar beyond earthly constraints. I ask for the veils of time and space to be lifted, allowing the spirit to embrace boundless existence. May the soul find freedom in the eternal realm, unbound by the limitations of the physical world."

Visualization:

✧ Visualize a vibrant and radiant light surrounding the deceased's soul, gently dissolving any remnants of time and space.
✧ Envision the soul becoming weightless and free, transcending any earthly boundaries and limitations.

- ✧ See the soul expanding and merging with the vastness of the cosmos, becoming one with the limitless expanse of the universe.
- ✧ Hold this image in your mind, offering support and love to the departed soul as it embraces its newfound freedom.

Affirmation:

- ✧ Speak the following affirmation or create your own words of empowerment:
"By the power of this spell, I declare that the departed soul is liberated from the confines of time and space. It is free to explore the infinite realms of existence, guided by divine love and light. As the soul transcends all limitations, it discovers the boundless beauty and wisdom that lie beyond. May this liberation bring peace and joy to the departed soul on its eternal journey."

Release and Gratitude:

- ✧ Release any attachment to the outcome of the spell, trusting in the divine wisdom and guidance.
- ✧ Express gratitude to the forces beyond time and space, the divine energies, and any spiritual beings or deities you invoked during the spell.
- ✧ Extinguish the candle, symbolizing the completion of the ritual and the continuation of the soul's journey.

Remember, this spell is intended to provide support and assistance in the liberation of the deceased's soul from the constraints of time and space. It is a way to honor their journey and offer them love and guidance in their transition. Trust in the power of the spell and the divine forces that are at work, and may the soul find ultimate liberation and boundless existence beyond the limitations of time and space.

afterlife.

death

www.ingramcontent.com/pod-product-compliance
Lightning Source LLC
Chambersburg PA
CBHW082139120626
46553CB00010B/2705